Post-Revolution Nonfiction Film

New Directions in National Cinemas

Jacqueline Reich, editor

Post-Revolution Nonfiction Film

BUILDING THE SOVIET AND CUBAN NATIONS

Joshua Malitsky

INDIANA UNIVERSITY PRESS

Bloomington & Indianapolis

This book is a publication of

Indiana University Press
601 North Morton Street
Bloomington, Indiana
47404-3797 USA

iupress.indiana.edu

Telephone orders 800-842-6796
Fax orders 812-855-7931

© 2013 by Joshua Malitsky

∞ The paper used in this publication
meets the minimum requirements of
the American National Standard for
Information Sciences—Permanence
of Paper for Printed Library Materials,
ANSI Z39.48-1992.

*Manufactured in the United States
of America*

*Library of Congress
Cataloging-in-Publication Data*

Malitsky, Joshua.
  Post-revolution nonfiction film : building the Soviet and Cuban nations /
Joshua Malitsky.
    p. cm. — (New directions in national
cinemas) 1. Documentary films—
Political aspects—Soviet Union.
2. Documentary films—Political
aspects—Cuba. I. Title.
  PN1995.9.D6M329 2013
  070.1'80947—dc22
                                    2012037385

1 2 3 4 5   18 17 16 15 14 13

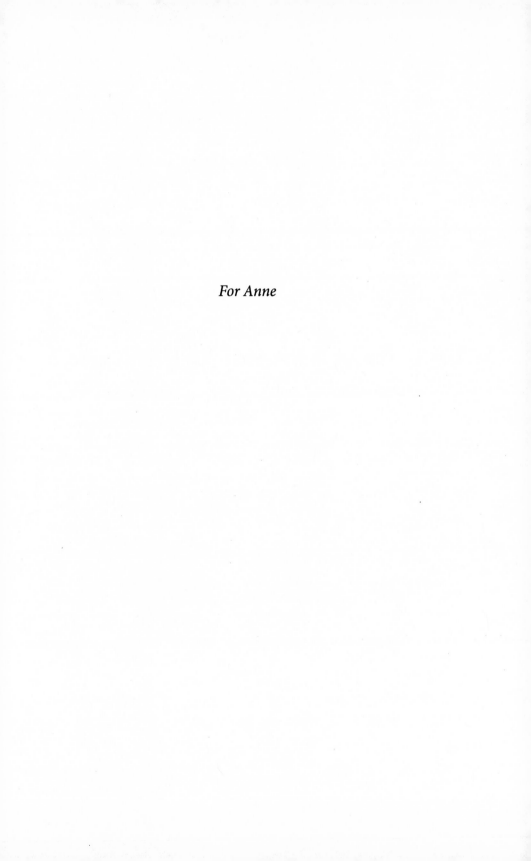

For Anne

CONTENTS

ACKNOWLEDGMENTS

Financial support for this book came from a variety of sources. My travel, research, and writing was supported by fellowships and grants from the graduate school and Center for International and Comparative Studies (CICS) at Northwestern University as well as by a summer Mellon Fellowship from the Russian and East European Institute (REEI) at Indiana University. In addition, the Department of Communication and Culture (CMCL) at Indiana University provided me a semester's leave to write.

Michael Chanan discussed Cuban (and Soviet) cinema with me at length, constantly responding to my queries, and helped establish my contacts in Havana. Those in Cuba with whom I worked and played and whom I would like to thank are Santiago Álvarez's widow, Lazara Herera; my translator, Vanessa Pedrosa; my social coordinator, Julia Cooke; Nelson Rodrigues; Pepin Rodriguez; Mario Piedra; Susan Lord; and my savior and hero, Maria Caridad Cumana. John Hess was thoughtful in his responses to my questions, and I thank him for his suggestions.

On the Soviet side, I would like to thank Ilya Kutik, Richard Taylor, Graham Roberts, Barbara Wurm, John MacKay, Masha Salazkina, and Seth Feldman for their work and correspondence. A special note of thanks goes to Yuri Tsivian, whose pragmatic and scholarly advice helped an earlier version of this work immensely and whose thinking continues to shape my own. Yuri curated the Vertov program at the 23rd Pordenone Silent Film Festival, making available the largest collection of Vertov's newsreels and silent features ever assembled. His accompanying collection of Vertov-related documents, *Lines of Resistance*, played no small part in making this and other studies of Vertov possible.

My research at the Österreichisches Filmmuseum in Vienna was supported by Michael Loebenstein, Dominik Tschütscher, and Alex Horwath. They provided me research copies of almost all of Vertov's and Shub's silent films and were thoughtful colleagues and friends.

I would like to thank two readers, Chuck Kleinhans and Scott Curtis, each of whom—though very differently—provided a model of academic scholarship and teaching that shapes my own today. I would also like to thank Andrew Wachtel, a wonderful mentor and friend. Mimi White always seemed to know what I needed, personally and intellectually, well before I did. She kept me focused while gently directing me to more fruitful areas of inquiry.

My father-in-law, Edward Brynn, deserves special recognition. Professor Brynn read every word of this book, going well beyond his apparent copyediting duties to offer substantive suggestions about the structure and focus of the argument. I want to thank both him and his wife, Jane, for their unconditional support throughout this process.

A number of people at Indiana University Press deserve thanks. Janet Rabinowitch, Jane Kupersmith, Raina Polivka, and Julie Bush have offered countless insights and demonstrated exceptional professionalism. I'm happy to be a part of what they are building.

I am extraordinarily fortunate to have the colleagues I do in CMCL at Indiana University. Joan Hawkins, Barb Klinger, Greg Waller, Alex Doty, Ted Striphas, Stephanie DeBoer, Michael Kaplan, and my occasional collaborator Ilana Gershon have, in various ways, enriched this book. I especially thank Ilana, who read a large chunk of this work, and Michael, who, in between Lionel Messi and Christiano Ronaldo exegeses, offered a number of critical directions I adopted. Michael Booth has been a wonderful friend and supporter during the writing of this book. His insights are sprinkled throughout. And Mark Kligerman provided a number of helpful comments early in the process.

Sara Friedman, Gardner Bovingdon, Sarah Knott, and Konstantin Dierks have all been amazing friends in Bloomington. In addition to their warm hospitality, I would like to thank Kon for his editorial work and Gardner, who not only read it all but put up with me throughout the process (no small task, I can assure).

Dan Morgan has read multiple versions of every chapter of this book, having been involved from the outset. Our conversations on film theory and film history have been invaluable. I cannot thank him enough for his extraordinary generosity. I only wish I were an ace southpaw for the Red Sox and could show my thanks every five days.

I want to thank my family—Gloria Caplan, Barry Malitsky, Jahna Gregory, Rodd Malitsky, and Denny Palmer. My son, Asher, made stepping away from Soviet and Cuban nonfiction film usually the best part of my day. I dedicate this book to my wife, Anne Brynn, who knows all the reasons why.

Post-Revolution Nonfiction Film

Introduction:
Revolutionary Rupture
and National Stability

The task of the total transformation of the world was not an end in itself—the end was ideal humanity, freedom from economic material necessity, and most important, freedom to create. Hence all avant-garde movements . . . however diverse their aesthetic sensibilities, were ultimately concerned with the identical problem: the development and implementation of a modern utopian science scheme that would affect the leap from the present to the future, or, in the idiom of the day, from the kingdom of necessity to the kingdom of freedom. But though Marx posited the fusion of art and life in *The German Ideology,* neither Marx and Engels nor the Bolsheviks articulated a coherent aesthetic theory. As a result, providing blueprints of the ideal future, particularly models of a new man, became the task of the artistic avant-garde.

—IRINA GUTKIN, *CULTURAL ORIGINS OF
THE SOCIALIST REALIST AESTHETIC* (1999)

Whenever a new social group, especially a new class, first appeared in history, it was seized for a time with a kind of fever to build. People would joyously start to remake the face of the earth in the image and likeness of their own conceptions of social justice, and their literature acquired an earthy, insistently urgent, and efficacious quality . . . a revolutionary form was invented that most hit the mark.

—NIKOLAI CHUZHAK, "PISATEL'SKAIA PAMIATKA" (1929)

It seems to me important that we advance by way of the very difficult combination of continuity and rupture. If you go too far ahead, nobody will follow you, you're not efficient because you don't communicate. If you limit yourself to respecting the level of the masses at a given moment, they may pass you by and leave you becalmed and paralyzed. If you go too far ahead in your search, you can become dangerously isolated from your audience—just as one runs a risk by choosing the well-traveled road and not achieving a personal advance. I think the will ought to be always to do violence to the public.

—MANUEL PEREZ, IN ISAAC LEON FRIAS'S,
"ENTREVISTA CON MANUEL PEREZ," *HABLEMOS DE CINÉ* (1979)

ENERGY, INNOVATION, AND AUDIENCES

Periods immediately following revolutions are often charged with artistic energy and creative experimentation. Industrial leaders, scholars, critics, and artists debate the value and role of artistic practice in a new society. They negotiate their own aesthetic theories with the politics of the victorious party and seek access to scant resources. Following the Russian Revolution of 1917 and the Cuban Revolution of 1959, the goals of political revolutionaries and revolutionary artists were complementary and integrated in ways never before experienced in each country. Each group supported political and aesthetic experimentation and believed that such practices could and would lead to a society of new men and women in the immediate future. Leon Trotsky envisioned an individual who "will become immeasurably stronger, wiser and subtler; his body will become more harmonized, his movements more rhythmic, his voice more musical. . . . The average human type will rise to the heights of an Aristotle, a Goethe, or a Marx. And above this ridge new peaks will rise."[1] And Che Guevara anticipated an individual who was "more complete, with much more inner wealth and much more responsibility," one with the potential to reach "total consciousness as a social being."[2] The duty of providing models of the new man, as Irina Gutkin describes in *Cultural Origins of the Socialist Realist Aesthetic*, fell in part to the artistic avant-garde.[3]

Even nonfiction film, associated with the communication of events and experiences of the everyday world, was drawn into the culture of experimentation. Soviet and Cuban leaders, in fact, privileged nonfiction film as a form uniquely capable of aiding the effort to shape the new man and to unify, edify, and modernize the citizenry as a whole. In the clarity of its language and in its visual and narrative pleasures, they saw considerable agitational, propagandistic, and economic potential. On-location shooting, use of found footage material, and limited need for elaborate sets and costumes: all this made documentaries and newsreels economically efficient in comparison to fiction films. And nonfiction film was thought to be consistent with Marxist-Leninist principles in that it grounded its artistic production in material reality.

But the dimensions and directions these forms should take were not at all self-evident, even to the Cubans, who at least had the privilege of exposure to other socialist nonfiction film projects (Soviet, Chinese, and Yugoslav, for example). Nikolai Chuzhak's essay "Pisatel'skaia pamiatka" captures the energy that infused these new cultural practices and asserts that new forms need to be invented to do the proper revolutionary work.[4] For Chuzhak, this is not a singular effort. Revolutionary art, he argues, has to exist in a state of *becoming*.[5] Because artistic forms have to correspond to the revolutionary social order if they are to "hit their mark," true revolutionary forms never stabilize. They must remain instead provisional aesthetic propositions. Guevara makes a similar point in discussing efforts to construct the image of the new man and woman through "indirect education." This image is one "not yet completely finished—it never will be, since the process goes forward hand and hand with the development of new economic forms."[6] Constructing, shaping, building, or painting an image of the new citizen—whatever metaphor they chose to employ—required constant aesthetic adjustment.

Whereas Gutkin captures the stakes involved in artistic production during these post-revolutionary moments and Chuzhak speaks to both the energy of the moment and the dynamic between revolutionary art and the contemporary social order, Manuel Perez articulates the extraordinary challenges facing an artistic vanguard that is supposed to simultaneously lead and respond to the people, who are its inspiration. The relationship between revolutionary art (Perez is discussing film) and its audiences (in this case mass audiences), he argues, must proceed by way of "continuity and rupture."[7] Political artistic communication must strike the balance between communicating efficiently in a clearly comprehensible fashion and offering innovative models of thought and vision capable of moving society forward. This challenge has been central to debates about Marxist aesthetics and politics, though no clear answers have emerged.

The Soviet and Cuban nonfiction film projects on which this book focuses were infused with extraordinary intellectual, artistic, and political energy, demonstrating a profound belief in the power of nonfiction film to contribute to the effort to build a new society. They were constantly innovating, formally and rhetorically, while also responding to shifting social, political, economic, cultural, and industrial contexts. And the choices they made were scrutinized by other artists, politicians, cultural leaders, industrial officials, and audiences. In each case they were granted financial, institutional, and political support. But with that support came significant pressure—a pressure that reveals a common set of dilemmas and possibilities facing leaders and artists in post-revolutionary socialist contexts.

This book is an analysis of state-sponsored newsreels and documentaries in case studies of two socialist revolutions: post-1917 Soviet film (1917–1928) and post-1959 Cuban film (1959–1974). I have chosen these cases based on the quality of the intellectual and creative work, their impact on film history, their importance on the national and international political stage, and their artistic and theoretical intersections. In addition to employing experimental nonfiction filmmakers—the most important being Dziga Vertov and Esfir Shub in the USSR and Santiago Álvarez in Cuba—to aid the nation-state building project, there were important parallels between the two states. Each state was intent on building socialism and modernizing an underdeveloped infrastructure. Each sought to forge a nation by carving a space for a national and international consciousness alongside particular local identities. Each deified revolutionary leaders. Each created mobile film units designed to reach all citizens. And each celebrated the potential of nonfiction film to counter the "false images" of imported fiction film and to address the specific needs of the nation-state.

Each project demonstrates a set of common themes and interests. They exhibit persistent attempts to transform how citizens see, feel, and understand their relation to the social world. They aim to project (materially and psychologically), model (through examples on-screen), and instill (through the emotional and visceral dimension) a socialist revolutionary mode of thought and being. They seek to reimagine the relationships between the individual and the collectivity as well as between subjects and leadership by providing new models of political economy, by generating new attitudes toward and experiences of labor, and by creating a new image of the nation while articulating citizens' roles within it. Filmmakers took advantage of these more "open" historical moments—when revolutionary achievement sparked utopian dreams capable of sustaining visions like Trotsky's "new man" and when many of the goals of leftist political and artistic revolutionaries converged—to create new social imaginaries and to do so at an accelerated rate. In the process, they provided people with visions of change, based on new social and political concepts and models of everyday life.

But more than that, these films and the networks through which they circulate do not just offer examples of new engagements with national space but *activate the process of imagining moving differently* through national space. They do not just offer virtual experiences of social and political change but create conditions for recognizing this as an active and urgent collective charge. In this way, they become part of a profound effort of bringing ideology—and the social imaginaries in which it is embedded—to consciousness. The decisive goal of these projects, therefore, was not only to participate in the accelerated development of subject construction but also to instill the desire for Soviet and Cuban subjectivity.

Understanding the relationship between nonfiction cinema, the state, and the shaping of a new national people (the paradigmatic case of modern social imaginary)[8] requires exploring it both as a synchronic snapshot and as a diachronic process. The combination enables me to identify an overall trajectory applicable to both cases, which can be roughly broken down into three periods. (The periods are divided according to the production of the films themselves.) The films of the immediate post-revolutionary period in both the Soviet Union (1917–1921) and Cuba (1959–1965) are realist in form and driven by a need to forge a space for the imagination of collective action. This required both visualizing a new collectivity and establishing reliable spaces of communication so that the people could begin to imagine themselves as a public, as a collective force. In the second period (1922–1927 and 1965–1971), key filmmakers developed new aesthetic strategies to expand the range of nonfiction film thought and experience. The films of this period urge new national, supranational, and international alignments; offer lessons in Marxist political economy (at the domestic and international/imperialist levels); establish a new hermeneutics of media culture; and, perhaps most significant, provide new understandings of the individual's role as a laboring citizen. The third period (1927–1928 and 1972–1974) marks the moment in post-revolutionary socialist contexts in which leaders appear to have recognized that the previous communication strategies were not working as they and the revolutionary artists had hoped. Leaders, critics, and artists responded by privileging a new rhetorical clarity, one that embraced new forms of historical discourse that rely on more realist, restrained approaches to directorial expressivity.

I do not define these periods in the service of a historiographical argument governed by a sense of history as monarchic succession. Rather, they allow me to refine the relevant features of the nonfiction film social imaginary at a series of moments—moments whose emergence depended on political-economic as well as social and cultural dynamics. To be sure, the borders of these periods are permeable. There are newsreels made in 1969 in Cuba that are more typical of Cuba's third period. Some of Vertov's early *Kino-Pravda* (Film-Truth) newsreel issues, made during the second period, have more in common with his earlier output than with his feature documentaries of the mid-1920s. But these periods allow me to identify the aesthetic and methodological strategies, as well as the individual voices, that became privileged—granted production, distribution, and exhibition support—by the state at a given time. These are the criteria that determine the focus of the chapters and the inclusion/exclusion of filmmakers and films.

In calling attention to the films, filmmakers, aesthetics, and methods that were financially and discursively privileged by the state at a given time, I do not intend to assert an ideologically overdetermined, top-down historical understanding of the relationship between the socialist state and cultural production. Rather, this book emphasizes the dynamic between the insistent and constant mandate from above and the (relative) open-endedness of the cinematic form. And it does so by recognizing that state-supported institutions, with their individual histories, shifts in policies, and dominant players, possessed varying levels of autonomy. From the establishment of the All-Russia Photographic and Cinematic Department (VFKO, which coordinated local cinematic activities and worked to nationalize individual film institutions), to the growth of Kultkino (the educational wing of the Moscow Cinema Committee), to the birth of Goskino (the first effort to centralize the film industry) and its transformation into Sovkino (which controlled distribution of all foreign films and subsidized domestic filmmaking), these institutions and the individuals who ran them shaped the direction Soviet nonfiction cinematic practice took. Such attention is also paid to changes that took place at Cuba's Institute of Cinematographic Art and Industry (ICAIC). Although a smaller institution that maintained a relatively stable structure during the period of study, ICAIC's shifts in priority, policy, and leadership informed the methods, aesthetics, and topics of both Cuban fiction and nonfiction film production.

In the Soviet Union, Dziga Vertov established himself as the dominant nonfiction filmmaker of the first two periods. He was the editorial voice of the *Kino-Nedelia* (Film-Week) newsreel series, the director and creator of the *Kino-Pravda* series, and the director of numerous state-sponsored found footage and live-action documentary features. At the end of 1926, Sovkino, the central state-sponsored film agency, and its head, Ilya Trainin, dismissed Vertov. In 1927 (the beginning of the third period), Esfir Shub's model of historical compilation documentary became privileged. Additionally, during the third period, newsreels themselves fell out of favor, waning considerably in financial and institutional support.

In Cuba, Santiago Álvarez was without question the leading voice of ICAIC's *Latin American Weekly Newsreel*. He was its director from its inception in 1960 until its final issue in 1991. He was also the foremost documentary filmmaker during most of the period under consideration. The exception was in the immediate post-revolutionary period, when Álvarez was one of a number of aspiring filmmakers developing his craft under the tutelage of established international documentarians such as Joris Ivens, Theodor Christensen, and Chris Marker. Perhaps at no time was Álvarez's position more evident than during the middle of the second period when Fidel Castro urgently requested that he make a film tribute to the life of Che Guevara to accompany Fidel's eulogy to the fallen revolutionary hero. It was Fidel's faith in Álvarez's politics and productivity that prompted him to commission a film (it would become *Hasta la victoria siempre* [Always until victory], 1967) that would be seen by hundreds of thousands of people assembled to mourn Che—moreover, Fidel allowed it to be seen without having first reviewed the film. Certainly there were other nonfiction filmmakers whose work was well-supported by the state, the most notable being Sara Gómez, José Massip, Octavio Cortázar, and Alejandro Saderman.[9] But Álvarez's influence and support was unmatched.

In focusing the majority of the book on Vertov, Shub, and Álvarez, however, I do not wish to silence the multiple conflicting and contesting voices that were active in nonfiction film culture in each context. Not only did the filmmakers on whom I am focusing (especially Vertov and Álvarez) constantly collaborate with other artists, but their methods and aesthetics were consistently challenged by others competing for resources and power. All three were part of an ambitious effort to rethink the role and practice of nonfiction film in post-revolutionary society. This book, therefore, does not conceive of Vertov's, Shub's, and Álvarez's work as totalizing visions of a more complex landscape but rather as paradigmatic of the shifting nonfiction film discourse. This centrality to their respective nonfiction film projects emerges both from the privileged positions they occupied in relation to the state and the attention they received in the critical discourse during each period under consideration.

These periods structure the argument of the book. Within each part, there is a chapter on the Soviet case and a chapter on the corresponding Cuban case. The chapters themselves highlight the synchronic element, outlining accounts of the forms of social imaginary that were sought through newsreel and documentary at a given time. They consist of close analyses of the body of films that make up the work of that period. But these analyses expand beyond the films' textuality. I argue that the nonfiction cinema network—the web of connections that makes up this cinematic practice—inevitably shapes the mode of address that, in part, figures the imagination. As I contend throughout, the array of exhibition and distribution practices is integral to the subject's comprehension of the role of the state, the map of the nation, and the appropriate performance of national citizenship. Within each of the periods, it becomes clear the direction nonfiction film took depended on how nonfiction film as a generic category, and documentary and newsreel as subgenres within that framework, were conceived by leaders, practitioners, critics, and viewers. Their attitudes about these practices were constantly shifting and elaborated both in relation to each other as well as in relation to other media. Fiction film, journalism, and even still photography were integral to the shape of the imagination Soviet and Cuban nonfiction film sought to project, model, and instill. In this way, Vertov's work is discussed in relation to journalism in both the first and the second period. And Vertov himself insistently celebrated the value of nonfiction film over fiction film in both writings and in his films. Fiction film's creation of imaginary worlds, for Vertov, amounted to a falsity akin to pre-revolutionary Russian culture. In Cuba as well, Álvarez saw himself as maintaining ties with journalism, even though he allied with a socialist journalism very much at odds with established Western standards.

My analysis of the beliefs these practitioners, critics, and audiences held about the meanings these mediums convey reveals both historically specific and persistent ideas about nonfiction film, and documentary in particular. In the late 1920s Soviet Union, for example, the value of documentary increasingly revolved around concerns about the rootedness and mobility of photographic signs. Critics, leaders, and cultural producers negotiated competing emphases on the object in the photograph's rootedness in a particular time and space versus the object's requirement to travel across contexts and speak agitationally to the vast and multinational Soviet citizenry. To understand how practitioners and audiences negotiate this relationship between text and context, I turn to linguistic anthropological work on language ideologies to derive a set of tools. I do this for two reasons. First, it opens to analysis how Soviet factographers such as Sergei Tret'iakov and Chuzhak conceived this work occurring in both moving and still-image photographic-based documentary. Second, it suggests a model of indexicality as both trace and deixis that is productive for understanding how meaning is made through multiple nonfiction film forms.

In addition to explicating the constitutive features of the social imaginary that nonfiction film sought to project, model, and instill, this book examines how those efforts developed over time. Doing so offers insight into Soviet and Cuban leaders' and filmmakers' stable and shifting social, political, cultural, and aesthetic priorities. In both the Soviet Union and Cuba, for example, increased efforts to collectivize and institutionalize ten to twelve years after the revolution prompted a shift in the cultural sphere from an emphasis on subjective inspiration to more objective organization. Soviet and Cuban cultural leaders began to promote a fascinating combination of diaries, reports, and other forms of representation of everyday experiences as well as new historical forms. I argue that combining Lorraine Daston and Peter Galison's work on the history of objectivity with recent scholarship in documentary studies provides necessary tools for nuancing changes in nonfiction film practices and their underlying ideologies. By charting the development of nonfiction film in each context, I aim to propose trajectories of each case study that will illuminate the social and political work those involved in the projects thought they could perform. But additionally, by mapping those trajectories in relation to each other, I endeavor to provide a framework against which other nonfiction film projects (socialist or not) can be located. My aim for the rest of the introduction is twofold. First, I will further develop the methodological and theoretical parameters that serve as a conceptual framework for the book. Second, I will offer more concrete detail about the contexts in which each revolutionary government assumed power and the impact of those foundations on nonfiction film. In the process, I will draw out the challenges and dilemmas facing socialist revolutionary governments looking to build new national cinemas with nonfiction film components. In so doing, I hope to provide a broader foundation for thinking about post-revolutionary nonfiction film in socialist contexts before delving into the specific realizations in the Soviet Union and Cuba.

NEW SOCIAL IMAGINARIES

Nonfiction film has a long history of challenging distinctions between official speech and common speech. It balances intellectual schemes with popular belief and does so in a way that allows citizens to understand, not just in an intellectual way but in an experiential way, the social and political consequences of their everyday thoughts and actions. Nonfiction film helps people grasp society as a set of identifiable categories while simultaneously prompting people to see themselves as belonging to new kinds of collective agency. In this way, nonfiction film participates in the effort to shape citizens' social imaginaries.

Social imaginaries, Charles Taylor argues, are broader and deeper than intellectual schemes people may hold when they try to conceive social reality in a disengaged mode. They are neither theories, which are more abstract and often held by a small minority, nor a set of ideas, which is too divorced from practice. Rather, they are "the ways people imagine their social existence, how they fit together with others, how things go on between them and their fellows, the expectations that are normally met, and the deeper normative notions and images that underlie these expectations." They are the "common understanding that makes possible common practices and a widely shared sense of legitimacy."[10] Social imaginaries shape the "repertory of collective actions" available to a group at a given time, which range from common actions like knowing what to say and not to say while standing in line, making an appointment with the cable company, or voting in a general election.

The relation between understandings and practices is pivotal because some self-understandings are not formulated in any kind of explicit frame. Instead, they are embedded in the narratives, symbols, modes of address, and systems of cognition that subtend and make possible everyday activities. As Dilip Gaonkar writes, "They are imaginary in a double sense: they exist by virtue of representation and implicit understandings, even when they acquire immense institutional force; and they are the means by which individuals understand their identities and their place in the world."[11] Without the context, it would be easy to imagine Gaonkar was referring to cinema itself. Cinema is both a representation open to interpretation by institutions, organizations, and individuals, and it is, to some, increasingly the means by which people understand their place in the world.[12] The social imaginary offers an important tool for thinking about the kind of work nonfiction filmmakers were aiming to do in these post-revolutionary periods.

Part 1 provides a telling example. The *Kino-Nedelia,* the early years of the ICAIC newsreel, and Vertov's and Álvarez's early documentaries have often been described as a prelude to their future development— that is, as a period of training. Alternately, the films have been seen as emphasizing the spontaneity of the revolutionary moment, their realist aesthetics entirely appropriate for such a purpose. Both arguments are valid. If one is interested in Vertov's or Álvarez's development as documentary artists with unique voices, ones that have a lot to offer to a history and theory of documentary, it makes sense to see the early period as merely preparation. If one is concerned with thinking about how documentary movements relate to drastic social and political change, it makes sense to emphasize the experience of spontaneity that is communicated. However, locating them within a larger project of shaping social imaginaries allows us to see how much more foundational they were to nation-state building goals and the specific political work they aimed to accomplish—in this case, establishing reliable spaces of communication, identifying new collectivities, and offering new models of movement through national space. It is a different way of understanding the project, one that I believe can account for how aesthetic and circulatory dimensions shaped the experiences people had with and knowledge they gained from engaging these films.

Transforming social imaginaries, as Taylor demonstrates, is an extremely long process. The Soviets and Cubans involved in this project sought an accelerated development of subject construction. Even banal newsreels covering an event at which rural citizens enter urban areas can be—and often were—understood as part of the utopian dream of rapidly remodeling society. These issues do not just redraw the makeup of the collectivity, in the process hoping to dismantle certain rural/urban divisions; they provide virtual experiences of what filmmakers and leaders hoped would become common practices.

CINEMA, NATION, STATE

Constructing a new coherent and communicable idea of the nation (the definitive case of modern social imaginary) following the assumption of power is one of the central concerns of post-revolutionary governments.

Benedict Anderson's modernist concept of the nation as an "imagined political community" offers an explanation of how a group of people highly unlikely to come into contact with one another identify themselves with a nation.[13] Emphasizing the impact of culture over political ideology, Anderson argues that nationalism "has to be understood by aligning it . . . with large cultural systems that preceded it."[14] Anderson's attention to the influence of print media on such identity formation has been usefully extended to cinema cultures, enabling media scholars to theorize how national cinemas and national media more generally help create those "imagined communities."

Many contemporary studies of cultural representation address what Homi Bhabha describes as a "particular ambivalence that haunts the idea of the nation, the language of those who write it, and the lives of those who live it."[15] As the roles of the nation and state increasingly diverge, and as nationalism requires situation in relation to terms such as "post-nationalism," "supra-nationalism," and "trans-nationalism," the idea of an essential ambivalence of the nation has taken hold. These studies highlight the differences between an official attempt to promote a sense of stable endurance and a social reality that continually manifests transitionality. Films produced in post-revolutionary contexts refigure that framework. These moments exacerbate the tension between the desire to present the nation as a permanent and progressive entity while conceding the need for rapid social change. At the same time, the association of the state primarily with the promotion of stability is problematized by the state's interest in stimulating radical social, economic, political, and cultural change. This tension between stability and transformation (at the locus of state-sponsored newsreels and documentaries), and how the elements that make up each side shift over time, is one of the objects of this study.

While at the broadest level the need to simultaneously promote stability and transformation is the raison d'être of these post-revolutionary nonfiction film projects (and that constitutes their basic similarities), this occurs through divergent processes in the Soviet Union and Cuba. Given some of the significant differences in their nation-building contexts and agendas, that is to be expected. While I have already addressed some of their similar goals and practices, I want to mark how their divergences shaped the conditions for filmic articulation.

The Soviet and Cuban revolutionary governments came to power in contrasting manners. The October Revolution of 1917 that brought the Bolsheviks to power had been preceded by the February Revolution, which occasioned the abdication of Tsar Nicholas II and left the Aleksandr Kerensky–led Provisional Government in power. The years immediately following the Bolshevik Revolution were marked by confusion, contention, and chaos on the political and cultural front and severe shortages on the economic front. The Soviet Union was simultaneously engaged in war with Poland, responding to German and Allied intervention, and surviving a brutal civil war. The impact of following the Provisional Government and of the deprivations of war can be seen, among other places, in the *Kino-Nedelia* newsreels' emphasis on the stability and problem-solving skills of the new Bolshevik government. Such an extended battle for control of Russia is contrasted by the remarkable ease with which the Cuban rebels came to power in January 1959. That is not to say that the overall process of assuming power was effortless for the Cuban rebels but that, following their seizing control of the formal institutions of power in 1959, they were not forced to engage in a lengthy military battle. Like the Bolsheviks, the Cuban rebels faced internal opposition to their authority, but unlike the Bolsheviks, the opposition never mounted a serious threat to their rule. Rather, as the Bay of Pigs invasion reveals, the gravest threat to the Castro government came externally from the United States.[16]

The differing military challenges to the revolutionary governments' power correlated to the initial overall levels of support for their rule. In the Soviet Union, the Bolsheviks did not enjoy the solid support of the peasants, especially in the peripheral regions. While peasant uprisings aided the Bolshevik Revolution and expressed their dreams for a transformed world, their hopes and identities clashed with an urban, Russian intelligentsia who sought to speak for them. The desire to unite the urban and peasant population and create in that unity a completely new sense of Soviet national identity, as I discuss in both chapter 1 and chapter 3, was one of the driving forces of the Soviet project. The Cuban rebels, however, had considerable support in the broad population of the island-nation at the time of their seizure of power. The construction of a new national identity in Cuba was less about creating something completely un-thought than about reconceiving and rearticulating the meaning of "Cuba" and "Cuban-ness."

The particular national, cultural, and ethnic makeup of the state in which the revolutionary governments found themselves of course influenced the nation-states they could build. Andrew Wachtel breaks states down on the basis of three "multis" potentially present in any state: multinationalism, multiethnicism, and multiculturalism. A multinational state is one created from a number of distinct nations. These distinctions continue to hold sway over individual identity as people see themselves primarily as part of their own nation rather than of the inclusive state. A multiethnic state is one whose citizens are drawn from a number of distinct backgrounds but see themselves as belonging to a single nation. A multicultural state is one in which citizens from different cultures see themselves as belonging to a state possessing a unifying culture that "each of its component parts recognizes as its own because each has made recognizable contributions to it."[17] Within this framework, we can identify the key difference between the Soviet Union and Cuba on the issue of multinationalism. Both states were composed of multiple ethnicities and sought to create a unified national culture—whether or not they actually achieved a single national culture is less important than the goal. But while the Soviet Union was multinational, Cuba is clearly a uninational state.[18]

Given these contexts, what emerged in the Soviet Union was a desire to create a unified national culture within a unified state. In the early 1920s, attempts were made to create a sense of Soviet national identity, and cinema was enlisted to aid in the process. By the mid- to late 1920s, however, aligned with changes in broader nation-building policy, we see in cinema subtle shifts from a utopian focus on creating a unified national identity to accepting multinationalism. Political expediency superseded more expansive and creative nation-building goals. In Cuba, the state's focus was on transforming what it defined as the previous idea of "Cuba"— one associated with American imperialism with Havana as the center of that impulse. In its place, the state sought to establish an essential Cuban spirit aligned with the rural and committed to national liberation. Therefore, continually drawing connections between the rebels of the War of Independence from Spain in 1898 (José Martí, Máximo Gómez) and the ouster of the dictator Gerardo Machado in 1933 was the new government's way of pointing to the timelessness of the Cuban national spirit as well as to the inevitability of the rebel victory. Moreover, as will become clear in chapter 2 and chapter 4, it is evident from how newsreels and documentaries showed the people "taking over" Havana that these films aimed to communicate a sense of a transformed urban space. As the literal and figurative home of the "party of the people," the city became capable of representing the nation. But that is not to say that Cuba's nation-building project was entirely inclusive. Cuba's active attempt to construct a unified nation-state in cinema did not exclude racial or sexual "others" per se but certainly denied the centrality of such identities.

DESIRING SUBJECTIVITY

Across the periods in this study, some features of the social imaginary that nonfiction film sought to shape (and the image of the nation and peoples therein) remained stable while others transformed. But from the revolutionary fervor of the 1920s in the Soviet Union through the Stalinist 1930s and from the politically and culturally experimental Cuba of the 1960s to the institutionalization policies of the 1970s, a preoccupation with internal transformation remained consistent. While I focus on the effort to shape interiority by filmmakers and revolutionary leaders, studies of both the Soviet Union and Cuba have demonstrated how citizens in each country lived the imperative to internalize these messages.[19] These studies do not aim to recover an authentic self that was repressed by ideology but to understand Soviet and Cuban subjects as being produced by power.

One of the defining efforts of these revolutionary projects was to bring ideology to consciousness. For Marxist revolutionary leaders, ideology was a critical idea that expressed the political consciousness of a class (most often: bourgeois ideology, proletarian ideology) or a group (Bolshevik ideology, "revolutionary" ideology, Marxist ideology). Instead of serving as an unconscious mechanism contributing to individual alienation, as it did in Western capitalist societies, ideology was seen as something that could be learned and felt by thinking and experiencing in an informed way. These efforts, many scholars argue, had a dramatic impact on the formation of individual identity. As Christina Kiaer and Eric Naiman write, "The coming of ideology to consciousness held powerful potential, seeming to promise individuals a magical scientific key to mastering their own destiny as they overcame the forces of oppression."[20] The effort to master ideology certainly had pragmatic aspects, as it contributed to professional advancement and even, at times, to survival. But more than that, what emerges through my analysis of the nonfiction films and the exhibition contexts through which they were engaged is an effort to instill a *desire* for subjecthood.[21] As I detail in part 1, the heightened, public mode of address within the films; the open, public spaces at which many of these screenings took place; and the introduction to and discussion of the films both at the screening venues and in mainstream publications all created a climate in which skilled performances of ideological mastery were sought. This initial foray remained in play throughout the periods under consideration in this book. Whether in urban public squares, workers' clubs, youth organizations, village centers, or even on the celluloid itself, these textual and extratextual dynamics not only strongly encouraged ideologically sound performances but reminded citizens that mastering the nuances of contemporary ideology required persistent vigilance.

That is not to say, however, that these efforts were necessarily successful and that evidence of proper Soviet and Cuban subjectivity was bound to emerge at a later date. But it is to say that these projects urged people to constantly refine their performances. In so doing, they held out promises of becoming part of an ideological community—of *belonging* to a political project—while recognizing their individual limitations. If sustaining desire requires an object always receding from reach, these nonfiction film projects sought to instill the desire for Soviet and Cuban subjectivity by reminding citizens of the standards that Lenin, Stalin, Che, Fidel, Martí, and each of their archetypal heroic workers set— standards to which they always needed to aspire yet by definition could never attain. Vigilance was required, but it was never enough. And, as I describe in each of the chapters, it was required not just of citizen-viewers but of the filmmakers themselves. This is evident both in the urgency embedded in the critical response to their films and in their own writings and remarks.

THE TASK OF FOUNDATION

Having outlined the conceptual and methodological parameters of the book as a whole, I will spend the remainder of the introduction focusing on the challenges of foundation in socialist revolutionary contexts—of the nation-state as a whole, of a national cinema industry, and of a viable nonfiction film project therein.

As Marx famously reminds, all revolutionary socialist leaderships have to account for societies "still stamped with the birthmark" of capitalism.[22] This is in fact one of the features of the first phase of the development of communist society. But the objects (be they political, economic, social, or cultural) and roles leaders chose to appropriate or transform and the manner in which they did so was an issue of ongoing negotiation. In 1917, the year of the Russian Revolution, no established model of socialist revolutionary behavior existed. Russian revolutionary leaders would likely have struggled to project a vision of daily privilege and power for themselves that became so standard in future socialist revolutionary regimes. The debates over what precisely to do with spaces associated with autocratic power (capitalist or not)—the Winter Palace, the Kremlin, and the Bolshoi Ballet being a few of the most notable—demonstrate their uncertainty. The Bolsheviks' decision to move from the recent home of the tsars in Saint Petersburg (the Winter Palace, residence of the tsars for over two centuries) to the previous home of the tsars and seat of the grand dukes in Moscow (the Kremlin) was neither inevitable, nor was the meaning of such a move self-evident. The same can be said about Fidel Castro's decision not to occupy a residence associated with power. His movements between the Hilton Hotel (shortly thereafter renamed Havana Libre) and various locales in and around Havana were pragmatic for a leader in constant and rightful fear of assassination. But they also pointed to a leader situating himself in opposition to the public displays of power and wealth associated with leaders of previous dictatorial regimes. Indeed, there was no natural revolutionary process for the development of socialism in an economically underdeveloped society. It was not at all inevitable that revolutionary leaders would adopt certain spaces and perform recognizable roles.

Hannah Arendt identifies a governing dynamic of stability and transformation when she describes the fundamental challenge revolutionary leaders faced when attempting to create a new order:

> The perplexity consisted in the task of foundation, the setting of a new beginning, which as such seemed to demand violence and violation, the repetition, as it were, of the old legendary crime (Romulus slew Remus, Cain slew Abel) at the beginning of all history. This task of foundation, moreover, was coupled with the task of lawgiving, of devising and imposing upon men a new authority, which, however, had to be designed in such a way that it would fit into the shoes of the old absolute.[23]

Revolutionary leaders, Arendt argues, must create a sense of newness (often through violence) that marks the moment of revolution as transformative, and they must also appropriate an old authority capable of providing the stability they need to realize their vision. This desire to negotiate anew the relationships between rupture and tradition and between national, supranational, and international identities gets to the core of the effort to build a new socialist post-revolutionary, and simultaneously *modern*, identity.

Masha Salazkina distinguishes the significance of the specific intentionality of this rupture in these modern post-revolutionary contexts:

> Their situation testified to the possibility of change that came with modernity, and even to the possibility of abrupt, revolutionary change, a rupture in the supposed logic of history brought about as an exercise in the will of the people rather than as some product of involuntary historical change thrown up by events such as invasion, war, or economic depression. It was the technostructure of communication, transportation, and the projection of the senses in various artificial media, all of them the result of intellectual invention, that made this kind of intentional rupture possible only in the modern age.[24]

This challenge—between intentional revolutionary rupture and historical stability—drove film projects and informed the answers to so many of the questions revolutionary leaders faced when trying to create not just a new nation-state but a new film industry and culture within it. Leaders had to ask: What is the political nature of the revolution, and how can cinema in general and nonfiction cinema in particular contribute to its realization? The answers to these questions were based in part on political and aesthetic philosophy and in part on the infrastructure in place at the moment of revolutionary transformation. But the answers are never self-evident and the conditions constantly in flux.

CINEMA BUILDING

Although revolutionary leaders' particular appropriation of bourgeois spaces and roles was not a necessary result of the assumption of power, the issue of how to deal with such resources was a question all revolutionary leaderships faced. And it applied not only to material resources but to human ones as well. This is perhaps especially true of cultural policy. Sheila Fitzpatrick argues that the major predicament facing the Bolsheviks when it came to cultural policy was a "dilemma of identity—to be or not to be proletarian—and, if to be proletarian, how."[25] In this regard, the Bolshevik Party was concerned about the domination of the cultural sphere by the intelligentsia, fearing that their bourgeois backgrounds and social attitudes would preclude the realization of a true proletarian culture. (For the intelligentsia, the issue concerned their freedom versus the fear of party autocracy.) Fitzpatrick claims that throughout most of the 1920s, the state decided that it needed the cultural services of the intelligentsia and would be willing to pay for them. Inherited culture and inherited skills had to be recognized. Specialists had to be supervised but not harassed. In time, the state hoped, a new authentic proletarian intelligentsia would emerge to replace them.

What Fitzpatrick describes as the Soviet government's "soft line"[26] toward culture is echoed in many initial post-revolutionary socialist governments' cultural policies. Building a new national cinema, however, poses a unique set of challenges, including necessitating a more active role by the government. As an industrial art, cinema requires a level of financial and organizational investment above that of more traditional arts (literature, painting, and sculpture, for example). States needed to establish standards for determining in whom to invest (youth versus established voices), in what models of production, circulation, and exhibition to invest (urban focus, theater-centered, fiction film versus peasant and worker focus, non-theatrical, experimental and nonfiction genres), in what technical equipment to invest, and to what ends. The debates over these decisions were shaped by each context's pre-revolutionary cinema industry, viewing practices, and circulation networks.

There was considerable variation in infrastructure across these contexts. Russia had a well-established tradition of private film production at the time of the revolution. It produced approximately 1,600 fiction films and screened films in 2,000 to 4,000 cinemas.[27] Cuba had produced very few films independently but in fact had the highest per capita filmgoing population in Latin America at the time of the revolution. It averaged a staggering one and a half million attendees per week (in a country of just under seven million people) despite having a primarily rural population.[28] Cuba's foremost production activity was as an exotic locale for Hollywood and Mexican producers, who controlled production, distribution, and exhibition on the island for most of the pre-revolutionary period.

One of the additional challenges facing Soviet leaders attempting to build the cinema industry was establishing a network of cinematic production and distribution that reflected both changing dynamics between center and periphery and their desire to balance promoting supranational (Soviet) and national (Russian, Ukrainian, and Georgian, for example) identities. Their multiple production centers and regional film agencies reflected these dynamics.[29] Moreover, both Soviet and Cuban leaders sought to reach their substantial rural populations by extensively and urgently developing mobile film units immediately after the revolution.

The infrastructural contexts these governments inherited shaped but did not determine the directions cinema took. Governments needed to decide what relationship they wanted the state and the party to have with film as an industry and as a cultural practice. The issue of nationalization was paramount. They had to evaluate whether nationalizing the film industry was necessary and, if so, how quickly it could be accomplished and at what cost. If they eliminated private production, distribution, and exhibition, in whose hands would power be placed? How would the industry be organized, vertically and horizontally? Would a nationalized film industry be subject to party demands or only to that of the representative agency? I will provide the answers to some of these questions in turn.

In the Soviet Union, Lenin had no plans to take over the film industry prior to assuming power, and once he did, there was little initiative to create a national system of state-run cinema. Twenty months later, Vance Kepley argues, he adopted a nationalization decree in response to events originating at the grassroots level and did so more for pragmatic than ideological purposes. Though intrigued by the possibility of a state-run cinema industry (especially the pedagogical aspect), neither Nadezhda Krupskaia (Lenin's wife and deputy commissar of Narkompros—the People's Commissariat of Enlightenment—in 1918) nor Anatoli Lunacharsky (commissar of Narkompros from 1917 to 1929) thought the administration had the power or skill to manage it effectively. Therefore, they established a system of authority in the initial years that was quite diffuse. A cinema committee in charge of producing educational and agitational films answered to its local commissariat, while another agency, the Central Executive Committee, controlled the agit-train production, an area assumed to require national coordination.[30] In the early years, these measures still did not ensure control, especially over the peripheral regions. The decree was a response to that challenge. However, the decree itself gave the government only the option to seize control of units; it did not automatically transfer ownership to the state. As a result, the state most often nationalized film units that had failed or been abandoned.[31]

Whereas the Bolsheviks had not prioritized a film industry systematically controlled by the government in the time leading up to the revolution, Cuban revolutionary leaders envisioned a centralized structure and took steps to implement it right away. The founding of ICAIC on March 24, 1959, is often cited as the first cultural act of the revolutionary government. ICAIC and the other major cultural institutions such as Dirección de Cultura, Casa de las Américas, and the Unión Nacional de Escritores y Artistas Cubanos had considerable power and answered directly to the government without a ministry of culture as an intermediary. The government was able to put in place and maintain such a structure on account of the relatively small size of the island, its uninationality, the fact that they had practically no established production infrastructure with which to deal, and their ability to mobilize preexisting revolutionary cultural collectives to organize activities. Moreover, their experiences shaping public opinion through mass communications during the revolutionary struggle had convinced them that the effort was worthwhile. But the Cubans paid much more explicit attention to balancing the artistic with their industrial and propagandistic goals than did many socialist revolutionary governments (for example, China and Yugoslavia). This commitment to artistic individuality as well as to the needs of the collective (as film workers and as audience) was reflected in the original organizational structure of ICAIC, which remained in place until 1975. "Artistic Programming" was a separate department from "Studios and Labor," "Technical Processes," and "Finances."

Lenin immediately established his faith in the propagandistic and agitational value of cinema. His pragmatic approach to industry nationalization, film importation, and private investment points to his belief in cinema's eventual financial sustainability despite the extraordinary shortages of the immediate post-revolutionary years.[32] The confidence that cinema was not only self-sustaining but held the potential to produce profits (and therefore sustain other cultural practices) pervaded both cases.

Financial viability, however, was not necessarily assumed for non-fiction film. Nonfiction film has a rich tradition of state sponsorship and has been held up consistently as having the power to shape public opinion.[33] But it has only rarely realized comparatively high profits or been expected to do so. Profitability depends, in part, on where nonfiction film is located institutionally. And that determination derives from attitudes about the nature and purpose of nonfiction film. Is it primarily a journalistic or an artistic practice?[34] Are newsreels the former and documentaries the latter? Are they commercially viable or only as part of a program that involves a fiction film? The institutional locations of nonfiction films influence their potential profitability as well as the degree of control the party and the state agency might wish to exert. Certainly both organs are more likely to limit the topical, methodological, political, and aesthetic flexibility of nonfiction film if they are understood as primarily or solely vehicles for communicating state priorities.

As a whole, these policy and organizational decisions both constitute and are constituted by beliefs about what cinema (and nonfiction film in particular) is, what it can do that is unique, and what leaders want it to achieve. Cultural leaders, state officials, critics, and producers debated these issues, constantly addressing and redefining the differences across cinema genres as well as between cinema and other cultural practices. They debated not only the essences of particular film genres but also the appropriate aesthetics and methods of production, circulation, and criticism for achieving their political-cultural ends.

For many proponents of nonfiction film, especially those committed to documentary, feature-length narrative fiction film became the primary object against which to situate their practice. They located their work in relation both to the dominant pre-revolutionary fiction films (Western or regional) that circulated in their countries and, to varying degrees, to the contemporary popular fiction films being produced within the country or region. Dziga Vertov, for one, vigorously promoted the value of nonfiction over fiction. He argued not only for nonfiction to receive considerable financial and institutional support but also for it to replace fiction film entirely. Like their Soviet predecessors, Cuban cultural workers at ICAIC privileged nonfiction film production for its economic efficiency and attention to material reality. The immediacy and authenticity of nonfiction film could expose the falsity of fiction film in the way that Marxism brought to light the ideological deceptiveness of Western capitalism. And it could do so by means of an affordable, entertaining practice.

But that is not to say that most nonfiction film supporters considered the truthfulness of their films as an automatic result of shooting moving images of the real world. Rather, the prominent Soviet and Cuban film workers saw nonfiction film truth as being constructed or, at minimum, actively revealed. As I detail in chapters 3 and 4, reflexive awareness of their own discursive authority is evident throughout Vertov's work, especially beginning with his *Kino-Pravda* newsreel series (1922–1925), and it is also a central premise of Álvarez's entire oeuvre. Moreover, they continually situated their work in relation to developments in other artistic practices—be it literature, painting, or music—and worked with writers, painters, and musicians to produce their work. In the Soviet Union, Vertov worked closely with Aleksandr Rodchenko on his intertitle design, and Esfir Shub worked on scripts with Viktor Shklovsky. In

Cuba, Álvarez worked directly with, among others, the composer Leo Brouwer.

Whereas feature-length fiction film was a touchstone against which nonfiction film workers consistently located themselves, they also explicitly articulated their projects in relation to journalism. Both Vertov and Álvarez called attention to their journalistic impulses while challenging the disinterested objectivity of established journalism. Jeremy Hicks asserts that Vertov's initial innovations were less the product of an inspired genius than a position "inconceivable outside the context of the Bolshevik approach to journalism."[35] Álvarez himself said, "I'm a journalist above all. My first vocation, before I thought about film, was journalism. And I've always craved to be doing journalism. I stumbled upon film and found out how to use it journalistically."[36] These filmmakers aligned themselves with the exhortatory tone and persuasive approach evident in the alternative journalist models each country adopted. They sought to shape the attitudes of the collective and did so avowedly. In part 1 and part 2, I account for these self-assertions while suggesting that the journalistic framework—even the alternative model on which Hicks focuses—might prove more limiting than productive. Rather than solely emphasizing reportage or the informational element, I argue that understanding how these projects endeavor to shape social, geographical, and political imaginaries accounts for the depth and breadth of their production and circulation practices.

The shape both newsreels and documentaries took in the Soviet Union and Cuba during these periods was informed not just by cultural workers' conceptions of nonfiction media but by pragmatic concerns as well. Shortages of film stock and human resources, underdeveloped transportation infrastructures, and large rural populations were just a few factors that challenged nonfiction film's potential as a timely, viable source of news information for citizens. The thematic interrelation of events and the self-conscious rhetorics that became the hallmark of these films both served as a valuable alternative to so much newspaper journalism and created the conditions for new uses of nonfiction film material.

But just because there was overlap in the conceptual approaches to representing the real world does not mean that documentaries and newsreels maintained stable relationships with each other in the decades immediately following the revolutions. Quite the opposite occurred. The common narrative of the development of the Soviet and Cuban nonfiction film describes the flowering of the newsreel in the work of Vertov and Álvarez until the differences between it and the feature documentaries they produced began to wane. Thematic interrelation, experimental audiovisuals, and rhetorical complexity emerged out of the less ideologically productive and aesthetically sophisticated newsreel practices of the initial post-revolutionary moment. To a certain extent, this narrative holds true. Vertov's *Kino-Pravda* newsreel series exhibits the first signs of the Vertov (as documentary filmmaker) we know today. And Álvarez's first few international festival award-winning documentaries (*Ciclón*, 1963, and *Now*, 1965) were both produced as newsreels. But I will argue that closer attention to these traditions demonstrates a multiplicity of aesthetics and purposes in these series over time, with the complexity of newsreel rhetoric and structure occasionally scaled back.

None of the distinctions now familiar to producers and viewers of newsreels and documentaries were in place at the time Vertov began to make films. Bill Nichols and Jeremy Hicks each have argued that Vertov was instrumental in defining the documentary by developing a distinct nonfiction film practice out of a newsreel tradition.[37] John MacKay likewise points to Vertov's continued relevance, remarking, "A striking feature of Vertov's films is the frequency with which they bring us almost immediately to the conceptual knot at the center of documentary theory and practice: the tension between relatively autonomous 'indexical traces of a real past,' and 'the control of pastness,' the sequencing and signifying work performed upon those (photographic) traces."[38] Álvarez is one of a number of directors who has carried forth the radical nonfiction film tradition.[39] While the relation between rhetorical complexity, stylistic innovation, and narrative structure in newsreels and documentaries respectively waxed and waned in the Soviet Union and Cuba, the different forms almost always functioned complementarily. The directions they took were shaped by the set of beliefs these practitioners, critics, and audiences held about the meanings these mediums convey. In other words, the dynamics between newsreels and documentaries both relied on and informed people's media ideologies.

COLLECTIVITY AND MOBILITY IN THE
NONFICTION FILM IMAGINATION

The Soviet and Cuban cases exhibit the complexity of attempting to shape a new imaginary of the nation (or "supranation") through media and the people's relation to it. But while the nation and its national people may be an exemplary case of modern social imaginary, other cases of social imaginary "are not articulated as a *we* but are third person objectifications of society."[40] Cuban newsreels and documentaries of the post-revolutionary period exhibit a dialectic between the first-person plural and third-person form of address.

Charles Taylor argues that this dynamic is in fact one of the features of modern social imaginaries. Subjects begin to see themselves as *belonging* to new kinds of collective agency and as being able to grasp society as an *objectified* set of processes. These two perspectives—feeling connected to this society wherein collective actions can have effects and being able to dissociate so that one can view society as a set of identifiable categories, each governed by a set of laws—have increasingly come to be seen as being incompatible. But Taylor insists that "these two standpoints cannot be dissociated. They are coeval; they belong to the same range of imaginings that derive from the modern moral order."[41] In this book, I analyze the shifting dynamics between the effort to communicate subjective belonging and objectified processes so as to better understand the form of social imaginary being sought at a given time.

In the immediate post-revolutionary moment, nonfiction films sought to shape new social imaginaries by speaking to these perspectives. However, they did so rather unevenly, with significantly more attention on sparking a sense of belonging to new kinds of collective agency. Whereas newsreels and documentaries participated in the broader effort to inspire radical changes in individual and collective identity, their most distinctive purpose during this period was to forge a space for the imagination of collective action. In the second period, select filmmakers became able to communicate simultaneously the sense of belonging to a collective capable of action and the objective qualities of a set of processes. The films of this first period, however, focused more on the activation of a collective imagination and less on the objectification of political and social categories. In both the Soviet Union and Cuba, the initial post-revolutionary moment was primarily concerned with establishing reliable spaces of communication so that the public could begin to imagine itself as a public, as a collective force, one that could act together but under the guidance of a new leadership.

What is distinctive about these initial moments (and perhaps what marks them as Marxist in their revolutionary endeavor) is that the films and their circulation through public space do not just visualize a collective; they activate the process of visualizing a collective. They do not just offer examples of new engagements with urban space, to mark one of the foremost examples; they activate the process of imagining moving differently through urban space. In turn, they become part of an initial effort, as I discussed above, of bringing ideology to consciousness.

But in addition to aiming to dramatically transform individual identity, they also refigured the individual's role in relation to the collectivity as they sought to reimagine the alignments that defined the collectivity. Nonfiction films participate in the process of bringing ideology to consciousness through their textual and extratextual mechanisms. At times this process is written on the filmstrip itself. At other times, it is realized through various marketing, exhibition, and distribution practices. These are as diverse as newly stylized movie posters in transformed public spaces, carefully chosen spaces of exhibition (often a labor union hall or a village edifice associated with political education), and leaders verbally framing the films themselves. As such, viewers are urged constantly to reassess their roles in the larger community and the expected actions that accompany those roles. Doing so manifests a recognition that their subjectivity is under surveillance. Thus, viewers do not simply locate themselves in relation to larger publics; they do so with the knowledge that such acts of location have a new political valence.

The two chapters in part 1 that follow outline an account of the forms of social imaginary that were sought through newsreel and documentary circulation in the initial post-revolutionary moments in the Soviet Union and Cuba. They sketch the overlapping effort to project, model, and instill ways of understanding and acting in the new revolutionary social world. This involved communicating the vision of a new collectivity with a basic sense of its goals and the requirements necessary to achieve those goals. The effort to imagine a new collectivity revolves most consistently around films, segments, and discussions of youth; rural/urban divides; internal and external enemies/comrades; and public performances such as parades, festivals, and speeches. Communicating the goals of revolutionary action requires reference to specific events and the social processes underlying them. Films most commonly invoked the goals by depicting shortages of human and material resources; natural disasters; and images of war/battle, broadly conceived. But whereas in the second period, these processes and the hermeneutics required to comprehend them are more fully elaborated, in the first stage this larger scope is only alluded to, not explained. That is not to say that filmmakers, critics, and political officials did not think viewers needed to understand the objective categories to which they referred in the films. Rather, they relied on the idea that viewers would obtain this information extratextually, either through public discussions or other media forms. Last, achieving these goals was possible by embracing two seemingly contradictory positions. First, the collective was a powerful, progressive force moving inevitably and creatively toward full liberation. Second, this power required direction from a vanguard with the moral authority, knowledge, and experience to lead.

In the nonfiction film project, however, these imaginaries were ultimately indissociable from the charge to reimagine selfhood. The decisive goal of these projects was not only to participate in the accelerated development of subject construction but also to instill the desire for Soviet and Cuban subjectivity. The newsreels and documentaries in the immediate post-revolutionary years are one example of the inauguration of that effort.

Chapters 3 and 4 from part 2 examine the subsequent post-revolutionary moment, a time in which a new set of socioeconomic and security challenges prompted a refining of the initially promoted social and geographical imaginations. If the first moment was characterized by the need to establish viable channels and acceptable practices of communication so as to forge a space for the imagination of collective action, this second moment developed further the relationship between collective action and individual identity. This period saw the increasing confluence of newsreel and documentary projects, as Vertov and Álvarez mobilized rapid montage, photographic trickery, expressive titling, and complex structuration with the aim of transforming the intellectual, perceptual, and moral lives of the viewer. These experiments manifested new nonfiction cinematic languages concerned with communicating revolutionary experience, inciting emotion, and modeling dialectical thought. If in the first period nonfiction filmmakers lacked the means by which to communicate social categories and processes, in the second period they developed new aesthetic strategies to expand the range of nonfiction film thought and sensorial experience. The films of this period urge new national, supranational, and international alignments; offer lessons in Marxist political economy (at the domestic and international/imperialist levels); establish a new hermeneutics of media culture; and, perhaps most significant, provide new understandings of the individual's role as a laboring citizen. By projecting the transference of revolutionary energy into the production sphere in an all-out effort to increase industrial and agricultural efficiency, these projects were thought capable of transforming citizens' work ethics and inspiring them to labor beyond traditional means.

Part 3 marks the moment in post-revolutionary socialist contexts in which leaders appear to have recognized that the previous communication strategies were not working as they and the revolutionary artists had assumed. Leaders, critics, and artists such as Shub and Álvarez responded by privileging a new rhetorical clarity, one that indicated a shift in the objects of transformation. Rather than aiming to transform perception or fundamental modes of thought, nonfiction cinema sought to transform how viewers read history. In the Cuban newsreels, this manifested in a more commemorative practice, one that celebrated transhistorical revolutionary achievements, and in lauding contemporary cultural production. In both Soviet and Cuban documentaries, this was realized by embracing new forms of historical discourse that relied on more restrained approaches to directorial expressivity: compilation documentary in the Soviet Union and chronicle films in Cuba. Whereas at first glance these films appear less radical than their predecessors, closer examination reveals something different. Embracing directorial restraints serves not to foreclose the possibility of expansive meaning but relocates it and transforms the process by which audiences engage texts and critically engage the material world.

NOTES ON TERMINOLOGY AND MATERIAL ACCESS

I have chosen to describe these films and their contexts as "post-revolutionary." One could certainly make the case that these are in fact "revolutionary" films produced in a "revolutionary" context. The point would echo Lenin's and Castro's position that the transfer of power does not "make" a socialist revolution. These films *are* revolutionary cinema because they are both *seen to be* and *articulated as* revolutionary. They did not prepare the groundwork for a transfer of power but participated in the process and contributed to making the revolution a reality. If a revolution does not sustain, history does not view it as a revolution but as a temporary coup. My use of the prefix "post" functions to describe a historical time period and to point toward some of the most critical questions I am hoping to answer about the relationship between cinema and the historical period following revolutions. For example, what *sustains* after the revolution? To what discourses do utopian longings attach? How are the utopian aspirations modified? How can nonfiction film contribute to the pragmatics of nation-building and socialist building, and, in so doing, how must they be seen to forge a new aesthetic (subject-object) relation between film and audience? The goal is to focus attention not just on the new, the utopian, and the revolutionary but simultaneously on the stable, the pragmatic, and the sustainable. Thinking about the "post" alongside the "revolution" figures the answers to these questions in a mutually determining rather than a mutually excluding framework.

I am also using "nonfiction" film as a term to categorize newsreels and documentaries. I do so in part because they were seen by both Soviets and Cubans as having related political, cultural, and social purposes. This was especially true in the first two periods. The Soviets in fact referred to both as "non-played" films; it was one of the ways to distinguish them from their main rival, "played" film.[42] Both Soviet and Cuban films incorporated pedagogical, scientific, and even industrial purposes and subjects. But in using the term I am not claiming to account for the totality of educational, scientific, and industrial films existing in the Soviet Union and Cuba during the period of study. I use it primarily because we are still developing a sufficient vocabulary for distinguishing these subgenres of nonfiction film both individually and in groupings. But I do believe that such efforts (and they are underway) are important for the field of documentary studies and for cinema and media studies as a discipline. It is a direction that requires thinking in historically rigorous ways about production contexts, film gauges, sponsorship, exhibition contexts, targeted audiences, and textuality, to name just a few issues. I hope that this book contributes to that body of work.

The reader will notice that I have chosen to translate certain film titles (*Shagai Soviet!* to *Stride, Soviet!*) but left others transliterated (*Kino-Nedelia, Kino-Pravda*) or untranslated (*Hanoi, martes 13*). My decision to do so derives from my experience with how people have been using the titles in written scholarship, in conference presentations, and in casual conversation. For example, scholars, whether native Russian speakers or not, most often refer to Vertov's newsreels either as *Kino-Nedelia* or *Kino-Pravda,* not as "Cine-Week" or "Film-Week" or "Cine-Truth" or "Film-Truth." Similarly, Álvarez's first award-winning documentary is repeatedly referred to as *Ciclón,* not "Hurricane."

Post-Revolution Nonfiction Film draws on viewings of approximately two hundred films and incorporates material written in Russian and Spanish as well as in English. Unless otherwise noted, the translations are mine. The primary archival research was carried out at the Österreichisches Filmmuseum in Vienna and the Cuban Institute of Cinematographic Art and Industry in Havana. For my study of the Soviet films, I had access to all of Vertov's and Shub's films that are currently available, including research copies of all but a few of Vertov's *Kino-Pravda* issues. At ICAIC, I had the opportunity to screen all of Álvarez's documentaries from the period and obtained research copies of most of them.[43] My access to newsreels was more limited. I was not allowed to choose topics. ICAIC gave me the opportunity to view five to six newsreels for each of the years under consideration, and I was granted research copies of some. I elected to view consecutive issues, which I believed would give me as strong a grasp of their focuses and forms as possible, given the restrictions. The arguments that I make about Cuban newsreels are informed by my more limited access. In addition, the reader will notice that at times I refer to a year of a newsreel issue and at times I refer to an actual newsreel issue number in addition to the year. When I was granted the issue number and was confident of the accuracy of the number, I used it. When I was not, I simply referred to the year of production.

PART ONE

ONE

Kino-Nedelia, Early Documentary, and the Performance of a New Collective, 1917–1921

TAKE ONE

The Red Star Literary-Instructional Agit-Steamer of the All-Russia Central Executive Committee was a propaganda ship that traveled down the Volga River in 1919. It was also the name (without question a most unwieldy one!) of a two-reel film that Dziga Vertov made in accordance with its voyage. *Red Star* is a political travelogue that follows the ship as it spreads propaganda in towns and villages along the river. The ship itself was a multipurpose vessel: it carried movie-barge; it was equipped with a radio station tuned to the national news service; it exchanged goods made in Moscow for peasants' grain; and it handed out propagandistic literature. Moreover, the ship was itself a piece of propaganda, as it was covered in banners and marquees championing political slogans.

To emphasize the importance of the mission, the *Red Star* bore celebrity leaders who would speak to citizens gathered along the way. Among the figures were Nadezhda Krupskaia (Lenin's wife) and Viatcheslav Molotov (Stalin's future minister of foreign affairs). The film captures the leaders in private moments—writing speeches, enjoying the sights, or conversing with comrades—and in public moments as they deliver speeches to crowds. In these latter cases, the emphasis is less on the individual speaking than on the crowd gathered. Close-ups of the speakers focusing on gestures quickly give way to long shots from the vantage point of, and covering, the crowd. The speech coverage, the handing out of propagandistic literature, and the political slogans marking the vessel contribute to the notion that the film is actually less about the content of the agit-prop than it is celebrating the propagandistic effort itself. It does not celebrate a speech; it celebrates speechmaking. It does not highlight a propagandistic message; it highlights propaganda.

But the film also visualizes the impact of the steamer on the populations it encounters. Two sequences in particular aim to demonstrate growing support for the Bolsheviks. The first is a striking scene of the ship leaving a large village. As it pulls away from shore, it appears that the *Red Star* has amassed hordes of new passengers. It is not clear why. Perhaps the captain agreed to transport locals down the river? Perhaps they just wanted to watch a film on board? Whatever the reason, the ship has apparently increased in population and energy. People wave good-bye, chat, and laugh. The vessel is full of vivacity and is reminiscent of a traveling show bringing joy to a town and moving on after its brief stay. It has a carnivalesque feel. Bolshevik propaganda appears not as a tedious thing but as an inevitable and pleasurable force sweeping the nation.

If this first sequence indicates the energy and optimism the film hopes to associate with Bolshevism, an additional example points to the organizational unity of the masses. Following a speech to a large crowd of people gathered on a hillside, we see a long shot of the group descending the hill. The shot is framed so that we see them gradually coming together as they make their way in organized yet urgent fashion between two obstacles (perhaps boulders, it is unclear), that cover the bottom left-hand and right-hand sides of the frame. Had Vertov immediately cut away from the scene, we would probably not have paid the sequence any attention. Instead, after slightly reframing, he cuts back to the same shot as the crowd has increased in density. Finally, he cuts to another slightly reframed image of the remnants of the crowd as the lingerers hustle to make their way down the bottom of the hill and along the path. In each instance, the condensed space does not have a suffocating effect on the crowd. The people convene in an organized fashion, with purpose and discipline. They adjust their personal positions to accommodate others. The cumulative effect of the three shots, like the previous scene of the people on the ship, is a sense of the inevitability of this national-ideological movement. It comes across not as an oppressive force but as an invitation, offering people a place on board, promising pleasure, excitement, and camaraderie, even as it requires a level of discipline and organization required for its efficacy. But it also implies a warning not to get left behind.

SHORT TAKE TWO

A complementary example comes in a sequence from a Swedish compilation film titled *Rysk Journal* (Russian newsreel). It may have been taken from another Vertov travelogue—the 1921 one-reel film *The Agit-Train of the All-Russia Central Executive Committee*—but this is not clear.[1] The film shows revolutionary leaders on a "kino-train," an agit-train equipped with a film camera and projector, arriving at a small village, handing out propagandistic literature, and speaking to the assembled crowds. Peasants peruse the literature, gaze at the train, and stare at the camera. When the train departs, newspapers are tossed from the window. The cameraman leans out the window, capturing on film the newspapers, which appear to have sprouted wings, as they float gently in the air. Peasants chase the train, reaching for the newspapers. One man snatches an issue out of the air.

The urgency with which the peasants pursue the newspapers speaks to nonfiction cinema's typical and unique role in the Russian/Soviet nation-building project. Like other nation-building endeavors, these films are examples of efforts by nonfiction filmmakers to communicate the transformation of life under the new Bolshevik leadership. They point to new peasant/worker, rural/urban, and national/transnational/global alliances. They communicate core agitational messages to a wide population. And they aim to create the new idea of a national collective—the kino-train film isolates the newspaper, which Benedict Anderson has demonstrated is the archetypal symbol of national belonging. In other words, they attempt the neat trick of showing that the nation has emerged while simultaneously calling it into being.

These two films—*Red Star* and *Rysk Journal*—highlight nonfiction film's uniqueness within the nation-building project. The peasants in these films are not static exemplars of new citizenries. Rather, their eager pursuit of the newspaper and longing to be on board the *Red Star* underscore twin aspects of the immediate post-revolutionary nonfiction film period. First, they call attention to an active effort to publicly perform citizenship. That is not to claim these performances as falsifications but to recognize—as the films themselves make plain—that acts of citizenship are increasingly visualized and visualizable. Second, they are not bland descriptions of participating in a collective. These films articulate the *sensible impact* of becoming part of a collective and participating in the effort to newly shape political, economic, social, and cultural life.[2]

How, then, are we to understand them as films with specific political purposes? Georgi Plekhanov distinguishes agitation from propaganda by claiming that propaganda is an attempt to communicate comprehensive explanations, often understandable only by a select portion of the population. At the turn of the century (and at the time of the Russian Revolution), it was associated with the written word and seen as a long-term process. In contrast, agitation presented a few ideas to a much wider population with the goal of rousing them to action.[3] It was associated with the spoken word and seen as a short-term process. Within this framework, the Russian/Soviet nonfiction films of the first period are more agitational than propagandistic. Vertov and other filmmakers had not yet developed the language to communicate cinematically the more sophisticated political, social, and even scientific concepts they eventually would. In fact, the most common way of describing the difference between Vertov's early work (the *Kino-Nedelia* series and his early documentaries from the late 1910s and early 1920s) and his more mature efforts (beginning with issues of *Kino-Pravda* and moving through his silent feature documentaries) is to locate the shift from reportage to documentary, or, as Jeremy Hicks describes it, from recording an already existing causal relation to creating it through editing.[4] From the vantage of the later films, these early films are described by scholars as striking in their lack of inventiveness and their passivity in relation to the material world.[5] But even if scholars are correct in claiming that this is the period "before Vertov became the Vertov we now know," as Philip

Rosen has described it,[6] I want to argue that marking these early films simply as reportage forecloses consideration of some of the productive capacities of the films, namely their effort to shape subjectivities and, in turn, build citizenries by projecting, modeling, and instilling new visions of collectivity.

The topics of these films and the rhetorics they employ seek to provide a foundation for the development of change in a socialist society. In this chapter, I argue that the films of the first period (1917–1921), conditioned by the circulatory practices and political-industrial context, sought to activate a collective imagination by forging a cinematic space for the imagination of collective action. Whereas the kino-train and agit-steamer are metonyms of these imaginary collective spaces, not all of the films are so explicit in their effort to bring Soviet ideology to consciousness. But even if agitation is understood as a limited intellectual engagement and thought to be valuable only for short-term practical goals, its effects on the imagination are far more lasting than Plekhanov's framework allows. The accumulation of moving images of a new Russian/Soviet citizenry, with transformed alignments and purposes, collecting and moving anew through urban spaces, wrought a powerful impact on the viewing subject's imagination. Combined with exhibition contexts in which these films were explicitly framed by a leadership both on display and available to reflection, they sought simultaneously to visualize the collectivity and to instill a desire for membership in that collectivity while making the effort itself an object of constant reflection.

PRE-REVOLUTIONARY NONFICTION FILM

The first regularly produced and distributed Russian newsreel was launched in 1908 by the State Duma's official photographer, Alexander Drankov. Only fragments of two issues remain. The material gives the impression that, like most foreign newsreel production the world over, many of the events were faked. Russian audiences displayed an immediate affinity for nonfiction film, and production increased accordingly. Most of the 1,800 newsreel films that were issued between 1907 and 1914 (the beginning of World War I) captured everyday life and official events throughout the empire. Considerable attention was paid to the grand occasions of the imperial state, notably the Romanovs' jubilee celebrations in the spring of 1913.[7]

During the war (1914–1917), the Skobelev Committee was appointed by the tsar to produce and distribute newsreels that reported on the fighting. The films focused on the Western Front in an attempt to rouse support for the war. However, there was little firsthand material to work with, and films regularly contained inserted dramatic footage.[8] But there were also numerous examples of films primarily concerned with identifying people, places, and events without drama or extensive description. The evidentiary capacity of nonfiction film was seemingly sufficient to attain the producers' objectives.[9]

While the Skobelev Committee did not cover the events of the February Revolution that overthrew the tsar, the Provisional Government immediately employed the committee to produce the newly established newsreel series *Free Russia,* with the hopes of using nonfiction film as a propaganda tool. By May, the series had become an aggressive vehicle for pro–Provisional Government propaganda, highlighting demonstrations against the Bolsheviks, solidarity with foreign governments, and Aleksandr Kerensky's military and civilian support. But owing to the combination of labor disputes, poor organization, and power shortages, there was little officially sponsored production, and private companies continued to profit from nonfiction film production.[10]

Upon seizing power, the Bolsheviks immediately sought to exploit the propagandistic potential of nonfiction film. Krupskaia was appointed the first head of the cinema subsection of the People's Commissariat (Narkompros), demonstrating the party's commitment to the medium. The commissariat did not immediately nationalize the industry for fear that doing so would alienate private industry and further contribute to the stock, equipment, and expertise shortage. Under the leadership of Grigory Boltiansky, a cameraman sympathetic to the Bolsheviks who worked during the Provisional Government's stint in power, the Skobelev Committee shifted *Free Russia* to a pro-Bolshevik stance. The importance of the series was short-lived, however. As the center of power shifted from Petrograd to Moscow, Anatoli Lunacharsky, head of the Commissariat of Enlightenment, established a newsreel section of the newly founded Moscow Cinema Committee.

He appointed Mikhail Koltsov to lead the division and create a weekly newsreel titled *Kino-Nedelia*. It was Koltsov who gave a young Dziga Vertov his first job in the cinema, offering him a position as a clerk in the spring of 1918.

BEGINNING TO SPIN

Dziga Vertov was born Denis Arkadievich Kaufman in Bialystok, Poland, then part of Russia, on January 2, 1896. He had two brothers, Mikhail (Moisei) and Boris Kaufman. His father was a bookstore owner, his mother a librarian. By the age of ten, Vertov began writing poetry and novels. He loved music, attending the Bialystok music school from 1912 to 1915, and was fascinated by science. In 1915, Vertov fled with his family to Moscow in order to escape the German onslaught in Poland. Boris was sent to France, Mikhail was drafted, and Dziga, exempted from military duty due to his chronic lung disease, studied law in Moscow and then psychoneurology in Petrograd.

It was in Petrograd that Vertov first connected with the Russian avant-garde that included such figures as Osip Brik, Aleksandr Rodchenko, and Vladimir Mayakovsky. The Russian Futurists, Vertov included, would have been familiar with the writings of the Italian Futurists. Filippo Marinetti's manifestos were distributed widely in Russia prior to his controversial visit in 1914. How Russian Futurism differed from Italian Futurism is cause for considerable debate. What seems clear is that both movements were interested in speed, youth, dynamism, and action. They were fascinated with the effects of motion and rejected conventional confines of space and time and any sort of contained or closed forms. They sought to shock bourgeois sensibilities by bringing the street into poetry, painting, and cinema. They were interested in the urban and the everyday, the formally experimental, and the use of mathematical and musical symbols. While absorbed with the energy of the contemporary moment, the Russians maintained links to the past and perhaps possessed more insight into the relation between aesthetic theory and radical politics than did the Italians. Rather than abandoning the past with its images, icons, and myths, they sought to transform them. The notion that producing anything new required working through the old undergirds most modernist Russian aesthetic thinking. Constructing new meaning in art required transforming older and deeply embedded epistemologies and habits. Politically, for the Italian Futurists, the revolutionary essence led to a reactionary politics linked to fascism and aggressive nationalism, while Russian Futurism immediately became linked with communism.

By 1917, the year of Vertov's arrival in Petrograd, the Russian Futurist movement had splintered into a number of factions. One of the dominant blocs was the Cubo-Futurist movement, led by David Burliuk and the two leading Russian modernist poets, Vladimir Mayakovsky and Velimir Khlebnikov. Cubo-Futurists sought to challenge the boundaries established by older artistic forms. They contended that Symbolist and Realist transcendentalism, eternalism, mysticism, religiosity, and psychologism reduced the meaning-making potential of art. Those aesthetic practices, they argued, trapped society in a bourgeois mentality and limited meaning to the semantic content of the word. In its place they sought to insert a "pure" form of word or image, one that was immediate, concrete, and actual. They felt that the verbal texture of the word, with its "pure" sound, could produce a liberating meaning, one capable of connecting to and forging a "New Age."[11]

Combining his childhood interest in sound with new Futurist conceptions of art, Vertov created a "Laboratory of Sound" in his room in Petrograd. There, he experimented with recording sounds in a straightforward manner, breaking them down into their smallest components and reediting them into a complete whole. As Seth Feldman argues, "in so doing, he was engaged in what was probably the first use of a recording device to compose a musical work."[12] Feldman concludes that Vertov's experiments in his "Laboratory of Sound" indicate not only his "continuing interest in editing but also a desire for the recording of non-staged reality that was to be fundamental to his later aesthetics." Moreover, "Vertov's insistence on real rather than imitated sound was, on the whole, far more characteristic of Russian Futurism's [compared to Italian Futurism's] demand for actuality."[13] It is with this aesthetic-theoretical foundation that Vertov, who had just the year before changed his name from Denis Kaufman to Dziga Vertov,[14] met Mikhail Koltsov and began his work in cinema.

THE NEW REVOLUTIONARY FILM INDUSTRY
AND THE BIRTH OF THE *KINO-NEDELIA*

Throughout his period in power, Lenin was far more interested in literacy than he was in any of the arts. He saw literacy as a precursor to any artistic flourishing and fundamental to the revolution's hopes for success. His famous quote "Of all the arts, for us cinema is the most important" was based on his belief that cinema had the most agitational and propagandistic potential of any artistic medium. The famous cinema kino-trains and agit-steamers not only were concerned with delivering films throughout the Union but distributed an extensive array of literary materials as well. Lenin always viewed the mobile cinema project in particular and cinema more generally as part of a broader public works propagandistic project.

During the immediate post-revolutionary years, the Russian cinema industry was in a state of flux. While Lenin signed the decree to nationalize the industry in August 1919, film production did not reflect a highly centralized and institutionalized structure.[15] Instead, while a few state-sponsored projects flourished (such as the *Kino-Nedelia*), most of the films were made by private firms and were not necessarily centered in Moscow or Petrograd. Overall production numbers decreased significantly from prewar figures, however, as many of the major firms relocated to Western Europe, taking their equipment and talent with them. The state of the industry was partly a result of inherited conditions, partly influenced by the loss of talent, partly due to Lunacharsky's gradualist approach, and always determined by the economic shortages that plagued Soviet society at the time. But whereas the industry as a whole remained decentralized and inclusive of private production, nonfiction film production was less diffuse (even though the infrastructures themselves were constantly in flux). The People's Commissariat of Enlightenment (Narkompros) established a cinema committee and gave it the task of making educational and agitational documentaries capable of serving the agency's needs.[16] Yet, instead of this setup becoming highly centralized, the individual cinema committees answered to their local commissariat government members. The Moscow Cinema Committee of the People's Commissariat of Education produced the *Kino-Nedelia* series.

The *Kino-Nedelia* newsreel ran for forty-three weeks and covered the period from May 20, 1918, until June 27, 1919.[17] At the time of the newsreel's origin in 1918, the Soviets were engaged in two wars: they were fighting a brutal civil war with the supporters of the tsarist regime (the Whites) and were trying to extricate themselves from World War I. In addition, they faced a major famine, worsened by extremely heavy snowfalls in the winter of 1918–1919. These concerns are all visible in the newsreels of the period.

The series marks the beginning of a concerted effort to distribute newsreels, especially to the European part of Russia. Prior to the war, there were often only four to five issues produced, on occasion only a single issue. However, the Moscow Cinema Committee produced forty to forty-five prints per week of the *Kino-Nedelia* series.[18] Mikhail Koltsov was placed in charge of the series. Initially, Vertov was only a clerk working administratively for the newsreel. But in the summer of 1918, when Koltsov was sent to the front to film the war, Vertov was asked to assume the responsibilities of chief editor. Clearly, he had impressed Koltsov and others with his enthusiasm and new ideas. He continually offered suggestions, such as setting up mobile cinema units, and worked tirelessly. Thus, it is important to understand in discussion of the newsreels that while Vertov selected and edited the material he was sent, he neither shot nor solely determined the topics covered. He relied on a wider array of coworkers for the newsreels than he later would for the feature documentaries he made with the *kinocs* in the 1920s.[19]

One of the foremost aims of the series was to inform the population about the progress of the war and to assure the citizenry that the Bolsheviks were making every effort to end Russian involvement. From the first to the last episode (#43), the *Kino-Nedelia* newsreels provide images of war refugees returning to their native lands. These are not only Russians coming home from abroad but Austrians and Germans returning to their homelands. Intertwined with this effort, and a related motivation, are calls for volunteers to fight against the counterrevolutionary Whites in the Russian civil war. The issues straddle a delicate line: they report extensively on a news story vital to the national interest (World War I) while trying to refocus citizens on a different enemy (the Whites). They show soldiers returning from battle while providing a new enemy for them to fight, one much more directly threatening. This shift in priorities was accompanied by increased reportage on the civil war efforts, making manifest the new focus of the nation-state and its citizenry. But in addition, the shift was not only about establishing Bolshevik-directed socialism in the USSR. At the time, many considered the war against the Whites to be the onset of the international revolutionary war against capitalism—the World Revolution predicted by Marx.[20] While the inclusion of refugees returning to other countries might have hinted at new transnational alignments focused on class instead of national identity, the Bolsheviks' dream of world socialism was not articulated in the series through intertitles or through montage juxtaposition. If viewers understood the refugee sequences as pointing in such directions, it would have been on account of the discourses available outside of the newsreel text. The effort to communicate concepts of World Revolution through newsreel montage was not yet the explicit concern of Vertov and his team.

The sequences on refugees returning from abroad and the calls for support in civil war efforts aim to shift understandings of national and international alignments while simultaneously refocusing energies on domestic priorities. But the effort to reimagine the makeup of the collectivity also had an urgent domestic dimension in the series. Bolsheviks were consistently and intensely invested in uniting the urban and rural citizen. These concerns are evident in sequences dealing with the impact of and reaction to natural disasters.

Many newsreels focused on the food shortages that plagued the country in the civil war period, either seeking to turn the painful lack into a sign of collective hope or, at minimum, acknowledging the struggles. Issue #3 begins by blandly introducing the food rationing commissars. The ensuing sequence captures an array of peasants and intellectuals planting cabbage and potatoes. Visually, the sequence focuses on a combination of the work and the land itself, as horizontal lines dominate an extended left-to-right pan of the field. The issue then states that those who worked the field are given dinner in exchange for their labor. This desire to unite the nation in the "struggle against hunger" is reinforced in episode #5. One sequence shows people waiting in long lines at a market in Moscow. Most important, like the attention to the farm labor of the intelligentsia and the peasants, the sequence indicates an attempt to dispel rural fears of unfair food distribution. Peasants are made aware that Muscovites had to stand in long lines and were not assured of bounty either. But in addition, these issues demonstrate collective efforts by organized citizens and governmental representatives to rectify the problems emanating from these disasters. The collaboration was evident not just in planting food and subsidizing meals (#3) but in a cooperative venture by military troops and local villagers to rebuild a bridge following its destruction (#33) and in parallel efforts by the Red Army and villagers to clear enormous snow drifts, thus enabling children to attend school (#34). This visible evidence of labor (and sharing suffering) aligns rural/urban and civilian/military citizens in a collective effort to fight the most daunting challenges facing civil war Russia.

While the films addressed rural citizens' concerns with fair treatment and articulated a vision of rural/urban and peasant/worker cooperation, they underrepresented rural citizens, who also had few opportunities to view the series. Although there is limited information about the distribution and exhibition of the *Kino-Nedelia* issues, an indication of the practices is evident in a response by the Eighth Party Congress as it demonstrated its frustrations with attempts to communicate with rural citizens. In March 1919, the Congress highlighted cinema's potential in this project while decrying previous agitational and propagandistic efforts. It stressed, "Cinema, theatre, concerts, exhibitions, etc. as far as possible in rural conditions must be used for communist propaganda." Mere speeches were insufficient and needed to be "strongly augmented by visual demonstrations with the aid of cinema."[21] To be sure, film stock shortages and the lack of transportation infrastructure affected the degree to which life in the countryside was represented. Most of the footage of the countryside is of military fronts and army garrisons, focusing more on the mundane activities of soldiers than on the strategic planning of military leaders. But on the whole, there is far more attention paid to daily life in urban areas than to that of the average peasant or rural worker. While we occasionally see footage of daily life or photographic proof of positive rural development, such as the newly built grain mill in Borisoglebsk (#21), more often the issues offer evidence of initial efforts to reach out to the rural citizenry. We see the agit-trains and steamers leaving Moscow to bring literature and cinema to the countryside (#17, #26, #32), and we see an irrigation team leaving Moscow for Turkestan (#16). These efforts demonstrate a commitment to a broad Soviet Union, even if they struggle to tender more concrete evidence of the projects' development. Just as it is not until the second period that nonfiction films communicated objective qualities of a set of social processes, the immediate post-revolutionary period required a certain amount of projection to envision a fully united rural and urban citizenry.

DYNAMICS OF STABILITY AND TRANSFORMATION IN NEW NATIONAL SPACE

Prior to the production of the *Kino-Nedelia* series, Russians had been exposed to numerous newsreels, but rarely did they contain images of Russian peoples. Following the failed 1905 revolution, the Russian state censor forbade images of real events filmed in Russia on screens. After a thaw, the production companies Pathé and Gaumont set up regional outfits that captured scenes of daily life, though much of it was staged. These films were extremely popular, but the companies lacked the capital for expansion.[22] Perhaps the most common method for showing citizens on film in the *Kino-Nedelia* newsreels was in funerals, parades, marches, inspections, and protest demonstrations.

Public celebrations have always performed a unique function in human societies.[23] But in the post-revolutionary moment, they took on a heightened power. Lenin himself suggested that "revolutions are festivals of the oppressed and the exploited. At no other time are people in a position to come forward so actively as creators of a new social order as at a time of revolution. At such times the people are capable of performing miracles."[24] Although not all of these examples exhibit the festivity associated with a carnival, they all visualize the movement of the masses through urban areas, transforming public space and, it was hoped, the viewers' relation to it. James von Geldern eloquently describes the impact in his study of Bolshevik Festivals from 1917 to 1920 (inclusive of the years of the *Kino-Nedelia* issues):

Festivals reshuffled the urban hierarchy by selecting new routes to be taken through the city, new places to be honored, and new spaces to be declared sacred. Space itself acquired new meaning. Revolutionaries spurned dusty urban squares for sprawling parks whose openness modeled egalitarian society and where fête participants were not divided by class or enclosed by the walls of authority. Time was reset inside the festive circle to show the revolution, and those monuments in it that organizers chose to emphasize, as a new beginning to history.[25]

Whether assembling to hear public speeches, marching through the streets of Moscow, or participating in May 1 celebrations, the crowd in the *Kino-Nedelia* newsreels occupies and overtakes city space. The city becomes emblematic of the nation as a whole, especially when, as in many of the examples, placards reveal that marchers have come from the outer regions to show support for a given project or to demonstrate their new organization. Such an effort to counter concerns in the periphery about the urban-centered, intelligentsia-led October Revolution can likewise be seen in the juxtaposition of protest demonstrations shown to be sweeping the nation following the murders of Rosa Luxemburg and Karl Liebnicht. In episode #35, we see people demonstrating in Moscow as well as in Kiev and Minsk. The importance of such sequences to the nation-building agenda of the *Kino-Nedelia* cannot be overestimated. It is in these sequences that the people not only could see themselves as such but could see themselves *actively* participating in the construction of the new nation. This is a sharp change from the Romanov jubilee celebrations or any other parade that dominated pre-revolutionary Russia in which the people statically and primarily watched the nobles pass by. The marches and celebrations create active, dynamic, integral spaces. They metonymize the nation by allowing the urban spaces to stand in for the nation as a whole, and they allegorize the nation by allowing the collective movement through space to symbolize the idea of a unified, new nation. But more than that, these films simultaneously gave people the opportunity to participate vicariously in the revolutionary activities and allowed them to see such participation at a distance. The repetition and accumulation of such performances throughout the *Kino-Nedelia* series provided an experience and a view. The combination, at this historical moment, urged citizens to draw a new cognitive map of Russian urban and national space.

FIGURE 1.1. Protest demonstrators take to the streets in *Kino-Nedelia* #35.

For Fredric Jameson, individuals depend on cognitive maps as a necessary practice for orienting themselves in the world. This is because of the utter dislocation of subjects from their conditions of existence, from their geographical imagination of the world, at the moment of the explosion of global capitalism (in other words, at a particular moment in time, one marked by dramatic changes in economic formations and relations).[26] The dislocation to which Jameson refers, rendering subjects incapable of recognizing their relations to the real conditions of the world, is akin to the dislocation of the post-revolutionary moment. And nonfiction films endeavor to provide a cognitive map by means of both the vision of a new world communicated and imagined in the films themselves and the network of distribution and exhibition through which they are framed and encountered. That is not to say, of course, that many peasants did not find the initial post-revolutionary moment dislocating at all. Certainly many did not experience it in such terms. But the *effort* to dislocate and relocate, to remap relations, to substitute the means and the people from their activities, expectations, and alignments in the pre-revolutionary world, was profound and insistent.

Cultural and political leaders' desire for subjective and material transformation was, of course, accompanied by a need for stability. In the *Kino-Nedelia* newsreels and in some of the early documentaries of the period, the rupture of revolutionary action, with its concomitant effort to transform collective imagination, was balanced by the need to establish an authority capable of realizing the goals of the people. In edifying and unifying the nation behind the government, the *Kino-Nedelia* series and the early documentaries turned to specific sites and symbols of power to ensure that the transformational was balanced by an image of stability, one capable of countering the "provisional" status of the Kerensky-led government.

National buildings strongly associated with the tsar and bourgeois culture were one such space. There was considerable debate among politicians and artists at the time about what should be done with iconic buildings. Some artists, like Vladimir Mayakovsky, argued that these relics should be destroyed because they were essentially infected and irredeemable. Each side could claim to be acting pragmatically. Those in the Mayakovsky camp who wanted to tear down what they saw as vestiges of elite and bourgeois culture argued that they were expensive to maintain. The preservationists contended that maintaining them might in the long run be cheaper than new construction.[27] In 1918–1919, however, the Bolsheviks were predominantly interested in laying claim to legitimate authority. To aid in the achievement of that goal, many issues dramatized the appropriation of tsarist or bourgeois spaces for socialist ends. Issue #23 demonstrates the transformation of the Hermitage from a tsarist palace to a museum, while issue #35 reveals how the estate of Prince Radzvill had been claimed by the Frontier Guard. By occupying and transforming these spaces, the Bolsheviks could both claim power and make plain its (re)distribution.

The appropriation of tsarist spaces allowed for the transfer, rather than total transformation, of power, thus offering a degree of stability. The creation of a number of new monuments (see #25 and #30, for example) pointed to the Bolsheviks' immediate interest in constructing a post-revolutionary history and claiming the authority that accompanies

FIGURE 1.2. Dedicating a monument to Danton in *Kino-Nedelia* #34.

such narratives. As Hannah Arendt argues, the relationship between stability and transformation is the fundamental dynamic facing revolutionary leaders attempting to create a new order.[28] Lunacharsky provides the guidelines to the initial cultural-historical picture they need to paint: "We must not be carried away by the full panoply of the past: we must concentrate only on moments that are important for agitation and propaganda. We must convey the history of the beginnings of the growth of the state in such a way that basic Communist ideas . . . are made clear to every viewer."[29] Such monumentalization intended to actively and avowedly construct the new national history for which Lunacharsky called. The monuments to heroes such as Robespierre, Danton, Bakunin, and Radischev (#25, #34) sought to create a new national collectivity both through imaginative inspiration and by reforming actual gathering spaces. Like the appropriation of the Hermitage or Prince Radzvill's estate, this practice responded to, and reworked, Russian history. Often, the new monuments were erected in place of previous heroes whose edifices were torn down. Thus, like the appropriation of tsarist buildings, the monumentalizing practice appropriated specific national spaces already forged in the Russian national memory. But, in the process of tearing down the old monuments and erecting new ones, the Bolsheviks actively and avowedly asserted the new. They announced the building of a new history for a new era. In the process of monumentalizing, we can see the negotiation between historical rupture, with its dream of the new, and historical appropriation, with its dual promises of power and stability—the fundamental dichotomy underlying this nation-building practice.[30]

SEEING THE STATE (AND THE SELF)

Whereas historical spaces provided the Bolsheviks opportunities for new national narratives and international alliances (for example, citing the French Revolution), the revolutionary government also required an image of leadership itself as permanent and identifiable. Cinema was seen as aiding this process. Throughout the series, new leaders are introduced, often as they are giving speeches. Title cards identify most of the leaders and occasionally refer to the content of the speech. The film that most directly communicates information about state leadership and the new institutions of power is *The Brain of Soviet Russia* (Vertov, 1919). A compilation documentary made entirely from bits of the *Kino-Nedelia* series, *The Brain of Soviet Russia* begins with long shots of the Kremlin in Moscow, the new seat of government. The massive buildings take up 90 percent of the screen space, but the vantage point provides more distanced perspective than in most previous examples. The image emphasizes the enormity of the buildings, and the screen time allows the viewer to reflect on the new site of power. The rest of the film consists entirely of shots of new Bolshevik leaders (including Trotsky, Sverdlov, Vatsetic, Lunacharsky, Pokrovsky, Karakhan, and Steklov). Other than Lenin, who is given longer screen time, each official appears on-screen for between ten and twenty seconds. He may speak to another person, stand silently looking at or away from the camera, or find some brief task to occupy him. Prior to his appearance, his title and name are announced

FIGURE 1.3 AND FIGURE 1.4. Lenin and Lunacharsky,
two of the "brains" of Soviet Russia.

on an intertitle card. After seeing the film, Lenin requested that it be sent to foreign governments to introduce them to the new leadership.[31]

The obverse of this "vision of leadership" is evident in the numerous inspections that occur in the newsreel series. Whether it is Trotsky firing up troops preparing for battle (#22), military leaders inspecting soldiers and viewing military maneuvers (#21), or an extended look at inspections of the documents of delegates attending a party conference (#24), the vision of leadership likewise entails a notion of how the state "sees" the citizenry and its representatives. If to be ruled means to be watched, regulated, and monitored, the *Kino-Nedelia* and the early documentaries of the period assert unquestionably that revolutionary transformation, while reliant on the efforts of a newly imagined and imaginative collectivity, proceeds under the guidance of a new authority.

The contexts of exhibition sustain and reinforce this alternative "vision of leadership," wherein the leadership possesses the power of the look. An announcement in *Kommunar* on November 3, 1918, asserted that a number of films about revolutionary action and the civil war effort would be screened as part of the celebrations of the October Revolution. The films included Vertov's *The Anniversary of the Revolution,* a four-reel film of which *The Brain of Soviet Russia* is the last part. The announcement states, "The films will be exhibited in the evening in five Moscow squares, and in most Moscow cinemas. Entry to cinemas will be free everywhere."[32] Nonfiction cinema, in these instances, became an integral part of these early public performances of revolutionary enthusiasm. These films are explicitly and discursively framed, at times serving as augmentations, as the Eighth Party Congress would assert, of speechmaking. Their exhibition was fully subsidized by the state ("Entry to cinemas will be free everywhere"), and the performance of viewing subjects was, in many cases, on display for leaders to see.[33]

The textuality and exhibition contexts of the *Kino-Nedelia* newsreels and the early documentaries of Dziga Vertov thus combined to communicate an urgent effort to address a citizenry. This thrust is visible on the celluloid itself in images of agit-trains, agit-steamers, projects that support transportation infrastructure, and those that explicitly address communications, such as issue #27, which conjures a communications system through a montage of transportation vehicles. But it is also evident in the exhibition contexts themselves. Such a conjuncture strongly encouraged an imaginative integration of performances of citizenship on-screen with Russian citizens' reflections of their own performances of citizenship both inside and outside exhibitionary spaces. As such, performances of citizenship on-screen were indissociable from the reflection on and (it was hoped) desire for Soviet subjecthood. While this was neither the Stalinist political theater of the ensuing decades nor the first step in an inevitable realization of such performances, it was one of the spaces (and a valuable one at that) in which the desire for Soviet subjectivity got cultivated and rehearsed.

TWO

A Cinema Looking for People: The Individual and the Collective in Immediate Post-Revolutionary Cuban Nonfiction Film

What is it that is hidden behind the Yankee's hatred of the Cuban Revolution? What is it that rationally explains the conspiracy which unites, for the same aggressive purpose, the most powerful and richest imperial power in the modern world and the oligarchies of an entire continent, which together are supposed to represent a population of 350 million human beings, against a small country of only seven million inhabitants, economically underdeveloped, without financial or military means to threaten the security or economy of any other country? What unites them and stirs them up in fear? What explains it is fear. Not fear of the Cuban Revolution but fear of the Latin American revolution. Not fear of the workers, peasants, intellectuals, students, and progressive sectors of the middle strata which, by revolutionary means, have taken power in Cuba; but fear that the workers, peasants, students, intellectuals, and progressive sectors of the middle strata will, by revolutionary means, take power in the oppressed and hungry countries exploited by the Yankee monopolies and reactionary oligarchies of America; fear that the plundered people of the continent will seize the arms from the oppressors and, like Cuba, declare themselves free people of America.

—FIDEL CASTRO, "THE SECOND DECLARATION OF HAVANA" (1962)

Shot rapidly in January of 1961, during the first period of alert . . . it
aims at communicating, if not the experience, at least the vibrations,
the rhythms of a revolution that will one day perhaps be held to
be the decisive moment of a whole era of contemporary history.

—CHRIS MARKER, PREFACE TO THE SCRIPT OF *CUBA SÍ!* (1961)

VISUALIZING COLLECTIVITIES AND EXPERIENCING MASSES

Fidel Castro delivered his extended exegesis on the history and philosophy of imperialism in Latin America to the Cuban people on February 4,
1962. The speech followed Cuba's expulsion from the Organization of
American States. A Cuban newsreel issue, which I describe in detail below, "covered" the events of the day.

Following the opening credit sequence and a title identifying this as
a "special issue," a patriotic anthem, sung by a chorus, runs over images
of hordes of people making their way through Havana to the National
Stadium for a major event. The camera shifts between long and medium shots of a mass moving in unison with tighter shots in the midst
of the marchers. As the voice-over of Julio Batista (the ICAIC newsreel
narrator at the time) begins, the camera captures people walking past
or milling around. It searches faces, zooms in on placards, and angles
down at ambulating feet. The different impact of the two shot lengths
and their objects is immediately striking. In the long shots, the crowd
usually appears as a unified force, marching with a purpose toward its
destination. In the tighter shots amid the crowd, people often appear to
be moving in varying directions if at all. There it becomes a scattered,
inquisitive camera, accumulating a breadth of detailed faces, gestures,
and costumes.

The newsreel issue then moves to the stadium. The initial shots
there are similar to the earlier tight shots of the crowd, only now the
gestures and movements are of Fidel Castro, Che Guevara, and President
Osvaldo Dorticos as they approach the stage. When he finally begins to
speak, Castro's voice assumes the narration, prompting a sharp change
in the cinematography. The camera moves to an extreme long shot and
stabilizes somewhat. It captures the massive crowd with gigantic banners of Karl Marx and José Martí looming as the backdrop. The camera

returns to Castro, shooting him from behind so that the immensity of the event is visible. After cutting to people in the crowd, the film returns to the shot behind Castro, only it has suddenly become dark. (Castro is known for his lengthy speeches; "The Second Declaration of Havana" is 13,470 words.) Upon returning to that view, Batista takes over the narration, filling in the missing content by means of a narrationally covered ellipsis.

Fidel reassumes the narration to finish his speech. As the event ends, the camera stays in an extreme long shot, capturing the spontaneous celebratory sway of the crowd and its chants of "Fidel, Fidel, Fidel." The anthem music that opens the issue returns, the camera points upward to the sky, and the film concludes.

This newsreel issue from 1962 manifests one of the central dynamics at work in the Cuban newsreels and documentaries of the immediate post-revolutionary period—that between individuals and their roles in the collective. The films of this period aim to project, model, and instill both a new concept of individuality and, balancing it, a new vision of the collective. In "The Declaration of Havana," distanced, seemingly objective views of the mass provide stable visions of the movement of collectivity and its relationship to authority. But such views are juxtaposed with tighter, mobile, seemingly subjective views that promise to offer a vision of the experience of individuals attending the event. This combination calls attention to the gap between the visualization of the collectivity from above and the experience of the mass from below. In this way, like the films from the initial post-revolutionary period in Russia, it partakes of the effort to communicate the sensory experience of modernity, namely the experience of participating in extraordinary mass demonstrations. But rather than countering a sensorial threat to the subject or acclimating the subject to sensorial overload, the dislocating experience of revolution is associated with spontaneity, pleasure, energy, enthusiasm, and improvisation. This is precisely the kind of experience—"the vibrations, the rhythms of a revolution"—that Chris Marker sought to communicate in the film *Cuba Sí!*[1]

These dynamics between individual and collective are also manifested in the film genres themselves during this period. As a "special issue" newsreel, "The Declaration of Havana" sits in an interstitial space between the ICAIC newsreel, more likely to focus on collectives or individuals as representatives of collectives, and the ICAIC documentary, more likely to personalize narratives. If in the first period in Russia the divisions between newsreel and documentary were still beginning to take shape, in Cuba filmmakers and critics had to respond to a set of generic expectations that had taken hold in the post–World War II period. This took two directions. First, viewers of nonfiction films (and especially documentaries) increasingly expected immediate and spontaneous access to individuals and their stories. Second, they were assumed to require a new vision of themselves *as mass*. The years between the Russian Revolution and the Cuban Revolution saw a new vision of authority and its relation to the mass. The cultural lexicon had been transformed by the visualization of the mass popularized by, among others, Nazi Germany and Fascist Italy. Their model of the de-individualized mass prompted filmmakers committed to collective action to reconceive aesthetic visions of the relation between the individual and the collective. This was especially true in Cuba, where leaders and cultural workers demonstrated sensitivity to any representational model that too closely aligned the Cuban people with a de-individualized (East European) mass.

This careful attention to the needs and positionality of the audience has been seen as one of the distinguishing aspects of post-revolutionary Cuban film. Castro established the terms for the discussion in 1961 in his famous "Words to the Intellectuals" ("Palabras a los intelectuales") speech. Castro contended that those in the vanguard had to both redeem and be redeemed by the masses. They had to cater to what was good for and beautiful to the masses and would, in turn, be redeemed by them. But how could they know what was beautiful, good, and useful to the people? And why should they play that role? The answer was that, because the masses were alienated from their conditions of existence, the vanguard must establish a revolutionary hermeneutics to distinguish that which was pure and noble from that which was alienated. As Hector Amaya describes, "This process of mutual education would result in different things for each group: through it, the people would acquire *conciencia*: exercising it, the vanguard would acquire a revolutionary hermeneutics and aesthetics."[2] From the outset, Cuban cineastes were

committed to addressing people where they were, simultaneously leading and following.

In their efforts to shape a social and geographical imaginary with
new national and international alignments, new visions of national and
international space, and new conceptions of history, filmmakers took
that principle exceedingly seriously. This chapter explores those efforts
to shape the new Cuban subject—and the proper public self he or she
was required to perform—through the establishment of institutional
policies and cultural principles and through the production, distribution, and exhibition of newsreels and documentaries between 1959 and
1965. These policies and the principles on which they depended were
informed by cultural accretions associated with the visualized mass
that were not in place at the time of the Russian Revolution. Thus, in
this chapter, I delineate the conceptual foundations and filmic traditions upon which the Cuban nonfiction film project was built. I do so
to provide historical rigor to the comparison that is at the heart of this
book and to demonstrate how the combination of these aesthetic shifts
and assumptions about Cuban national character shaped the conditions for articulating the pivotal relationship between the individual and
collective in post-revolutionary Cuban nonfiction film. It was a vision
of a people acquiring *conciencia*—a consciousness or subjectivity that
motivates social action—projected to an audience in the hopes of providing it the tools and sparking the desire to obtain (a uniquely Cuban)
revolutionary freedom.

THE ESTABLISHMENT OF ICAIC AND THE
FOUNDATIONS OF CUBAN CINEMA

The founding of the Cuban Institute of Cinematographic Art and Industry on March 24, 1959, often cited as the first cultural act of the revolutionary government, was both a generative and sustaining moment.
While marking cinema as a unique communications and artistic medium, it continued the guerrilla leadership's appreciation of the educational and propagandistic potential of mass communications. During
the guerrilla struggle, leaders such as Carlos Franqui mobilized Radio
Rebelde and the rebel newspaper *Revolución* to educate the Cuban popu-

lation about the intentions and progress of the Fidel Castro–led 26th of July Movement and to unify the people behind them. Two weeks after seizing power on January 1, 1959, the rebels, led by Che Guevara, founded Cine Rebelde as part of the rebel army's National Board of Culture. The organization produced two documentary shorts, Tomás Gutiérrez Alea's *Esta tierra nuestra* (This is our land) and Julio García Espinosa's *La vivienda* (Housing), prior to becoming part of the newly founded ICAIC.[3]

The body of the ICAIC charter begins by defining cinema first and foremost as a singularly effective mass communications and artistic medium. The first line identifies cinema as an art. The second line, tellingly, attempts to redefine what an "art" can be during this post-revolutionary period. Here, the drafters mark cinema as an "instrument of public opinion" capable of successfully communicating particular messages to a diverse audience (mass communicative aspect) and as possessing the "*power* to prove and make transparent the *spirit* of the revolution" (artistic element).[4] The astonishing history of ICAIC and Cuban cinema itself is partially legible in these terms. While insisting that cinema is always and necessarily ideological, the filmmakers and leadership of ICAIC have consistently voiced the opinion that the artistic element is fundamental to cinema's success. Artistic experimentation was not judged a priori to be indulgent, decadent, or anti-revolutionary, nor was celebrating the achievements and vision of individual directors seen to be bourgeois. The aesthetics, ideology, and institutional structure of cinema in Cuba were all seen to be capable of answering such criticisms.

Alfredo Guevara, ICAIC's first president, summarized Cuban cineastes' position on the sticky relationship between revolutionary art and revolutionary politics when he said in reference to Castro that "we are the same people he's always trusted, loyal to the Revolution, critics like him, not more critical than him, capable of holding back, if it's necessary to hold back; but not to abandon our language, because the *language of the cinema is either the language of the cinema or it isn't cinema.*"[5] Guevara's insistence on the simultaneous interrelation and separation of revolutionary politics and art demonstrates the critical sophistication of the Cubans as they continually rethought and reworked this fundamental relationship. He hints at the uneven development, the power inequalities, the diverging goals, and the uniting principles fundamental to understanding the connection between state revolutionary politics and state-sponsored cinema.

Adolfo Sánchez Vázquez provided many of the aesthetic principles on which the artistic elements were based. A Spanish philosopher who spent most of his life in Mexico, Sánchez Vázquez's work on Marxist aesthetics was widely published in Cuba from the early 1960s to the 1980s. He was a strong supporter of the Cuban Revolution and visited the island many times. Sánchez Vázquez was committed to the idea of the transformational power of art. If, according to Marx, aesthetics is a subject-object relation between man and reality, Sánchez Vázquez believed that a proper aesthetic approach could help man assimilate reality. This was possible, however, only in conditions where the self was knowable and objectifiable. Because subjects are still alienated from their labor (a condition against which the revolution continually fought), aesthetic experience became a primary means of self-knowledge.

But what artistic methods and styles are appropriate for achieving such ends? Sánchez Vázquez was insistent that art remain an "open conception," one that allows for flexibility and experimentation. That is not to say that he embraced experimentation for its own sake. Rather, he urged the creation of new forms that shape a critical consciousness. Artists had to relate their work to the contemporary struggle for transformation. Instead of representing or imagining the future development of society (as in Socialist Realism), revolutionary artists had to concern themselves with what was happening in the particular situation.[6] And they had to do so by employing "multiple realisms for a diverse reality." In addition to the foundational idea that art, under certain conditions, can serve a vital transformational function, three core principles of Sánchez Vázquez's thought shaped the discussion of how Cuban filmmakers, producers, and critics should develop a new national, revolutionary cinema. The first was the effort to create an artistic situation in which the self is objectifiable or in some way knowable. Second, Cuban filmmakers had to develop a deep realism by maintaining awareness of the potential deceptiveness of surface reality. Third (and related to both the second principle and Sánchez Vázquez's celebration of the creative), artists had to understand the Cuban Revolution as a creative act itself, one in which rigid dichotomies about the progressive and the reactionary, the realist and the experimental, and the dogmatic and the idealist could be overcome.[7]

EARLY CINEMATIC INFLUENCES ON
CUBAN NONFICTION FILM

Post-revolutionary Cuban cinema did not emerge in a vacuum but took shape from a wide range of cinematic influences. These influences did not simply unconsciously inform the development of Cuban cinema—their strengths, weaknesses, and overall political, ethical, methodological, and aesthetic applicability were cause for considerable debate. Italian neorealism affected Cuban cinema production most broadly by offering a novel method of capturing and communicating social and political change. But both Fernando Birri and the British Free Cinema movement had a more substantial effect on the development of documentary. Birri provided guidance on efforts to apprehend a genuine national identity, and Free Cinema suggested a new model for visualizing how workers function as subjects and makers of culture in their everyday lives. In this section, I break down how Cuban cineastes engaged these traditions' potential for registering and communicating political and social reality. The process by which this occurs began to establish a field within which Álvarez and others operated, informing how they sought to shape new revolutionary, national subjectivities.

Michael Chanan identifies the unexpectedly similar contexts in which Italian neorealism (fifteen years earlier) and Cuban cinema emerged:

> The Italians had needed to make a virtue of the lack of resources they suffered as they emerged from the war, just as the Cubans did in setting up a film industry in an underdeveloped country going through a revolution. And then the kind of movie both groups of filmmakers were seeking to counter was closely similar. Both had suffered the domination of Hollywood. The Italians had decided to take their cameras out into the immediate photogenic real world in order to counter the fanciful studio space of the "white telephone" film, the Italian fascist equivalent of the Latin American melodrama.[8]

Like Italian neorealists, Cuban revolutionary filmmakers sought to newly visualize the nation and its spatial landscape by rejecting the formerly dominant aesthetic. Both found that photographing the immediate world best captured the significant changes taking place. They often shot on location, used non-professional actors (though usually alongside professionals), and dealt with stories of everyday life. The rhythm of the films was slow in comparison to Hollywood production, and they chose to emphasize moments in people's lives and in the social world previously thought unimportant. Such an approach responded to economic and political needs as well. Filmmakers saved money on costumes, professional actors, and elaborate sets, while their emphasis on the everyday lives of the urban poor centered attention on subjects and lives most often deemed unworthy of film drama.

The influence of Italian neorealism was also felt in part because Cuba's two most celebrated fiction filmmakers, Tomás Gutiérrez Alea and Julio García Espinosa, trained at the Centro Sperimentale in Rome in the early 1950s and continued to work with Italians in Cuba. In 1955, García Espinosa made *El Megano,* a neorealist reconstruction of the terrible conditions facing charcoal workers in the Zapata swamps. Batista officials seized the film after its first screening and interrogated García Espinosa. In 1960, Gutiérrez Alea made the first post-revolution Cuban feature film, *Historias de la revolución* (Stories of the revolution), with a neorealist cinematographer and in a neorealist style. While neorealism appealed to the Cubans' need to get out on the street and film the energy and spirit of what was happening after the revolution, it may have been, as Chanan describes it, a "default aesthetic." It was thought capable of registering change but was limited in its potential to meet revolutionary needs. Gutiérrez Alea and García Espinosa contended that once Cuban society began to transform in more complex ways, they needed a different framework. As Gutiérrez Alea writes, "The Revolution implies a fundamental change in the structure of society, but the appearance of things also changes from day to day. A billboard announcing a luxury hotel in Miami and inviting Cubans to spend their vacation there is substituted by another which declares Cuba a territory free of illiteracy."[9] While capable of capturing the physical transformations of Cuban society, to Gutiérrez Alea, neorealism struggled to connect those surface changes to deeper, more complex structural changes. Gutiérrez Alea's position aligns with that of Italian filmmaker Pier Paolo Pasolini, who critiqued neorealism as a "superstructural phenomenon." Neorealism, according to Pasolini, was able to imagine (and capture) something new—something superstructurally new—but it never moved through the contradictions of contemporary society to get there.[10] Pasolini's argument is similar to Gutiérrez Alea's and García Espinosa's in that all three laud the ethical value of the neorealist paradigm and yet question its aesthetic potential as an intellectual and revolutionary cinema. Italian neorealism thus served a temporary and pragmatic solution, one that fulfilled certain needs yet failed to align with the developing revolutionary aesthetic principles.

Like Gutiérrez Alea and García Espinosa, Fernando Birri studied at the Centro Sperimentale in Rome in the early 1950s. Returning to his native Argentina, Birri founded the Latin American Documentary Film School in Santa Fé, Argentina, in 1956. There he emphasized documentary's applicability to Latin America and the need to train filmmakers and film technicians for documentary work. Birri's thinking was influenced by the ethics and aesthetics of Italian neorealism and the political commitment of John Grierson's social documentary movement. He celebrated neorealism for two reasons. First, he found its attention to the hidden underbelly of society absolutely necessary for a frequently overlooked Latin America. Second, he thought its realist representations an appropriate vehicle to counter the false images Latin Americans had been forced to digest. He argued that combining those aspects of the neorealist approach with the political commitments of the Griersonian social documentary and applying them to Latin American ends could serve to eliminate any sense of naive realism associated with neorealism and Western humanism associated with the Griersonian tradition. Turning the camera to the underrepresented and misrepresented within Latin America created a dialectical edge and bore critical witness. Birri described the new documentary paradigm as a process of "successive approximations *to* reality," indicating he embraced critical realism, not an unproblematic relation between filmed and lived reality.[11]

Perhaps the underlying thread linking Birri and many that followed in the Latin American social documentary tradition was their attempt to apprehend an essential national reality, be it Cuban-ness, Brazilian-ness, Bolivian-ness, or Argentine-ness. They became, as Julianne Burton describes, "self-appointed ethnographers in search of the 'true face' of their people, of the true custodians of national culture, of the true exemplars of national identity."[12] Such a face was to be found in the traditionally invisible and inaudible and relied on a Manichaean view of society. Burton summarizes the position:

> The world at large, and specific countries within it, were clearly divided into the haves and have nots. Purity and authenticity resided only in the latter.... These militant filmmakers opted for misery over opulence, rural over urban, primitive over modern, artisanal over industrial, indigenous and/or African-derived over European, pre-literate over literate and folk over elite. The key to a *realidad nacional* was thought to reside in a simple operation of inversion: turning the official version of nationhood and national culture on its head.[13]

Cuban state-sponsored film production required a more multidimensional view of national identity to realize its nation-building goals. Rather than establishing binaries between authentic and inauthentic national culture, citizens, and identities, Cuban filmmakers sought to build a unified image of a nation with new rural/urban, gender, economic, and national/transnational/international alliances. They projected a view of an energetic, determined, mobilized collective in the process of realizing revolutionary goals. This image functioned as a response to what Damián Fernandez describes as a pervasive and historically enduring sense of elusiveness that accompanied the intense desire Cubans felt for their nation and the ideals it represented (or had the potential to represent). According to Fernandez, the conflict between the normative and rationalizing logic of modernity and the "anything goes" instrumentality of Cuban informal personal relations had led to a loss of faith in models of the nation, democracy, revolution, and socialism they continued to desire.[14] Cuban nonfiction films sought to provide a vision and experience of transformation, one that established a new dynamic between the individual and the collective that was capable of overcoming such intransigence and frustrations.

The British Free Cinema movement was another tradition in relation to which Cubans began to define their own political and aesthetic filmmaking project. Between 1956 and 1959, a group of young British filmmakers put together six film programs under the heading "Free Cinema."[15] The manifesto accompanying the original program was written after the quite diverse body of films was already made. Nevertheless, as Gavin Lambert writes in his review of the program, "it was clear that people desirous in spirit were working together, by a combination of accident and design."[16] Though contrasting in subject matter, the films all took to the streets of Britain in an attempt to bring to the public an awareness of working and social conditions in urban settings. They examined the complexities of modern life—analyzing the role of work, the role of community, and the role of the artist in navigating these terrains. They had in common a devotion to the subjects of their films, who, they argued, needed to be treated with respect and listened to if British society was to move forward intelligently. If Grierson chose to speak for the public and look out for its interest in the earlier documentary movement, Free Cinema sought to provide a space for more autonomous public articulation.

In the years immediately following the revolution, Free Cinema stimulated lively critical discussion among Cuban film critics and artists. Some critiqued it and some supported it, but few denied that it was an important idea. The Cubans saw the movement as offering up a model of an improvisational, agile cinema, one that escaped the traditional confines of technical perfection, the costs associated with it, and the expectations that come with traditional exhibition practices. Cubans approved of Free Cinema's attention to the working class not just as objects but as subjects and makers of culture. Gutiérrez Alea offered the most sustained critique of the Free Cinema approach in *Cine Cubano* in 1960.[17] He argued that the Free Cinema filmmakers saw films as most effective when they expressed individual poetic sensibilities. In addition, they saw truth emanate most forcefully from the image when it functioned as a fragment of reality. On the contrary, Gutiérrez Alea contended, Cubans must be attentive to audiences in multiple ways: first, by not emphasizing the role of individual artistic expression at the expense of audience interest, and second, by being avowedly political and making judgments. The latter required the interventions of editing and narration instead of the observation of spontaneous fragments of everyday life. Cuban cinema had to be critical and didactic and speak with more forceful voices than Free Cinema did. This last point sharply distinguished the respective political underpinnings of each practice. Whereas Free Cinema film-makers were consistently antiestablishment and oppositional (Lambert even refers to them as "revolutionary" as opposed to "evolutionary"), they were revolutionary only within a liberal humanist framework. Thus, while Free Cinema was of great value to the Cuban project, Gutiérrez Alea warned cineastes of overlooking its inherent dangers.

INTRODUCTION TO ICAIC'S *LATIN AMERICAN WEEKLY NEWSREEL*

Santiago Álvarez presided over ICAIC's *Latin American Weekly Newsreel* from its inception in 1960 until its last issue in June 1991—overseeing 1,500 editions and personally directing more than 600.[18] Álvarez shot footage himself, coordinated multiple camerapersons, edited or oversaw the editing, and, most important, served as the guiding force behind the numerous aesthetic and discursive transformations that took place. While he was best known internationally for the politically and aestheti-cally radical documentaries he made in the mid- to late 1960s, Álvarez's experimentalism never ranged far from everyday political realities. This attitude is evident in his thirty-one year commitment to ICAIC's newsreel division.

Álvarez was born in 1919 in Havana, the son of Spanish immigrants. His father was arrested for anarchist activities when Álvarez was a young child. At the age of fifteen, Santiago began working as a printer's ap-prentice and soon thereafter participated in strikes organized by the Union of Graphic Arts. In 1939, he lived and worked in Pennsylvania as a dishwasher and coal miner. It was this stint, he claims, that politically radicalized him. He explains, "It was here in the United States that I started to become politically conscious and when I went back to Cuba I became a communist. American imperialism is the greatest promoter of communism in the world. In fact, it was my experiences here that form the roots of *NOW*, my film against racial discrimination in the U.S. That film grew directly out of my experiences here [in the United States]."[19] Returning to Cuba, Álvarez's political involvement grew and he returned to school, studying philosophy and literature at the Univer-sity of Havana.

During the 1950s, Álvarez belonged to the leftist political-cultural society Nuestro Tiempo (Our times). The society had a ciné-club where Álvarez and other eventual ICAIC mainstays such as Gutiérrez Alea, Garcia Espinosa, Alfredo Guevara, José Massip, and Manuel Octavio Gómez were able to watch films and discuss them in theoretical terms. They saw classic Soviet films and read books on cinema by Bela Balazs, Georges Sadoul, Lev Kuleshov, Alexander Pudovkin, and Luigi Chiarini. More than providing a political-cultural education, Nuestro Tiempo can be seen as a forerunner to ICAIC with its radical collective forming a ready-made revolutionary cultural faction. The society was a combination of revolutionary-artists and artist-revolutionaries. Some members prioritized political over aesthetic ambitions and others aesthetic over political ambitions. Abstract art was not seen as apolitical but as a viable expression of protest. In addition, the society performed many cultural functions in support of the Communist Party. Its exhibits, various publications, and self-titled magazine heightened ideological conflict in the cultural sphere. This political-cultural foundation is visible in many of ICAIC's tenets. The need to counter official culture united artists and revolutionaries, creating friendships and an openness to debate the complicated relationship between revolutionary art and revolutionary politics. It also established culture in general and cinema in particular as a battle zone—one not simply responding to political change but actively and avowedly bringing about revolutionary communism.[20]

Although he lacked formal training, Álvarez was appointed to direct the ICAIC newsreel from its founding in 1960. During the immediate post-revolutionary period and throughout the history of its newsreel, Cuba was not equipped for the rapid distribution and exhibition of 35mm weekly issues. Neither the transportation nor the theatrical (or even nontheatrical exhibition) infrastructure was in place for such a practice. Because it was easier for audiences to obtain up-to-date information through other mass media sources such as the newspaper, radio, or television, it was determined that newsreels should provide more in-depth coverage of fewer stories than replicate, in film form, newspapers.[21] Thus, newsreels functioned similarly to news magazines in that they reported issues in-depth and provided commentary on the news. While this practice (and the reputation of the ICAIC newsreel throughout the world) did not reach its acme until the latter half of the decade, the initial post-revolutionary period saw gestures in such directions. From the outset, the Cuban newsreel eschewed pretenses of objectivity and avowed its political partiality. Its overriding discursive message was one of transformation and unification. Newsreels informed Cubans about the steps the government was taking to stabilize the nation, and they communicated a message of sacrifice required from citizens to build the new nation. They most often employed a single authoritative voice-over narrator and a fragmented narrative structure. With the rare exception of the occasional "special issue" that focused on a single topic (I discuss examples below), the newsreel was divided into four to eight fragmented sections and ran for ten minutes. Occasionally, Álvarez ran a brief story on a political or cultural issue, moved to one or two stories completely disconnected from the original one, and then returned to the initial subject. He explained this editorial practice as "anticipatory," arguing that by citing a story and then returning to it, audiences were energized and engaged with the issue. Whereas his early application of such principles created confusion and came across somewhat awkwardly, Álvarez in due time developed a sophisticated language for directing viewers' intellectual and emotional energies toward new nation-building needs.

IDENTIFYING THE COLLECTIVE

In his role as director of the ICAIC newsreel, Álvarez became part of a larger effort to, as Homi Bhabha puts it, "narrate the nation."[22] As in practically all post-revolutionary contexts, Cuban leaders in the immediate post-revolutionary period proposed a new definition of the nation—one that was accepted, rejected, or modified by the population at large. Newsreels and documentaries contributed to this political process by connecting locations, events, and the figures associated with them to shared public narratives. In the Cuban nonfiction films of the first period, such efforts involved transforming the spaces associated with power and the concomitant inequities they signified. But unlike in Birri's early work, these films did not envision a straightforward reversal of dichotomies such that the poor, primitive, rural peasant became the single archetype of the nation. Rather, the films and the circulatory means by which they were distributed and exhibited demonstrated a commitment to a new collective makeup, one that urged new national and international alignments while radically transforming previous class, and power, relations.

Although based in Havana and lacking the resources and networks to consistently produce images of events in the countryside, the ICAIC newsreel continually articulated a new relationship between rural and urban citizens. Most often this involved rural citizens coming to Havana to participate in events such as the July 26th celebrations or the meetings of the Federation of Cuban Women (1960)—opportunities that would not have been available to them previously. Images of developments in agriculture were present throughout 1960 (the "Year of Agrarian Reform") and 1964 (the "Year of Economics"), which focused on the modernization of agricultural production. Beyond labor, these issues also highlighted cultural activities in the rural areas. A story from 1960 covers the art and music produced in accordance with the "festival of fishermen," while another from 1961 showcases rural wood carvings ("Culturating the Forest"). These issues also presented leaders assembling in the countryside. Whether it is Che cutting sugar cane (1961) or Fidel returning to the Sierras, the issues make plain that "all will be united in the hills" (1960).

The project that most clearly represented leaders' efforts to transform conceptions of the makeup of the citizenry—and in turn received considerable attention in the newsreels and documentaries of the initial period—was the National Literacy Campaign of 1961. After achieving power, the Castro government named the years by honoring revolutionary efforts or identifying revolutionary goals. The year 1961 was called the "Year of Education," with the primary focus on eliminating illiteracy and teaching rural Cubans to write.[23] The government sought to bring educational opportunities to the traditionally neglected rural areas, shantytowns, and urban slums. The most celebrated education campaign was the literacy campaign, an operation designed to achieve the dual objectives of youth involvement in the revolution and adult literacy. The campaign hoped to instill a sense of revolutionary fervor in the student *brigadistas* (their first real opportunity to participate in the struggle) and unite urban and rural citizens not only by having the urban-educated teach the rural but also by creating a situation in which the urban could learn about rural daily life and work. By all accounts, the campaign was remarkably successful.[24] More than 100,000 mostly urban student volunteers lived with rural families for six months, imparting reading and writing skills as well as lessons in revolutionary politics. The campaign raised the adult literacy rate from approximately 74 percent to 96 percent and was hailed as a victory for the nation of Cuba.[25]

The year 1961 was important not only for the literacy campaign; it was also the year of the U.S. invasion at the Bay of Pigs (Cubans refer to it as Playa Girón).[26] Both the newsreels and documentaries of the period link these stories, interrelating their urgency and success. In a newsreel story from 1961 titled "Bay of Pigs: Invaders of Peace," Cuban teachers reenact the Bay of Pigs invasion, but with a twist. This time the Cuban teachers are the invaders, and they are "attacking illiteracy." By equating a successful military campaign with a social works campaign, the segment hopes to demonstrate that these campaigns are not just highly valued in revolutionary society but are of a similar order. But in addition, the metaphor proposes to infuse a social works project with the vitality of a successful war effort.[27] The story is one of the earliest examples in either newsreel or documentary of a governmental call for sacrifice in the population. Rather than a plea for help, here the message is steeped in vibrancy, commitment, and inevitability—the kind of activity undertaken by the "new man." The Bay of Pigs had thus become a resource of collective knowledge, one capable of being mobilized by Álvarez for other ends. The segment enacts a role reversal (or perhaps a "role replacement"), with the Cuban teachers occupying the position of the mercenaries. By placing the teachers in the position of the attackers, the film promotes a political ethic driven not by the binary attacker/ attacked or even rural/urban but by one informed by the nobility of the cause. The merits of such a position are determined not by geographical location or by ability to access historical information but by the participant's commitment to *patria*.

The documentary that celebrates the literacy campaign—Manuel Octavio Gómez's *Historia de una batalla* (Story of a battle, 1961)—is organized in a related fashion and yet also points to some of the discrepan-

cies between how newsreels and documentaries articulate the dynamics
between individual and collective. The film envisions the campaign as
a series of waves of political and social activity. After successfully participating in the campaign, *brigadistas* (almost entirely young women)
return home to Havana where they are met with adoring and highly
emotional mothers. In turn, new cadres head off to the provinces to
continue their efforts, leaving nervous but accepting mothers in their
wakes. During these sequences, the voice-over is limited. The film is
dominated by a sense of festivity and youthfulness. Teenagers move
through the streets of the city, at times in alignment, at other times as
part of a disorganized crowd. They sing and dance on trucks returning
to Havana and in the city streets. The film is rapidly cut for the period
and aligns urban and rural spaces by visually matching the movement
of a busy street with the movement through the thick vegetation and
steep hills of the countryside.

The middle part of the film develops the metaphor established in the
newsreel story from the same period. It explicitly equates this battle with
Playa Girón, providing visible evidence of the attacks and demonstrating
the Cuban population's preparedness for battle. The argument expands
beyond Cuba's borders by incorporating newsreel footage from around
the world as Chinese, Soviet, Polish, and Brazilian masses demonstrate
support for the Cuban position. But the most compelling aspect of the
film, and that which is commented on most frequently by critics, is the
personal element. The emotional intensity of mothers watching their
children depart or greeting them upon return and the vibrancy of the
youth brigade (shaped by the rapid editing, fairly tight cinematography,
and array of musical selections) present a vision of a population prepared, determined, and yet human. Family sacrifices are not glossed
over but registered. The youth—energized, transformed, and productive—signal a new revolutionary moment and a new revolutionary space.
It is one driven not by antiquated class, gender, and racial divisions but
united by new rural/urban alignments.

While the films about literacy in 1961 work to create a newly constituted image of the national collective, they also situate the alignments
driving such orientations within an international landscape. The newsreels of the early 1960s devote more time and space to this issue than

FIGURE 2.1. A family reunited after a *brigadista's* return from the literacy front in *Historia de una batalla* (Story of a battle).

perhaps to any other. They constantly invoke "new friendships" with other countries, providing evidence in the form of the newly established political relations (with Bulgaria, China, and Serbia in 1960) and cultural exchanges (ballerina exchanges in Riga, Latvia, and film exchanges with the USSR, to name just two).

An issue from 1961 is aesthetically and thematically typical of the discourse on new international alliances. The issue begins (after the title sequence) with the title "Czechoslovakia, a Country of Friends" (in 1961, Álvarez began to title individual story sections). The emphasis is on Czechoslovak technology and culture, with the message being that in a great socialist country like Czechoslovakia, elegance and culture is within the reach of everyone. Images of a puppet show are interspersed with shots of the audience enjoying the entertainment. The second part of this story is connected to the first and shows young Czechoslovaks folk dancing. The second story reveals Cuban youth on their way to study in Moscow and young Soviet students arriving in Havana. The focus is not only on traditional educational exchange but on how such programs promote cultural dialogues as well, in this case, through music. The section ends with young Cuban agricultural workers preparing to leave for Moscow, demonstrating again that the knowledge and pleasures that come with such exchanges are not reserved for the elite. The sixth story returns to the topic of international relations and is titled "Friendship without Conditions." Interestingly, Cuba is visibly absent as the voice-over discusses a cultural and economic exchange between Brazil and the USSR. The critical issue comes through when the narrator Batista, fulfilling the promise of the title, points out that Brazil is a nonaligned country.

The emphasis on international solidarity in these segments is indicative of Cuban political concerns during this period. By the middle of the decade, Álvarez was running more stories on Latin American and Caribbean affairs. During the first years, however, Cubans sought to increase ties with the Soviet Union and its allies in the hope of securing support for the revolution from the other superpower. This is frequently evidenced in the newsreels. Edward González writes that in the aftermath of the revolution, the Cubans had two primary foreign policy objectives. First, they aimed to overcome the hostility of their neighbors and the isolation the United States imposed. Second, they hoped to do so without relinquishing their independent status.[28] Cuba was in fact able to obtain the political, military, and economic support it desperately needed during the 1960s from the Soviets while largely maintaining its independence within the socialist faction. The goal of intimate friendship with independence is visible in this newsreel issue. The segments on cultural exchange across population and discipline point to Cuban-Soviet amiability and respect. But the sixth segment (on Brazil-USSR relations) is perhaps intended to qualify that message to the Cuban people. The ICAIC newsreel spoke directly to the Cuban people, asserting the state's positions, providing information on governmental action, offering pleasurable images and sounds of cultural activity, and responding to perceived insecurities about the nation's direction. By couching these stories within a framework of nonalignment, the newsreel emphasized the Cuban authority's diplomatic position vis-à-vis the

Soviet Union and hoped to quell concerns that Cuba was handing over its sovereignty to a superpower with whom few Cubans saw themselves as having anything in common.

No relationship, however, was more central to the new sense of national autonomy than Cuba's relationship with the United States. If the literacy campaign was the defining project for reconceiving the makeup of the citizenry, Playa Girón drove the reorientation of international alliances even as it focused almost entirely on the Cuban response to the invasion. But more than continuing to shape the national imagination—determining with whom the collective was aligned and with whom it was opposed—Playa Girón and the discourse associated with it urged Cubans to adopt a defiant, prepared, alert attitude to ensure the security and continued viability of the nation.

Immediately following the invasion, Álvarez teamed up with Gutiérrez Alea to produce a special issue newsreel titled *Muerte al invasor* (Death to the invader) (establishing its position rather unambiguously). The issue runs sixteen minutes, incorporates footage shot by ICAIC and Cuban television, and has a confident and defiant tone. It demonstrates both the strong leadership necessary to overcome an economically and militarily superior foe and the unity and determination of the Cuban people. But the film is also highly agitational, designed to increase nationalistic intensity while unequivocally establishing a new enemy. The film points to a shift in the threat from the counterrevolutionaries within the country (ones potentially visible) to forces outside the national bounds, namely the United States CIA. Two examples, each of which highlights the film's innovative use of sound, reveal the dynamics between establishing a definable enemy and the vigilance the Cuban citizen was required to adopt in relation to the enemy.

The main body of the film is a combination of actuality footage of the results of the attack, genuine battle sequences, and troops mobilizing to join the fight (primarily in that order). The images of the violence are gruesome. They reveal the intensity of the struggle and the resulting civilian deaths while the voice-over condemns the immorality of killing civilians. As the People's Militia rushes to the front in response to the attack, the intensity of the soundscape matches the energy of the soldiers. Álvarez and Gutiérrez Alea raise the volume of the synchronized sound,

the voice-over describes the mobilization, and a patriotic anthem under-
scores the process. Sequences are shot from military trucks, placing the
viewer in the position of the soldier going to battle. The visual and aural
perspectives during the battle sequences are entirely from the positions
of Cuban soldiers. Invading planes are heard overhead. Wounded Cuban
soldiers are carried away. Artillery is fired. The enemy is not seen but is
felt and heard.

The ensuing sequence captures the victory of the Cubans. It begins
with celebratory newspaper headlines and moves to a sequence of the
invading forces surrendering their weapons. The music accompanying the surrender is ironic and reminiscent of dramatic Hollywood
film sound. The audio choice seems even more poignant after hearing
Rafael Quintero, a member of Brigade 2506 who was captured during
the invasion, remark on the impact of American film (and the mythol-
ogy it supports) on the Cuban psyche. Quintero says, "In those days,
the Cubans thought of the Americans in what I call the 'John Wayne
syndrome.'... We thought the Americans worked the way John Wayne
worked in his movies. Of course, this was naïve, but this was the way
most of us felt. I mean, the Americans hated communism and, like
John Wayne, they never lost—ever."[29] The choice of the music thus has
two functions. First, it exposes and destabilizes the myth of American
invincibility, in the process locating one of its foremost enunciations in
popular culture.[30] Second, it establishes without question the identity
of the invaders. This last point explains the primary visual focus of the
sequence—the uniforms of the captured soldiers. By zooming in on the
particularities of the uniform, the film hopes to provide evidence for its
assertion that the invading force was trained by the CIA. The voice-over
eventually confirms this position, explaining in more detail what the
evidence means.

Muerte al invasor aims to shift the battle lines from an internal
struggle with counterrevolutionary forces to an external one with an
imperialist aggressor. Tacking back and forth between direct address
and a subjective soundscape and image-scape, the film locates the enemy
outside of this representational framework. It identifies the source of the
attack (the CIA) while hoping to increase passion for the revolutionary
cause and the actions required to ensure its security.

NEW VISIONS OF THE SELF AND LEADERSHIP

The effort to create a new image of and sense in the national collective was visible not only on the celluloid of the newsreels and documentaries themselves. It was also evident in distribution and exhibition practices established during this same period. Like the literacy campaign, the *cines movíles* (mobile cinemas) were part of a larger public works agenda designed to modernize, educate, and, especially in this case, entertain rural audiences while integrating them into the national project. Transporting 16mm films, projectors, and screens by trucks, boats, and even mules, mobile cinema workers had organized 4,603 screenings for 1.2 million people (in a population of approximately 7 million) by 1962.[31] The screenings consisted of a weekly ICAIC newsreel, an animated film, a documentary, and a feature film, most often from Cuba, the Soviet Union, Czechoslovakia, Germany, Spain, or China. ICAIC created the Department of Film Dissemination (Divulgación) to coordinate this effort. But unlike the literacy campaign, which employed urban volunteers, the mobile cinema projectionists and discussion leaders were from the provinces. ICAIC trained these workers in projection as well as in film history, theory (from a Marxist perspective, of course), criticism, and production.[32] Through such circulation practices, cinema distinguished itself from literacy (and literature) and presented a new model of the nation and its citizenry. Serving as a symbol of modernization and development, cinema—and nonfiction cinema as an integral part of this project—became a site of integration, one in which a new vision of a democratic collective was produced, framed, and interpreted by all of its citizens.

The mobile cinemas—whether transporting films by truck, boat, or mule—were linked in the rural imagination with new networks of transportation and communication that aimed to more fully integrate the country. As such, they became part of the effort to shape a new geographical imagination of the nation. Although I would hesitate to characterize this remapping as a full-blown decentering of Cuban national space akin to the Soviet film project of the 1920s, it was a signal of less centralization.[33] It aimed to create new vectors of communication and networks of production.

This move to reimagine the relationship between Havana and the countryside as well as across provinces themselves developed at the same time that ICAIC sought to become a burgeoning center of Latin American and Caribbean leftist film culture. Those involved with ICAIC were especially interested in working with and getting training from European filmmakers. They welcomed, among others, the Italians Cesare Zavattini and Armand Gatti; the Soviets Roman Karmen and Mikhail Kalatazov; the French Chris Marker, Claude Barret, and Claude Otzenberger; the British Ricky Leacock; the Dane Theodor Christensen; and a number of East German and Czechoslovak filmmakers. But the filmmaker who influenced the shape of documentary production in Cuba more than any other was the Dutch socialist documentary filmmaker Joris Ivens.

Ivens shot two documentaries during his visit to Cuba in 1960—*Carnet de viaje* (Travel notebook) and *Cuba pueblo armado* (A people armed). He also had a special issue of *Cine Cubano* dedicated to his work.[34] Both films capture the assemblage of masses and highlight the improvisational aspect of the Cuban Revolution. *Carnet de viaje* does so by surveying the accomplishments of the revolution in its first two years and *Cuba pueblo armado* by focusing on a militia's offensive against counterrevolutionary threats.

Carnet de viaje is a travelogue that literally tracks Ivens's tour of the island, identifying each location with a different aspect of revolutionary transformation: education, culture, health care, defense, agriculture, industry, and political organization.[35] The structure is one of "before and after." The film provides proof of revolutionary progress by juxtaposing vestiges of pre-revolutionary life with transformations in everyday life and the architectural landscape in which it takes place. Social change, as Ivens always maintained, needed to be visualized in material terms.

But Ivens's role in Cuba was not that of a celebrated filmmaker who transformed Cuban attitudes toward filmmaking. Rather, one of the reasons he was so beloved was because he came to Cuba not to make his films but, as the director José Massip would attest, to help Cubans make theirs.[36] As Thomas Waugh describes, Ivens performed an "activism that lends solidarity and resources to local initiatives without imposing external models of any kind." He "encouraged them to rely on their own instinctual feelings about a task, to trust in their own innate human sympathies and interactions with their fellow Cubans in a dialectical relation with their own clearly defined ideological aims."[37] This effort to integrate the personal with the structural became a foundational principle for early Cuban documentary. As a filmmaking *method,* Ivens's model celebrated the collaborative aspect (between filmmakers and subjects) of documentary production, always demonstrating sincere respect for the individual human being. As an *aesthetic,* in addition to asserting the dignity of the individual, it urged Cuban citizens to rethink their roles as individuals in relation to regional and national collectives. Notions of autonomy and privacy required rethinking. Negotiating these components of individualism in a proper fashioning of revolutionary selfhood required recognizing them not as pure domains of the self but as constantly shifting tenets coordinated with the needs of the nation. Viewers would thus realize a *conciencia* imbued with a new model of revolutionary identity while the vanguard would acquire the hermeneutics and aesthetics thought to assure effective intellectual and emotional communication. As this framework indicates, it was both individual citizens and the vanguard that had to engage in this process of self-perfection. But each had to do so by drawing on the model of a small core of revolutionary leaders. Nonfiction films of the period build an image of this group (most prominent of whom was, of course, Fidel Castro) that is quite distinct from that of the Soviet leaders. In both newsreels and documentaries, speechmaking becomes a prime vehicle for the assertion of authority. The content of speeches was less important than the act of speechmaking. Likewise, the films exhibit the government's ability to control spaces associated with previous regimes. But they do so differently than in the Soviet example. Whether it is assuming control over the Yacht Club (1961), organizing the Cuba Cup Regatta (1960), or opening up the Presidential Palace to evening stays for regular citizens (1961), the issues focus attention on the redistribution of power, the elimination of privilege, and the command required to make such changes.

Perhaps the most distinctive aspect of the image of governmental power these films convey is their projection of a new model of leadership. Fidel, Che, Raul Castro, and Osvaldo Dorticos are not presented as stiff bureaucrats removed from the people. They are represented as spontaneous, responsive, intimate, and yet authoritative. They possess the power of vision and voice to justify the positions they occupy. Natural disasters and the responses to them became sites for this articulation of leadership, one in which individual and collective mobilization is most clearly situated in relation to leadership.

In 1963, Álvarez directed *Ciclón*, a double-length newsreel (twenty-two minutes) covering the devastation of and response to Hurricane Flora in Camagüey and Oriente Provinces in the southeastern section of the island. The film uses an array of footage shot by ICAIC, the armed forces, and Cuban television. It was produced as a special issue newsreel. Like "The Declaration of Havana" issue and *Muerte al invasor*, the film garnered considerable praise and was significant in establishing Álvarez's international reputation.[38]

The first section of the film runs about four and a half minutes and catalogs daily working life in Camagüey and Oriente Provinces. Men and women build houses, work in factories and electrical plants, fish, raise poultry, and cultivate cocoa, coffee, and potatoes. The audio track consists of Cuban music and a dominant voice-over describing the work and the region. The framing is moderately tight, often immersed in the work. The editing rhythm is consistent and somewhat fast, evoking a sense of continuity and productivity.

The second section begins with a sharp transition. With a forewarning indicated by silence on the audio track, a succession of images of working life, each selected from those already shown, runs for two seconds and then freezes for another two. Immediately thereafter we see actual hurricane footage—massive floods, trees at their breaking points, people struggling to walk against the high winds, boats barely staying afloat. The voice-over narration continues to describe the situation at hand, although it intervenes less frequently during this section. The sequences alternate between shots of exterior spaces and interior spaces. The exterior sequences capture the hurricane, its violent sounds, and its devastating impact on the landscape and infrastructure. The interior sequences depict people surveying the storm, waiting for loved ones, or receiving medical attention. The quiet piano music (with interspersed, regular drumbeats) reflects the tense mood of the people.

Eight minutes into the film, Fidel Castro, Vice-Premier Raul Castro, President Osvaldo Dorticos, and other officials arrive at the scene. The voice-over ceases entirely, and on-screen come shots of the devastation from the perspective of airplanes and helicopters. For the remainder of the film, three types of sequences predominate: Fidel and others taking action to organize relief efforts (though the fewest sequences are devoted to this); the results of this action, such as organized medical care and the dropping of supplies; and continued coverage of the damage the hurricane has inflicted, now focusing more on dead humans, animals, and plants and the visible impact of these deaths on human faces. The film concludes in a personal tone, with Álvarez's camera lingering on children being carried by their parents. The last image is of a toddler staring back at the lens unflinchingly as his mother soberly carries him down the road.

The first section serves as a prologue to the main body of the film. The idealized productivity of Camagüey and Oriente highlights new and traditional Cuban labor. The old and the new blend seamlessly, appearing not in conflict but indicative of the unity of post-revolutionary Cuban society. The voice-over provides information on the region, the people, and the work. The first section is not unlike many of the early newsreels of the first period in that it offers evidence of positive Cuban economic transformation and seeks to unite people from various regions of the country.

The multiple freeze-frames at the end of the first section and the actuality footage of the hurricane indicate a transformation in the responsibility of the Cuban citizen. Whereas the first sections emphasize labor productivity in support of the local and national economies, the second section requires a unified and urgent response to a natural disaster. The succession of freeze-frames is a clever way of creating a sense of simultaneous urgency, suspending each worker's efforts at one symbolic moment. The transition is a move from individualized labor (albeit as part of a socialist effort) to a more communally organized and focused reaction.

The key juxtaposition in the second section is between the actuality footage of the hurricane (its dramatic impact heightened by the audio track) and the distanced perspective given by maps and aerial footage. Whereas the actuality footage and corresponding narration testify to the reality and drama of the natural disaster, the graphics and extreme long shots place the viewer above the landscape, situating the subject within and outside the fray. Immediately thereafter, however, the maps of the storm's movement become associated with the positionality and view of the revolutionary leadership. As leaders arrive on the scene, they are capable of charting the storm and, though not overcoming it, providing the necessary relief and support to weather it. They are discursively equated with the helicopters and airplanes, which not only help to follow the storm but also provide supplies to people desperate for help. They are above the landscape, above the storm, and part of the heavens, but at the same time on the ground, in the muck, and with the people. The spatial dynamics and discourse of the film visually embody this dual relation between the leaders and nation as the attention to rural and urban spaces allows the provinces to stand in for the nation as a whole. This metonymic relationship articulates the film's address to a united collectivity in the throes of a *national experience*. The leaders can therefore be seen as the reason for the new Cuban economic prosperity, as embodying responsible, hands-on leadership, and as the center of Cuban unity and community.

MEDIA HERMENEUTICS AND THE NEW NATIONAL GAZE

It is important to remember that Cubans, like the Russians at the moment of their revolution, had rarely seen themselves on cinema screens. There was little domestic production to speak of, and the work that did exist seldom offered a vision of Cubans as collective bodies and as makers of history. The revolution changed all that. Not only did they see themselves (including a newly imaginable collective self) on-screen, they saw themselves being watched by the world. Whether it was the Soviet public reading a reprint of Fidel's UN speech in *Pravda* (1960) or the presence of mass gatherings in support of Cuba's position on the Bay of Pigs in China (1961) and Poland (1961), the ICAIC newsreel communicated to Cuban citizens in no uncertain terms that their efforts, their performances, were being viewed as models to be emulated. As Fidel insists in his "Declaration of Havana" speech, the Cuban Revolution of seven million people was not imagined as the end of a national process but as the beginning of an international revolution.

The immediate post-revolutionary period also saw an increase in attention on media hermeneutics. In addition to ironic references to Hollywood music as a strategy for exposing the myth of American invincibility *Muerte al invasor* (Death to the invader), the newsreels of the period began to introduce citizens to the mechanisms by which Western imperial powers used media to shape subjectivities. Whether it was demonstrating how the revolution breaks down stereotypes of blacks established in Hollywood films (1960) or marking itself as news in relation to "Hollywood entertainment" by means of witty cartoons (1961), the ICAIC newsreel began to instruct Cuban citizens in Marxist models of media analysis. And the stakes for cinematic activity was high. Film's increasing importance was indicated by references to it in the bodies of ICAIC newsreels themselves: interviews with Ivens and celebration of his visit; numerous revolutionary leaders attending a screening of Gutiérrez Alea's *Historias de la revolución;* and Fidel himself attending a screening of newly imported *Soviet* film.

But it is not just on-screen that such acts of cinematic reflection were encouraged. The effort to produce, distribute, and exhibit films throughout the country by means of mobile cinemas makes that plain. As in the Soviet Union, the textual and extratextual conjuncture strongly encourages an imaginative integration of performances of citizenship on-screen with reflections of viewers' performances of citizenship both inside and outside exhibitionary spaces. An appropriately "anonymous" article in *Cine Cubano* captures the thrust. The writer describes the process of bringing cinema to people who had not experienced it before as an effort "to inculcate values, to educate, and to help create the revolutionary 'new man' via the cinema in addition to education and other forms of socialization. *It is the cinema, then, who looks for these people* in the mountains or in the plains."[39] Cinema and its sponsoring institutions here obtain the look, aiming to instill in people the urgency of seeing and the stakes in being seen. It is with this dynamic that Cuban nonfiction film of the immediate post-revolutionary period hopes to enact a shift in conceptions of Cuban identity from the "elusive" to the attainable.

PART TWO

THREE

The Dialectics of Thought and Vision in the Films of Dziga Vertov, 1922–1927

We therefore take as the point of departure the use of the camera as a kino-eye, more perfect than the human eye, for the exploration of the chaos of visual phenomena that fills space.

The kino-eye lives and moves in time and space; it gathers and records impressions in a manner wholly different from that of the human eye. . . .

We are preparing a system, a deliberate system of such occurrences, a system of such seeming irregularities to investigate and organize phenomena.

Until now, we have violated the movie camera and forced it to copy the work of our eye. And the better the copy, the better the shooting was thought to be. Starting today we are liberating the camera and making it work in the opposite direction—away from copying.

—DZIGA VERTOV, "KINOCS: A REVOLUTION" (1922)

CIRCULATING MEAT

The Young Pioneers was a Soviet version of the Boy Scouts and Girl Scouts. In the spring and summer of 1924, Dziga Vertov chronicled the activities of one Pioneer unit in a six-reel film that was to serve as the first part in a six-part documentary series about post-revolutionary activity called *Life Off-Guard*.[1] The title of this installment, *Kino-Eye on Its First Reconnaissance: First Episode of the Cycle "Life Off-Guard"* (1924), offers a hint at its primary focus. The title does not mention the apparent object of the film—the Pioneers. Rather, it reveals the film's interest in experimenting with a new theory of production ("kino-eye").

A little over five and a half minutes into the film, it becomes apparent that Vertov's camera has no intention of merely following his young heroes' activities. The sequence begins with some Young Pioneers and one of their mothers separately inquiring about the cost of a piece of meat at a private, open market. Both gather the necessary information. A step behind (as older generations are likely to be), the mother sniffs the meat, walks away, and reads a sign the Pioneers have posted urging people to buy meat from the workers' cooperative.[2] In a sudden and disorienting move, the film begins to reverse time. The mother walks backward, but not toward the private market. In reverse direction, she arrives at the cooperative, where we see the meat quiver and return, along with the entrails, into the bull. The hide is reattached. The bull comes back to life. From the stockyards, he is loaded onto a train and sent back to the countryside, where he and the other members of the herd are raised by cattle farmers. The Young Pioneer Latishov hands a farmer a letter. When he eventually reads it, the image (seemingly from his perspective) cuts to handwritten script that reads "End of the first reel"—a playful and witty way to end.

The most immediately striking aspect of the sequence (and the one most remarked on by viewers) is the reversal in time. Is Vertov simply demonstrating cinema's capacity to reverse the flow of time? Had that been the goal, he likely would have returned the woman to the private market. But instead, as he does to the woman on-screen, he urges the viewer to go in another direction—the direction of political economy. We see that the piece of meat from the cooperative is better not just because it is fresher but because it was produced through socialist practices. In the competing economies, the socialist meat with its collective farming and cooperative distribution wins out over the capitalist meat with its private farms and market distribution.

The sequence does not stop with its reminder of the Marxist lesson that the nature of any commodity is determined by its process of

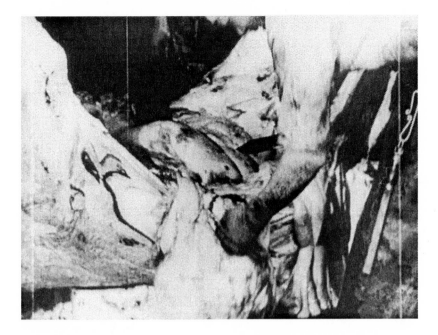

FIGURE 3.1. A cooperative worker "returning the entrails"
to a bull in Vertov's *Kino-Eye.*

production. Had that been the only goal, Vertov could have cut directly
to the collective farm. Instead, he emphasizes cinema's ability to offer
new conceptions of space in addition to time. The camera boards the
train and rides, along with the steer, to the countryside. Those icons
of modernity—the cinema and the train—combine to link the efforts
of the urban with those of the rural. In the early years of the USSR, it
was not just the socialist nature of the meat that was important but also
the identities of those who cooperatively produced it. Moreover, the effort to link the urban and the rural through modern technologies not
only produced a new understanding of commodity value. As the letter
changing hands indicates, the technologies that both materially and
imaginatively produce *smychka* (alliance between worker and peasant)
have real personal value as well.

   As Vertov makes clear in the title of the film and in his writings that
preceded the film (such as his essay "Kinocs: A Revolution"),[3] transform-

ing the thought of the spectator is not to be achieved through verbal language (in intertitles) nor merely by offering a copy of people's vision of the material world. The "kino-eye" experiment aims to combine the vision available through the camera with natural human vision. And it does so *systematically,* through a series of innovative methods of capture and montage. In the process, it aims to produce new relations between thought and vision such as the ones described above. People have to learn to make sense of "chaos of visual phenomena" to which Vertov refers.[4] They have to see the material objects (including people) and processes taking place in the Soviet Union differently, recognizing *relations* across them in ways not theretofore encouraged. Cinema has the potential to train the eye and mind for such integration precisely because of its ability to reconfigure the world.

But *Kino-Eye* is not a dry, intellectual illustrated lecture of Marxist concepts. The sequence I described above is jarring and speaks to the creative force capable in cinema (it can even restore life to a dead bull!). It urges viewers to take notice of its efforts, becoming, in turn, an authored, "voiced" cinema. Its lesson in political economy depends on an inter-relation of cinematic perception and human perception, on represented objects and objects that exist in the material world, and on recognizing this relationship as such. In this way the meat becomes neither wholly image nor wholly object but what Jonathan Beller describes as an *object-image* whose value depends on its industrial-cinematic circulation and the thoughtful, critical experience it engenders.[5]

This sequence from *Kino-Eye,* the film whose name refers to a foundational concept underlying Vertov's cinematic practice,[6] offers a glimpse of Vertov's efforts to shape the social and geographical imaginaries of the new Soviet citizen from 1922 to 1927. It presents a new vision of the collectivity, a new recognition of the relations that connect them and new sensorial and intellectual modes of apprehending these connections and insists on a critical, reflective engagement with this process. Vertov's film project—for he insisted he had no individual films but one continuous film that functioned as a critical, scientific experiment[7]— from this period aimed to produce both a model of social totality and a critical, active, creative subject capable of comprehending the totality. If Sergei Eisenstein's cinema from the period sought to work directly and automatically on the viewer, Vertov's cinema sought to work with the viewer. He required a level of fierce sensorial, intellectual, and critical attentiveness—the kind of subject, he believed, required to properly participate in revolutionary transformation. His efforts to achieve this new vision and the epistemological foundations necessary for its realization, as well as the responses he encountered to his *Kino-Pravda* newsreel series, *Kino-Eye, Stride, Soviet!,* and *A Sixth Part of the World,* are the subject of this chapter.

INDUSTRIAL AND AESTHETIC (RE)ORGANIZATION

A number of important pronouncements and policy decisions that shaped the direction of cinema occurred in the years between the end of the *Kino-Nedelia* newsreel (1919) and the birth of Vertov's second newsreel project, *Kino-Pravda* (1922–1925). At the beginning of 1922, Lenin offered his "Directive on Cinema Affairs," which marked a new political and artistic interest in cinema. Lenin wanted to get Soviet cinema on its feet and believed it would be self-sustainable. His strong reiteration of the goals of the Ninth Party Congress set the agenda for nonfiction film. Lenin wanted "to pay special attention to the organization of cinemas in the countryside and in the East, where they are novelties and where, therefore, our propaganda will be particularly successful."[8] Later that year Lunacharsky famously reported his conversation with Lenin in which he claimed Lenin said to him, "You must remember that of all the arts, for us cinema is the most important." Equally important for nonfiction film was Lunacharsky's report that Lenin wanted a "definite proportion between entertainment films and scientific ones" with "newsreel" as the starting point.[9] Vertov and others continually referred to this statement as evidence of Lenin's commitment to nonfiction film and sought to quantify the "definite proportion" in a way that increased funding for newsreel and documentary production.

Although most of the civil war fighting had ended in 1920, it was not until 1922 that the final uprisings were quashed. As a result, the Union of Soviet Socialist Republics was founded in December 1922. Centralized organization on the political front was echoed by another effort to establish centralized control over the film industry.[10] In December 1922, Sovnarkom, the Council of People's Commissars, established the first centralized cinema organization, Goskino, at the behest of Lenin. Reflecting Lenin's conviction about the commercial viability of cinema, Goskino was expected to be self-financed.[11] Unfortunately, Goskino's economic potential was not soon realized. Like Soviet society as a whole, state-sponsored cinema continued to be plagued by shortages of every kind. Goskino and the private companies lacked film stock, technical equipment, skilled workers, and even scripts for new projects.

These conditions affected the kinds of projects in which Vertov engaged. In the period immediately following the revolution, Vertov had remained in Moscow editing material he received from the front for the *Kino-Nedelia* series and for some of his early documentaries. In the years between the *Kino-Nedelia* and *Kino-Pravda* newsreels, however, he spent significant time traveling throughout the Union working on the agit-trains himself. The trains were composed of sixteen to eighteen coaches and were connected by telephone and radio to Moscow. On average, they employed fifteen to eighteen political workers and eighty to eighty-five technical assistants. They were decorated with paintings and futurist slogans by artists such as El Lissitzky and Vladimir Mayakovsky. They housed a political department, an information department, a complaints office, a Russian telegraph agency department, a film department, a bookshop, and an exhibition space. Workers screened agit-films from Moscow and Petrograd and filmed activity in the countryside.[12] Richard Taylor sums up their importance for the establishment of the Soviet Union and for cinema history:

> The agit-trains represented a spontaneous and temporary response to an emergency situation.... Their greatest importance though lies in a longer term historical perspective: the agit-trains represented one of the earliest attempts at the creation and manipulation of a mass communications medium for political purposes and their requirements and techniques exerted a formative influence on the future development of the medium, the cinema, in both artistic and economic terms. Without the challenge of the Civil War it is unlikely that the Soviet cinema would have developed the forceful, distinctive and revolutionary visual style of the 1920s, and without that style the effectiveness of the cinema in transmitting the Bolshevik world-view both within and beyond the frontiers of the U.S.S.R. would have been severely restricted.[13]

Vertov's experience on the agit-trains shaped both his conception of the new national, supranational, and international collective and the formal possibilities for envisioning that collective. Beginning with a concerted effort at *smychka,* or "alliance," between the rural peasant and the urban proletariat (with which the intelligentsia often aligned itself) in *Kino-Pravda* and ending with his celebration of the ethnic and cultural diversity of the Union in *A Sixth Part of the World,* Vertov's films of this period advanced the effort to newly envision the mass described in part 1. His work of this period does so through a series of increasingly creative formal experiments designed to instantiate not just a new vision of the Soviet collective but a new conceptual apparatus for making sense of its role in revolutionary society.

SMYCHKA AND SUPRANATIONAL HETEROGENEITY

In late spring of 1922, Vertov was given the opportunity by Kultkino, Goskino's educational or documentary section, to direct the newly established newsreel series *Kino-Pravda.* Vertov himself declared that the lack of film stock and adequate contributors kept the newsreel from being a "Cine-Gazette" ("a survey of the world every few hours") and required it to be a "periodical film magazine."[14] A "magazine" would be released less frequently than a gazette and would concentrate on fewer issues. Whereas Vertov was very much in favor of the interrelation of a magazine and of the requirement that it have a greater permanence, he was also drawn to the speed with which a gazette could go from production to exhibition. This commitment to interrelation—of thematic as well as of thought and sensorial experience—and speed of circulation remained core concerns throughout the series.

The "Pravda" in the name of the series should be read as an allusion not to literal truth but to the name of the Communist Party's daily newspaper. But rather than report the news in a traditional sense, Vertov's effort at interrelation speaks to a different concern. Whether it is, as Yuri Tsivian contends, the effort to "string facts into sequences, and make sequences into statements," or as Hicks claims a shift from recording "an already existing causal relation" to *creating* that relation, *Kino-Pravda* might be the birth not only of the "Vertov we now know" but of the Soviet avant-garde cinema itself.[15]

Throughout the series, Vertov endeavors to establish an image of the collectivity that aligns with the party's unity-building efforts but that also preserves identity within each category. The image of the mass itself is reminiscent of the spontaneous and energetic yet disciplined model visualized in the first period of films. Issue #16 captures the Moscow May Day celebrations and the funeral of the Soviet delegate Vaslav Vorovsky in 1923. The camera moves throughout the city with parade participants and mourners, witnessing and experiencing the events from a range of views and spaces. Once again we see a mobile, youthful, growing mass assuming power over urban space and building communities in the process.

But if issue #16 labors to communicate a sense of the collective as a mass, the ensuing issues more carefully delineate the makeup of the collective. Developing more fully the central thematic of unity between worker and peasant, issue #17 celebrates the realization of *smychka* at the All-Union Agricultural Exhibition in Moscow that brought peasants into the city. Elizaveta Svilova's rapidly edited montage connects the worker and peasant as they labor to build the exhibition together (sawing a log) and enjoy leisure together (having a smoke). Vertov announces the dates and location, encouraging all to attend an event built in unity that will celebrate unity.

Issue #18 follows up on the story of the exhibition and the thematic it establishes.[16] While again focusing on *smychka,* the issue offers a tour and experience of the city from the peasant Vasilii Siriakov's point of view. He travels on a tram, goes to see Lenin's grave, and even ends up at a Goskino workshop.[17] The montage aims to realize a new image of the peasant and his relation to modern spaces and technologies. Siriakov's son is born and partakes in an "Octoberism" (a kind of revolutionary baptism). In a rapidly edited scene that builds rhythmic momentum, the child's name (Vladimir) is superimposed over various parts of cameras and machine tools. The peasant emerges from the issue transformed— his experience of the city (with its emblems of modernity) and his relinquishing of backward religious practices testifying, in cinematic terms, to his inclusion in the national revolutionary project.

Vertov continues to attend to the multiplicity of identity categories in issue #19. If #16 offers a vision of the mass, #17 celebrates the unity of worker and peasant, and #18 delves deeper into the experience of identity by providing access to the subjectivity of the peasant, #19 promotes gender equality across these newly established bounds. Women do secretarial work, agricultural work, political work, and even cultural work. Four years before the release of *Man with a Movie Camera*, Vertov presents an image of Svilova, his wife, editing issue #19.

The topic of inclusion in the Soviet project, like so many of Vertov's efforts to shape political views, is at times infused with a sense of playfulness. We see examples in issue #20 of non-humans allied with the Young Pioneers—*smychka s zvermi* ("alliance with animals"!)—as our young heroes embrace a wolf and play with snakes. *Stride, Soviet!*, a feature film from 1927 that likewise aims to promote *smychka*, even extends the purview of *smychka* to machines themselves. In a wildly innovative sequence centered on a Mossoviet election rally in 1925, Vertov replaces the supporters at the event with buses that listen to (established through a cone motif), watch (circular motif), and applaud (horns and pulsing images) the Mossoviet leaders. As if that substitution were not enough, Vertov expands the metaphor geographically by cutting to buses outside the city-space that also respond with approval. Rural buses need not take a backseat to any in the Union!

Issues #18 and #19 are structured as a cine-race (*kino-probeg*), a travel genre Vertov and the *kinocs* developed to counter hierarchical and colonialist models of representing the traditionally unrepresented. An earlier example of the genre can be seen in #7. The issue shows Siberians responding to the defeat of Admiral Aleksandr Kolchack (leader of the counterrevolutionary White forces during the civil war) by rebuilding and establishing a commune. But unlike issue #19, issue #7 extends beyond the borders of the Union. Within the Union, the issue offers glimpses of mica pits near Lake Baikal, the health resorts of the "Caucasian Riviera," a beach on the Black Sea, and people loading silk onto a boat destined for Baku. Extending beyond the variety of landscape and wealth of mineral resources, the borders of the Union provide an opportunity to focus more on cultural activity. Muslims in Persia and at a bazaar in Kabul, Afghanistan labor, partake in cultural festivities and exhibit a range of habits and dress. But if in these issues Vertov is interested in representing a wide range of customs and peoples, the *Kino-Pravda* series as a whole focuses much more on the unity of the worker and peasant. The non-Russian peoples function more as extensions than fully integrated participants in a supranational project. It is in *A Sixth Part of the World* that Vertov articulates an image of a collectivity as expansive as that of the Union.

A Sixth Part of the World was commissioned in 1925 by Gostorg, the central State Trading Organization. Vertov was charged with creating a film capable of promoting Soviet products abroad and representing Gostorg as an active force within the New Economic Policy (NEP). To the Soviet citizen, it was also supposed to demonstrate how the NEP would create a trade surplus and allow the Soviet Union to purchase industrial and agricultural machinery to modernize the nation. Thus, even as a celebration of the most exotic borderlands of the Union, the film was to recognize the crucial link Gostorg played between Soviet producers and the foreign (mostly capitalist) world, with whom they remained (unfortunately) connected.[18]

The second reel of the film proposes a new vision of the makeup of the supranational collective while instructing the viewer in the proper mode of analysis. While the first reel establishes capitalism as an overall system of inequality whose exploitation is visible in people's gestures, performances, and visual pleasures, the second reel then contrasts CAPITAL with the Soviet land and its masters—the Tartars, Buriats, Uzbeks, Khakkass, people of the Caucuses, and Komi. The inspirational titles shift into a direct address mode, commending the herdsmen, hunters, fishermen, and factory workers as we see them perform their duties. This section not only focuses on the range of labor but concludes by showing cultural festivals, musical traditions, and eating habits. The Samoyeds of the Arctic north get the most attention as they are seen eating their "venison raw" and racing reindeer. It ends with the direct declaration:

IN YOUR HANDS
IS A SIXTH
PART OF THE WORLD

The governing concept behind this reel is the establishment of a visual bond that aims to create a sense of unity between citizens and ethnic groups from across the vast Union.[19] Throughout these sections we see a fairly rapidly cut collection of static images, usually in medium or long shots. Often, only one image will capture a particular subject. For example, we see one or two shots of a man bathing his sheep in a body of water followed by one or two shots of another man bathing his sheep in an entirely different body of water. The emphasis is less on documenting the event taking place, in its specific time and space, than on its value as representative of the larger community. Prior to each is a title with a direct address and grammatical regularity ("You, who bathe your sheep in the surf of the sea" followed by the image; "and you, who bathe your sheep in a brook" followed by the image). The titles serve to establish an idea of collectivity and a continuous rhythm while the Whitmanesque direct address serves to create a sense of urgency and inclusivity.[20]

The film as a whole presents an image of national particularity that focuses, as Emma Widdis describes, "on the *specificity* and differ- ence of all the cultures represented as part of the Soviet Union."[21] It is a celebration of ethnic diversity and part of a larger effort to identify the major determinants of nationality that, Francine Hirsch argues, were seen to ensure its cultural autonomy.[22] Terry Martin in fact marks the "systematic support of national forms: territory, culture, language, and elites" as the distinctive feature of Soviet nationalities policy.[23] A *Sixth Part of the World* thus presents a vision of a heterogeneous and unified collectivity—a vision that expands on the notion of *smychka* so predominant throughout the 1920s. Whereas Vertov may not entirely escape the hierarchical and dominating effects so often attributed to ethnographic models of visualization (and he does not question his own representational authority), he does exhibit an awareness of many of the inherent political dangers. His vision of the collective is both clas- sificatory and expansive—identifying the constituents of the citizenry while urging that citizenry to maintain both a supranational and in- ternational perspective. It is in the relations across the collectivity that the expansiveness of Vertov's visions and thought become apparent and contentious.

CINEMATIC SPACE, VIRTUAL MOBILITY, AND THE (SUPRA)NATIONAL COLLECTIVE

The new image of the collective that Vertov proposes is always accompa- nied by an analysis of the relations subtending it. In *Man with a Movie*

Camera, as Annette Michelson and Jonathan Beller (among others) have argued, Vertov mobilizes an extraordinary range of cinematic devices— acceleration, deceleration, double exposure, optical printing of single frames, shots of the editing process intercut with the resultant final film, split screens, extreme close-ups, and use of still images—as a way of revealing the forces governing the production and reproduction of social life. It is, as Beller describes, above all "a way of seeing through matter," a method of making the unthought relations of capital thinkable.[24] Whereas in *Man with a Movie Camera* political economic relations are revealed primarily through a "virtual city" (a combination of Moscow, Kiev, and Odessa), in the films from the mid-1920s these relations are often revealed through a mobilized gaze in which the *experience* of visualizing the Union is inseparable from political economic analysis of the social relations governing it. Vertov describes kino-eye as "documentary cinematic decoding of both the visible world and that which is invisible to the naked eye. . . . Kino-eye means the conquest of space, the visual linkage of people throughout the entire world based on the continuous exchange of visible fact."[25] The goal was to create a model of vision that would unify (with a presumption of equality) and provide a foundation for an analysis of social totality. It is the dynamic between a sensory experience of the world (achieved through vision) and the decoding of the relations governing that world that drives these efforts at unification and political edification.

One of the primary means through which Vertov sought to achieve this goal in his films from the mid-1920s was by creating a new relationship between the Soviet citizen and supranational space. This was not an uncommon approach in the Soviet Union at the time. Political leaders and numerous types of cultural producers—from filmmakers, journalists, and novelists to cartographers and architects—saw such a project as crucial to instilling Soviet identity and modeling a proper way to live in the world. Widdis describes the stakes: "Understanding Sovietness . . . means understanding the space of Sovietness. . . . The success of any social or political project depends on the provision of an 'imaginary' map of the social and spatial totality within which the individual is to function: in the case of the Soviet Union, the sheer scale of the territory made this a monumental, and crucial, task. . . . Social revolution demands spatial revolution: the new regime needed a new map."[26] Vertov employs varying degrees of direct and symbolic representation of national and supranational space in his films, but all depend on the simultaneous experience and imagination of this new map of social and spatial totality.

No object in Vertov's films carries more symbolic weight and experiential power than the train. It is a recurrent image and a motif that sustains many of the dominant themes of the films (mobility, communication, travel, technological progress, leisure, speed, and urbanism). It carries propaganda from center to periphery and between peripheries and connects them through tracks. It is a symbol of economic progress, transporting new technical equipment to the countryside and increased yields back to the cities. It is also a symbol of social progress, standing in for the speed and mobility of revolutionary life. It integrates the citizenry; its "railway lines facilitated the new 'blood circulation' of the nation."[27] And it does so while reinforcing a sense of strong leadership (the name *Lenin* is given to certain trains and highlighted in the titles).[28] Like the agit-steamer I described in part 1, it is a powerful *movement* that has marched into the countryside. It is gaining momentum, its reach broad, its encroachment inevitable.

But in addition to providing an image of a unified national body operating under the guidance of visionary leadership, the train offers a *dynamic experience* of travel. In this way it conjoins any "decoding of the visible world" with an accounting of the new subjective experiences it offers. For Vertov and many other artists in the USSR in the 1920s, any effort to liberate citizens ideologically rested on their ability to emancipate the senses of the viewer through artistic means. Vertov's effort to instill *oshchushchenie* (a "cinematic feeling" that incorporates both sensation and experience), like that of many filmmakers, revolved around the issue of mobility. The view from the window, the back, the front, or the roof of a train offered this dynamic experience, one in which both the object of vision and the perspective from which one saw was in flux. This experience is vital to encouraging a collective reimagination of what was occurring in new revolutionary space. Viewers encountered landscapes anew, whether it was their first exposure to them or whether the train newly connected them. And they saw new everyday activities within these spaces. Whether it was the journey to Lake Baikal, the "Caucasian

Riviera," and Azerbaijan in #7, the excursion into Moscow and through Moscow from the peasant perspective in #18 and #22, the rapid rushing through landscape and village in #20, or the expansion of the visible modes of perception beyond the train to that of the horse and car (#9) and even the sled, ski, and steamer (#19), mobile perception created a sense of a dynamic space to which a visually dynamic subject must attend.

These issues of *Kino-Pravda* provide examples of urban, national, and supranational space experienced through fairly stable spatiotemporal relations. Other examples were not nearly as direct or continuous. *Stride, Soviet!,* for example, focuses its attention on Moscow as the symbolic center of the country. Its logic is that familiar one of the old and new—the achievements of the past eight years contrasted with the nightmare of the pre-revolutionary (or at times, the pre-USSR) period. The first series of the first reel exhibits shots of a well-functioning modern industrial city—skyline, mass gathering, illuminated light bulb, working factory, functioning plumbing. The second series reveals the long lines, bus crashes, idle factories, faulty plumbing, famine victims, dead animals, and lack of firewood that characterized the past. The reel concludes with title cards such as TOWARD A VICTORY OVER COLD, TOWARD A VICTORY OVER HUNGER and TOWARD A COMPLETE VICTORY FOR THE REVOLUTION interspersed between shots of a man splitting wood, a soup kitchen, and a political parade. The section is visibly affective, with extreme close-ups heightening the diseased figures, and rhythmically consistent, which may aim to establish the continuous progress the Union had seen under the Mossoviet's guidance.

In contrast to the first reel, which begins with the positive results, the second reel begins with scenes of devastation caused by the civil war. Intercut with those images are shots of Lenin speaking at the Mossoviet. He calls FOR GREAT SACRIFICES, TO THE STRUGGLE, FOR THE REVOLUTION as soldiers heed his call. The section then focuses on the military and civic role of the Mossoviet in aiding the fighting and overcoming the devastation caused by the war. Evidence of the shift from devastation to construction is visible in contrasting scenes of idle and working factories as well as in scenes of the ELECTRIFICATION OF THE VILLAGES and building of schools. Framing the section is a superimposed close-up of Lenin over the newly lit lightbulb.

The logical structure—whether positive to negative or negative to positive—highlights differentiation between the two times. In turn, it creates a sense of contiguous space for the achievements of the present. The focus on Moscow serves to indicate that the capital stands in for the Union as a whole. Although the electrification of the village serves an integrative function, pointing to the interconnected energy of the people and space they inhabit, *Stride, Soviet!*, like the *Kino-Pravda* series and much more than *A Sixth Part of the World*, asserts unity in different measure than equality. The city is both synecdoche and privileged space in the Union.

In addition to the continuous mobile perception of urban, national, and supranational space and the synecdochical relation between city and periphery, Vertov also offers an image of a virtual event that serves to shape the imaginary geography of the country. Developing further an idea he tries out in the *Kino-Nedelia* series (#35, for example), Vertov intercuts October celebrations and funeral proceedings in *Kino-Pravda* #13 so that the represented audiences appear to experience them as single events. Marchers celebrate the national revolution together, while mourners recognize the losses to all citizens. By means of a singular close-up image of a mouth screaming "Hurrah!" and an image of Red Troops marching through an unspecified square, Vertov situates viewers in a united virtual space by foregoing the common usage of chronological time.

A Sixth Part of the World builds on this strategy. In *Kino-Pravda* #13, a unified space communicates a sense of a national event with shared feelings of celebration and sadness. In *A Sixth Part of the World*, however, this virtual, unified space and the shared sense of a cooperative project extend beyond such boundaries. The third reel of the film explores the geographical range of the Union (and expands the second reel's emphasis on national peoples) by highlighting its various natural resources. FROM THE KREMLIN to THE CHINESE BORDER, and FROM A LIGHTHOUSE ABOVE THE ARCTIC CIRCLE to THE CAUCUSES are animals such as the silver fox, bear, and polar owl. Continuing with the direct address, ALL IN YOUR HANDS is wool, fish, tobacco, oil, cotton, and the most important national export, grain. The fourth reel demonstrates how they circulate throughout the Union ALONG ALL THE ROADS OF THE SOVIET NATION.

Boxes, trains, and barrels move along waterways, railways, and country roads, ending up at Gostorg trading posts, where they are EXPORTED TO THE LANDS OF CAPITAL. The fifth reel proposes that through the network established by Gostorg, all of the Soviet people are working toward the construction of socialism. Titles explain that the goods they produce are being exported abroad and bring not just machines, but MACHINES TO BUILD MACHINES. Here, citizens of the Union are afforded a new understanding of how the New Economic Policy structures the economy. Vertov demonstrates Gostorg's coordination of enterprises from around the Union, noting how these efforts position them to accumulate capital and reinvest in and thus modernize the Union.

If, as Vertov claims, these films are a series of experiments that offer a new vision of the world so that the world can be newly thought in Marxist political economic terms, the films from 1922 to 1927 demonstrate the development of this idea. Viewers see how, what, and where goods are produced. They see how their model is different from both the old model (*Stride, Soviet!*) and from alternative models (the capitalism of the first reel of *A Sixth Part of the World*). And they see how their country is transformed as a result of these efforts. This transformation provides visible evidence of the validity of their approach, one in which community-serving state organizations do not extract the difference between cost and revenue but reinvest it in the people responsible for the creation of value.

SENSORIUM AND THE SUBJECT

In the above section, I have explicated the complex address that infuses Vertov's films of the period, one that aims to instill a sense of belonging to a collective while providing political economic tools (and evidence) for understanding the revolutionary project. But these films also work to transform individual subjectivities. They not only aim to imbue Soviet citizens with a sense of and reason for belonging but also educate citizens in the proper way of behaving *as individuals* in post-revolutionary society. And they provide the tools necessary to begin transforming the self.

The role of individual subjectivity was a point of interrogation for art in the years following the Bolshevik Revolution—not least for the artists themselves. Artists sought to seize the world from the past, with its binds to mysticism, spirituality, and the natural itself, and replace it with an art focused on building and synthesizing both materials and previously autonomous artistic forms. Constructivists such as Vladimir Tatlin and Aleksandr Rodchenko insisted that the artist be a technician and use the tools and materials of contemporary production. The artist was obligated to work to benefit the proletariat and build harmony into life by transforming "work into art and art into work."[29] In cinema this interest was realized in the effort to rethink the nature and experience of space and time. Harmonizing the body with the new revolutionary world required acclimating the citizen to a level of kineticism and speed theretofore unimaginable. Such an achievement was considered absolutely vital to the modernization project, for it was only by transforming the Soviet work ethic from one of laziness, wildness, and inefficiency to one of attentiveness, precision, and even grace of movement that the USSR could catch up to and bypass the West.

For both artists and government officials, these efforts coalesced around citizens' engagements with machines.[30] Machines of mobility, machines in the factory, and of course the machine of cinema—all these possessed the potential to transform subjects' experiences of work and everyday life. The endeavor to harmonize and in turn transform the sensorium of the Soviet subject aligns with the Soviet government's simultaneous endeavor to incorporate a model of American scientific management theory. Lenin himself established the stakes for the future of the revolution, maintaining that "those who have the best technology, organization, discipline, and the best machines emerge on top."[31] Machines could transform Soviet citizens from lazy, panicky, and wild to energized, organized, and well trained. And cinema could help arm them with the sharpness of vision, attention to detail, and recognition of precision necessary to enter the new Soviet factory.

The adoption of Frederick W. Taylor's experiments to increase the efficiency of machine shop production was one of the more curious, experimental, and utopian projects undertaken in the post-revolutionary period. By the time of the Russian Revolution, Taylorism had become a series or synthesis of tools, methods, and organizational arrangements to increase efficiency and speed.[32] Taylorism's time-saving claims thus had obvious resonances in the Soviet Union, where increasing productivity and the eventual abolition of private property were supposed to aid a massively underdeveloped nation realize its aims.[33] Productivity itself, or what Anson Rabinbach refers to as the "ideology of 'productivism'—the balancing of expanded output with social reform"—became adaptable to "liberal, socialist, authoritarian, and even communist and fascist solutions."[34] While increasing the efficiency of the shop had obvious financial benefits, a utopian social impulse subtended Taylorism's utilitarianism. Taylorism sought to eliminate the conflict between workers and management by establishing scientifically "what constitutes a fair day's work" through various timing procedures. Most important, Taylorism (herein I am including the bonus plans devised by Gantt, the organization of machine speeds by Barth, and the time and motion studies conducted by the Gilbreths) first introduced a management-oriented industrial ideology that could bring harmony to a relation traditionally rife with conflict. Greater productivity, Taylor claimed, made both sides happy as the focus moved from concerns over the division of the surplus toward a joint effort to increase the surplus. Taylor understood his system as nothing short of a mental revolution.

The sense that Taylor's politics were radically anti-worker prompted Judith Merkle to describe the absorption of Taylorist principles by the Bolsheviks as "one of the most curious episodes in the history of Taylorism."[35] Nikolai Sukhanov was one of many at the time to react ambivalently to the possibility, weighing the technical benefits against the potential social exploitation. But with the support of Lenin, the belief that Taylorism had the potential to harmonize relations across the production process won out. Moreover, it was accompanied by a concomitant desire to transform relations between individuals and their external worlds.

The pivotal figure in the relationship between Taylorism and Soviet policy was Alexei Gastev. He attained this status not simply on account of his influence on industrial policy; his interest in Taylorism was both social and cultural as he himself was both an industrial and artistic figure. Gastev was one of the most popular "worker-poets" at the time of the revolution.[36] During stints in prison and Siberian exile for revolutionary activity, Gastev wrote poems about a new industrial Russia, incorporating aural symbols such as the factory whistle, steel lathe, and blast furnace. Gastev was a skilled laborer and organizer who claimed he turned to poetry only because other revolutionary opportunities were unavailable to him. In 1920, Gastev became head of the Central Labor Institute and imbued the organization with his romanticism and ideological beliefs. More than anything, he was concerned with the transformation of Russian culture and believed that Taylorism could create a "type" of proletariat characterized by a specific psychology. He envisioned Taylorism as a form of social engineering that would transform every aspect of the proletariat's existence: "even his intimate life, including his aesthetic, intellectual and sexual values."[37] Gastev highlights the two sides of Taylorism—its emphasis on discipline, control, and social mobilization and its emphasis on the transformation of individual psychology. As Richard Stites argues, although Gastev spoke in the idiom of the former, his "aim was to 'free' the Russian population from its enslaving lassitude and to transform it into a spontaneously functioning army of producers."[38] It was this liberatory element that aligned with Vertov's efforts to transform the sensorium of the subject in the mid-1920s.

One of the profound shifts from Vertov's films of the first period to his films of the second period is his increased attention to the issue of speed. The camera races or "cine-races" that I have described were, of course, not just about transforming notions of the space through which one moved (and the relations engendered by that movement) but also about the speed with which it was traversed. *Kino-Pravda #9* is the archetypal example.

In this regard, *Kino-Pravda #9* (August 1922) is thematically, visually, and formally integrated. The issue focuses on new technology, urban mobility, and the transformation of urban space—all linked by the attention to and visualization of speed. The first sequence breaks down a bus ride in Moscow into ten shots that last a total of thirty seconds. The sequence establishes a rhythm for the issue and offers a new perspective on the workings of bus travel. A later section insists that mobile cinemas are not just disseminated on agit-trains and agit-steamers with the goal of linking the countryside to the city but exist within urban areas themselves. In 1922, most of the urban theaters were in the hands of the private companies. Goskino had few of its own theaters, and as a result they could not reach a large number of people theatrically. Thus, they exhibited many films, issues of *Kino-Pravda* included, in city squares and workers' clubs.[39] After a demonstration of the technologically advanced American movie cameras VFKO had recently acquired, *Kino-Pravda #9* visualizes the process of setting up an urban mobile cinema. It begins with a call to the central office to strike up a screening in Strastnaia Square. The mobile cinema team departs for the square immediately, requiring only themselves and a horse-drawn cab to transport their equipment. Once they arrive at the square, a countdown begins that demonstrates that they can set up the equipment in only eight minutes. The square fills up with both viewers preparing for the show and marchers, who are seemingly disconnected from the anticipated screening. The marchers are granted extended screen time, pointing to social mobilization as the flip side of the transformation of the individual sensorium. But it is clearly the importance of speed itself that dominates the issue.

The Constructivist artist and theorist Alexei Gan identifies the ideological imperative behind such experiments.[40] Gan critiques the individualism of other leftist artists at the time, whom he claims produce "only one thing: an endless series of formal experiments," disconnected from proletarian ideology.[41] In contrast, Vertov links "people, machines, and the material environment" in a cinematic way that allows viewers to see differently. The crux of the issue for Gan is Vertov's skill in capturing and organizing images of daily life. He argues that the swiftness of the revolution is visible only through a machine since humans are not currently conditioned to perceive it. The cinematic apparatus will then give our human eyes perspective, a new way of seeing, which will allow people to return to material reality and see the incredible pace with insight and clarity. Thus, cinema organizes revolutionary consciousness by allowing citizens to see the pace of the revolution as it is.[42] Whereas other issues of *Kino-Pravda* (including #7) and the feature films provide examples of people engaging machines on the factory floor, here Vertov offers examples of people engaging machines that move people quickly (buses, cars) and machines through which people move (cinema). Each case serves to acclimate people to the pace of revolutionary life while reminding that speed is not synonymous with the haphazard but requires precision and expertise for proper functioning.

In issue #9, speed is both the apparent topic and a subjective experience that prepares individuals in the proper mode of apprehending the world. Or perhaps, put differently, speed is both the object lesson and the subject lesson. It is communicated through the referential activities and visual qualities of the image and through editing rhythms. Throughout his work, Vertov employed precise, regulated rhythms to the point that his editing has been described as "metrical." His careful attention to the specificity of frame lengths in individual images as well as relations of frame lengths across sequences can be seen as equivalent to and preparation for engagement with factory machines. Their regularity and precision matches that of the machines on the shop floor. Cinema thus imbues people with what the Taylorist enthusiast Platon Mikhailovich Kerzhentsev calls a "feeling for time."[43]

But for Vertov, this feeling for time, this desire for speed, and this larger effort to transform the sensoria of the Soviet citizen are never removed from a sense of playfulness, of liberation, of inspiration. Soviet Taylorism as a scientific and ideological system was simultaneously concerned with restructuring the shop floor, its relation to management, and individuals' subjective experiences (both inside and outside of work). In this large-scale restructuring, Vertov does not adopt the position of the worker. Rather, he becomes the new Soviet engineer, organizing the material and people's engagements with it. However, if the Taylorist engineer seeks organization and intuitive senses of movement and time in the hopes of achieving maximum efficiency and standardization, Vertov's application is for different purposes. While likewise aiming to counter the apparent laziness and wildness of the worker, Vertov seeks to instill a sharpness of vision, a feeling of inspiration, and an attentiveness to as well as sense of the environment—especially the urban environment. If his experiments on the body of the viewer sought to produce mechanized subjects, it was ones with fierce creativity.

THE *ICE-BREAKER LENIN* AND THE OBSERVATION OF MEASURE

Vertov's commitment to projecting, instilling, and modeling a sense of belonging to, an understanding of, and a feeling for the revolutionary socialist project reaches its acme during this period in *A Sixth Part of the World*. The film provides a sensory experience of the world and its dialectic with analytical thought. If, as I discussed above, the middle section of the film is concerned with linking people and their relation to the world through affective and analytical addresses to citizens as members of a unified collective, the beginning and ending of the film offer a visual hermeneutic, one that implores viewers to see isolated facts and objects anew and then situate them within a larger Marxist framework. The film thus encapsulates many of the aesthetic, political, and conceptual concerns Vertov had during his time in Moscow working for the dominant state-run film organizations. But this ambition turned out to instigate considerable debate. The problem for many cultural critics was not Vertov's goal of providing viewers with a perspective on the nation and the world but the aesthetics and method he employed in doing so. The thematic structure and range of dialectical montage techniques confounded many reviewers and everyday citizens. As Vertov continually sought to expand the boundaries for nonfiction film, state officials and critics alike increasingly sought to define its methodological and aesthetic limits.

The film opens with a couple of rapid shots from an airplane offering views of the city below. This perspective sets the stage for the analysis of CAPITAL in the first reel, encouraging a visual-analytical stance toward the material. Vertov's position that vision is less a static perspective than a conscious act is made apparent through the intertitle I SEE, which appears on-screen immediately prior to images of the capitalist world.[44] The distanced perspective of the airplane is followed by fragmented views of objects, gestures, and movements of the world dominated by "capital." In lightning-fast montage, we see people dance the foxtrot, get served by chambermaids, eat, and laugh IN A NATION OF CAPITALISTS. We see a black jazz band performing, followed by SLAVES IN THE COLONIES. The CHOCOLATE BOYS dance number is intercut with ethnographic footage of Africans emerging from a hut. Except for the African footage, the other images are all rapidly cut and usually exhibit only fragments of body parts, instruments, or performances. The viewer is asked to approach the images within the scope of "capital," an overall system of inequality whose exploitation is visible in people's gestures, performances, and visual pleasures.

The interrelation of the experience of visual fragmentation and encouragement of analysis of social totality is picked up at the end of the film. Reel six centers on the transformation of reactionary social and cultural practices. We see a peasant who works the soil with a stick, a woman in her yashmak, shamanist rituals, a man counting beads, and a woman dancing in traditional costume. The sequence begins to take shape as the massive vessel *Ice-Breaker Lenin* drives through the partially frozen Black Sea, helping ships that are stuck and bringing modern goods to citizens. At the beginning of the *Ice-Breaker Lenin* sequence, the camera shoots from alongside the massive ship just above sea level. It is an impressive angle from which to view the ice bounding off the front of the ship (and likely would have impressed an audience aware of the danger involved in getting the shot). While this shot lasts for a considerable length of time (for Vertov), the majority of the sequence consists of a rapid array of sharp angles and perspectives of the ship from the side and from high above. As in the opening of the "capital" scene, the perspective that we are given functions not to locate us spatially within the Black Sea or to provide the view of the *Ice-Breaker*'s place within that landscape. Instead, the rapidity of a range of oblique and unexpected perspectives promises a new vision of the represented objects.

For Constructivists like Aleksandr Rodchenko and for the *kinocs* themselves, this was not a minor point. Transforming vision, they argued, required looking at objects both from a range of vantage points and from uncommon ones. The goal of this strategy was to make familiar objects look strange so that once people encountered them in the real world, they would see them anew (Viktor Shklovsky's well-known effect of *ostrannenie* or "defamiliarization"). Doing so, Tsivian argues, "was tantamount to making it more real."[45]

This is not simply a formalist gesture, as it is the integration of the "defamiliarization" effect with the content that is key to understanding Vertov's aesthetic. Here, "defamiliarization" is accompanied by the symbolic meaning of the *Ice-Breaker Lenin* as a revolutionary force for progressive change. To fully appreciate how this works, we need to return to an earlier sequence in the film. Throughout *A Sixth Part of the World*, images of water come to symbolize regularity, stability, force, rhythm, power, beauty, and even eroticism as they stand in for the revolution

FIGURE 3.2 AND FIGURE 3.3. Oblique and unexpected perspectives of the *Ice-Breaker Lenin* in *A Sixth Part of the World*.

itself.[46] Vertov effectively conveys such meanings in the rhythmic and emotional consistency of his metrical montage and titling. If the train is the prevailing motif in many of Vertov's films, water takes its place in *A Sixth Part of the World*. In one section of the film, Vertov makes this connection explicit. Approximately thirty-four minutes in, we see a low-angle shot of a train at track level. The wheels spin rapidly, and the image gradually becomes more and more abstract. As the figurative aspect of the image dissipates into pure form, Vertov cuts to a serene but highly contrasting shot of the Arctic Ocean at night. The left side of the screen is illuminated by the moon, the right side barely visible in darkness. Each image remains on the screen for seven to eight seconds. The formal and connotative contrast is sharp (socialist world versus capitalist world) and one to which Vertov returns in the *Ice-Breaker Lenin* scene. As the great ship moves through the sea, its symbolic impact is evident in the progressive responses by citizens. Instead of old prejudices and super-stitions, the *Ice-Breaker Lenin* has cleared the path for Arabic women to throw off their veils, Buriats to read party newspapers, and Mongol children to join a Pioneer camp. We see a lightbulb switch on in a hut and smoke rise from factory chimneys, two predominant symbols of progress for the peasant and worker population. With the water already established as a symbol of the unity and breadth of the nation, we now understand the great vessel forging through it is the idea, the power, the momentum of revolutionary socialism. We see that unity is not an end in itself but is valuable only when situated within a socialist framework. It was Lenin, of course, who united the people initially and who continued to do so, marking the lightness of the socialist world from the darkness of the capitalist world.

These experiments provoked considerable debate in the responses to *A Sixth Part of the World*—conversations that profoundly shaped the future direction of Soviet documentary. The slower-paced alterna-tion of related images designed to create a visual bond prompted an ambivalent reaction. Critics were moved by the film's power to create a sense of connection across the Union. But these sections of the film also frustrated critics, who argued that they were semiotically imprecise—a fault intolerable in a documentary. The hyper-rapidity of the fragmented sequences with their corresponding distanced perspectives designed to spur a reflexive, analytic approach to the world also posed a problem. They were deemed to be cognitively overwhelming and even, at times, irritating.

Reels two, three, and four are dominated by the goal of establishing a visual bond or unity between citizens and ethnic groups. Supporters of the film commended these sections by arguing that their montage rhythm and topical similarities allowed viewers to feel their essential likenesses and valuable differences with other Soviet citizens. Izmail Urazov, always interested in the performative, felt "the connection of such things—the common character of which cannot be proved by any calculations."[47] The vehemently argued counterpoint claimed that the images' lack of context, both visual and situational, caused them to function as symbols rather than as real examples. Shklovsky contended that in *A Sixth Part of the World,* "the factual nature of the shot has disappeared . . . the thing has lost its materiality and become transparent, like a work by the Symbolists."[48] Similarly, Osip Brik claimed that Vertov "has turned real footage . . . into a conventional cinematic sign. . . . Instead of a real deer, we get a deer as a symbolic sign with a vague conventional meaning."[49] Shklovsky and Brik are saying that the filmmaker who has most vigilantly supported the use of "facts" has lost track of their fundamental value in his attempt to expand their meaning-making potential. By 1927, this position was well entrenched in the leftist art community, with many critics (even those who loved the film) claiming that Vertov's facts functioned as symbols in the film and that it therefore no longer qualified as "newsreel."[50]

Critics strongly emphasized the context of the film image or document in *A Sixth Part of the World* in part because of its ethnographic content. An extended quote from A. Zorich is absolutely archetypal of the critical response to the film:

> Of course the very nature of cinema is such that it cannot stand sluggishness and immobility, but in the dynamism and tension which the cinema demands some sort of measure must be observed, which would after all let you concentrate your attention on the individual objects which pass by the viewer on the screen. And this must apply in the first place and particularly to ethnographic film. In *A Sixth Part of the World* this barricade is crossed and this measure not observed. . . .

> For all that, however, it must be admitted that *A Sixth Part of the World*
> is an extremely interesting experiment and an undoubted achievement
> for our cinema.[51]

Zorich's quote demonstrates the ambivalence that almost all of the re-
spondents expressed. On the one hand, they were frustrated by their
inability to *learn more* about the geography and inhabitants of their
vast new nation. On the other hand, they were moved by the emotional
power of the film. But perhaps the most critical question for an understanding of the *direction* of Soviet nonfiction film is, "What would a
proper 'measurement' of an ethnographic documentary film be?" The
answer (one I explore in depth in the chapter 5), evident from the critical responses, is that it would require two interrelated changes—a more
legible defining structure and an aesthetic that offers a more objective,
distanced perspective.

This need for distance is evident in the fact that it was not simply
the lack of established context that troubled the critics. Many felt that
the rapidity of Vertov's montage did not provide sufficient time and his
images enough spatial proximity for the viewer to digest the image or
collection of images. Nikolai Aseev did not "have time to assimilate
the type of bird; your eye doesn't manage to take the impression to the
stage of remembering it."[52] Another reviewer remarked, "This montage
is so feverish, or to put it more precisely, so disordered, that it irritates
the viewer by introducing confusion."[53] Sosnovsky is one of a few to ad-
mit embarrassment, explaining, "The viewer feels dumbfounded, a bit
stupid, because he cannot explain either to himself or to others what is
going on."[54] At this point in time, it is clear that both the value of the film
document itself and the comprehensibility of the montage were deemed
of utmost importance.

The need for a transformation in structure is clear from the considerable criticism of Vertov's method. In other words, Vertov's approach
required total transformation. Instead of filming "life caught unaware"
(and editing according to the internal rhythms of the material), Vertov
was urged to create an organized plan for the film prior to his and his
cameramen's entering the field. This question of organization became
linked to economic efficiency. Following *A Sixth Part of the World*, Ver-

tov was fired from Sovkino.[55] A series of contentious debates among Ilya Trainin (head of Sovkino from 1926 to 1929), those who did his bidding, and Vertov in 1927 revealed the primary reasons for the firing. First, it was determined that *A Sixth Part of the World* cost three to four times as much as it would have had Vertov shot according to a preconceived plan. Second, Sovkino claimed that Vertov did not abide authority, as evident by the fact that *Stride, Soviet!* was never accepted by the Moscow Soviet, the group that commissioned the film. Third, the fact that Vertov would not submit a plan for *Man with the Movie Camera* was a plain indication that this insubordination was likely to continue.[56] While Vertov believed that Trainin inaccurately represented him because he considered nonfiction film unprofitable, among both the leftist avant-garde and the state authorities Vertov had clearly fallen far out of favor.

What emerges from the film and discourse surrounding it is that Vertov's attempt to expand the meaning-making possibilities for nonfiction film—and in the process expand dimensions of thought and experience—had increasingly come up against those in power (cultural or political) wanting to limit its potential for the sake of efficiency and clarity. Sosnovsky argued that such transformative propaganda should not even be Vertov's aim.[57] The complex relationship between the individual and the nation, between a national and an international revolution, and between objects of thought and thought itself was not now, if it ever really had been, Vertov's to articulate.

FOUR

(Non)Alignments and the New Revolutionary Man

The difficult thing to understand for someone not living through the experience of the revolution is this close dialectical unity between the individual and the mass, in which both are interrelated and, at the same time, in which the mass, as an aggregate of individuals, interacts with its leaders.

—CHE GUEVARA, "SOCIALISM AND MAN IN CUBA" (1965)

Che Guevara opens his famous essay "Socialism and Man in Cuba" by countering the characterization of socialism as "the abolition of the individual for the sake of the state."[1] Instead of the elimination of the individual, he argues that socialism seeks a new interrelation not only between the individual and the mass but between that mass and revolutionary leadership. The new configuration serves to overcome the "individual's quality of incompleteness" endemic to capitalist societies (and its colonial legacies) but does so only if it is accompanied by a simultaneous increase in technological production and a deepening of consciousness. The achievement and sustenance of socialism, Che argues, requires continual material and ideological transformation. In his newsreels and documentaries from 1965 to 1971, Santiago Álvarez sought to effect this Guevaran vision by projecting, modeling, and instilling a new technological, ideological, ethical, and sensorial *conciencia* (a consciousness or subjectivity that motivates social action).

A nonfiction genre that commonly articulates the role of the individual in both shaping and responding to social conditions is the biography. Álvarez's "biography" of the Vietnamese leader Ho Chi Minh, however, offers an alternative, socialist model of relationships between individuals and collectives and collectives and leadership. Moreover, it serves as a constellation of Álvarez's efforts during this period to deepen moral and critical consciousness and transform the sensorium of the Cuban citizen by educating citizens in the proper ways to behave as individuals in post-revolutionary society. If as Che describes, individuals have consistently turned to art and culture as tools for freeing themselves (albeit temporarily) from the alienating conditions of capitalist labor, Álvarez's *79 primaveras* (79 springtimes, 1969) develops Che's vision of an ideologically and morally edifying socialist culture. The film provides a vision and an experience of a non-alienated existence. Ho's life and work exemplifies meaningful labor, while Álvarez's expansive vision deepens consciousness by providing core foundations for locating the individual in the world.

Álvarez's *79 primaveras* is both socialist biography and elegy to the Vietnamese leader, who died in 1969. The film begins by chronicling the foremost events in Ho's political development. Ho's achievements are conveyed through beautiful intertitle cards that state the date and his accomplishment (for example, thirty-five *"primaveras"* had passed when he founded the League of Oppressed Peoples in Asia). Archival footage of the different types of labor Ho performed—manual labor with the people, political labor leading meetings, and intellectual labor at the typewriter—supports the titles. This section of the film concludes after the victory of Dien Bien Phu and an abrupt shift to the funeral, where international leaders and Vietnamese citizens mourn Ho's passing.

Álvarez's chronology of the political life of Ho is far removed from dominant Western generic models and serves a pedagogical function as it provides instead an exemplary model of socialist labor. It is in the climactic section of the film that the extent of his effort to deepen consciousness—and his skill in assembling extraordinarily disparate music, imagery, and slogans—fully emerges. Immediately prior to the climactic section, Álvarez inserts a brief juxtaposition that aligns

FIGURE 4.1. Cinematic war in *79 primaveras*.

American antiwar protesters and the North Vietnamese on one side of the international struggle against capitalist imperialism. In the first sequence, protesters burn their draft cards as police in riot gear initiate violence. Rock music predominates as the camera presents an immersive view from the vantage point of protesters. In the second sequence, an older Ho Chi Minh warmly communicates with an old peasant woman attending what appears to be a press conference. At the transition between the sequences, the music shifts to the electric keyboards and drums of Iron Butterfly.[2] Scratchy guitar music begins to merge with Iron Butterfly and gradually becomes dominant as a new title appears on-screen. It states one of Ho's last wishes—DON'T LET DISUNITY IN THE SOCIALIST CAMP DARKEN THE FUTURE. Through animation, the title breaks apart, spins, and gives way to black screen. The film then enacts its most abrupt shift. The discordant guitar gives way to loud battle sounds of bombs, explosions, gunfire, and helicopters as the image track offers a dizzying assortment of rapidly edited images of battle footage. What distinguishes the montage sequence from the rest of the film is that during the subsequent two minutes, the film images are covered with scratches; seen to burn; shot with visible frame edges, sprocket holes, and tears; seen in freeze frame; repeated; and vertically aligned with a frame. The sounds of the battle are joined by inharmonious keyboard music halfway through the sequence. One minute and fifty seconds in, the frame hastily freezes, the audio goes silent, and white screen appears. The title DON'T LET DISUNITY IN THE SOCIALIST CAMP DARKEN THE FUTURE reassembles on the screen. The film concludes with a brief coda. Bach plays energetically to firing rockets, flowers bloom, and a final set of titles read THE YANKEES DEFEATED / WE WILL CONSTRUCT A HOMELAND TEN TIMES MORE BEAUTIFUL. The blooming flower reappears, and the film fades out.

The montage sequence problematizes any notion of cinema's capacity to *represent* war or anything else objectively. In exposing the machinations of cinema, Álvarez asserts the partiality and the situatedness of his vision and that of the socialist camp as it engages in war. The sequence establishes an array of alignments and emphasizes the *intensity* of connection. It visualizes transnational alignments with the Vietnamese, commitment to the nonaligned movement, and even alliance with American antiwar demonstrators. Álvarez paints a virtual image of a multiracial, anti-imperialist collective uniting in its efforts. But he also offers an experience of that positionality by immersing the viewer in the chaos of battle—the utter confusion, the dominance of earsplitting explosions, the inability to get any sort of distanced perspective. But as the last title in the montage (a repeat of the DON'T LET DISUNITY IN THE SOCIALIST CAMP DARKEN THE FUTURE title) demonstrates, this chaos, fragmentation, and intense action need to be reassembled into the larger ideas of the film. The graphic composition of the title literally enacts this coming together. Making sense of this synthesis requires juxtaposing the earlier reflective aspects of the film—monumental images of Ho Chi Minh, poetic quotations from Ho and José Martí on living a meaningful life, and the emotional mourning of loss—with the war sequences and its corresponding protest footage. In this new synthesis, Ho Chi Minh emerges as a paragon of determination and moral commitment who creates unity out of disunity and fluidity out of chaos and provides a different perspective on and vision of the war. The final coda does not condemn the chaos of war but represents it as manageable, elegant disorder through a combination of Bach, exploding rockets, and, eventually, the beautiful rebuilding of the Vietnamese homeland. It presents Cubans with a strategy for negotiating reflection and action. It addresses them as individual and collective subjects, teaching them to situate the chaos of war and violence and even the disruption of mass mobilizations into their contemporary lives with a steeled heart and utopian vision.

This extraordinary and deeply arresting section both is the climactic scene in Álvarez's body of work from 1965 to 1971, the period often considered the height of Cuban nonfiction film artistic experimentation, and reflects his political, artistic, and ethical commitments of the period. He presents a new model of and relationship to leadership. He delineates transnational, transhistorical, and multiracial alignments, in this case insisting that it is the U.S. government and military, not the entirety of its citizenry, which is the enemy. He emphasizes the principles of racial justice, hard work, and mutual loyalty between leaders and those led and also the need to live a critically aware, moral life—the foundations upon which these alignments depend. And he does so by means of a viscerally and emotionally intense, affective aesthetic that responds to a shifting political, social, and economic climate.

This chapter identifies and situates these core aspects of Álvarez's documentaries and newsreels in relation to the constantly changing national and international political-economic landscape. I argue that Álvarez's films and statements of this period are strikingly congruent with Che's vision of the new man and his dreams of international revolution. They are internationally focused and present ideological and moral commitments as intertwined. But whereas Dziga Vertov sought to articulate social totality and the political economics governing it during the second period in the Soviet Union, Álvarez at this time was more concerned with *intensifying* commitment to core revolutionary principles. That is not to deny the critical acuity of Álvarez's films of the period. But it is to say that he was less focused on *explaining* core Marxist ideas than on *mobilizing* a population behind core ideas articulated in detail elsewhere. At the same time, like Vertov, Álvarez developed sophisticated strategies to transform the sensorium of the viewing subject. It is in this aspect of his work, in particular, that divergences between his newsreel and documentary endeavors begin to emerge. The newsreels exhibit an extraordinary attention to detail and offer a mechanistic model of subjectivity (akin to that found in the USSR, as discussed in chapter 3) that sought to transform Cuban citizens' work ethics and sense of collectivity. The documentaries, however, often make use of collage aesthetics and employ abrupt structural, tonal, visual, and metrical shifts. These disjunctures serve an intellectual purpose by requiring viewers to synthesize elements from across the film. But in addition, the intensity of such disjunctures aims to create a subject that is committed, responsive, adaptable, and attentive to the dramatic changes taking place in Cuban society—changes that saw a Cuban government constantly adapting to various international and domestic threats and alliances.

NEWSREEL AND DOCUMENTARY
CONVERGENCES AND DISTINCTIONS

As I discussed in chapter 2, distinctions traditionally understood in the West between newsreel and documentary did not obtain in post-revolutionary Cuba. The relation between these two forms continued to develop during the latter half of the 1960s. The ICAIC newsreel, especially during this period, was known domestically and internationally for blurring the boundaries between newsreel and documentary. Its emphasis on depth of coverage, interrelation of stories, and formal experimentation (including destabilizing traditional narration strategies) was seen to be irreconcilable with common assumptions about newsreel (and even journalistic) practice. Professor Mario Piedra of the University of Havana, who worked in the newsreel division as a writer and journalist from 1974 to 1976, related to me in 2004 that the university had recently held a symposium to discuss the question, "Was the Cuban newsreel actually news?" A number of scholars, critics, film workers, and students concluded that it was not, in fact, news. The key issue, I determined based on our discussion, was that of timeliness.[3] Contemporaneity is one of the traits traditionally used to distinguish newsreels from documentaries, with newsreels having shorter shooting schedules, briefer editing periods, and more rapid circulation. The ICAIC newsreel did not follow this model.

As in the Soviet Union, both pragmatic and ideological factors shaped the direction the ICAIC newsreel took. Cuba had neither the film stock nor the transportation or exhibition infrastructure in place for the rapid distribution and exhibition of 35mm weekly issues. But, more than that, Cubans saw the Western newsreel as hypocritical. Álvarez and others felt that claims of entertainment through story fragmentation attempted to mask what they saw as ideologically laden films.[4] By contrast, the Cubans made their ideological position clear by interrelating the stories. Linking stories was considered to be ethically responsible and politically efficacious. In contrast to capitalist journalism, where the principal aim is "to be the first with the news," Álvarez argued that this "doesn't mean that all journalism has to be like that. I prefer a kind of journalism that gets across, and is more enduring, so that when I make a newsreel, it won't grow old, it will be viewable with equal interest today, in a year, and longer."[5]

Although many of these ICAIC newsreel issues transcend the contrast between newsreel and documentary, they were still produced, distributed, marketed, and exhibited in film programs as newsreels, with prescribed production periods, ten-minute running times, and a need to communicate information on a timely basis. A number of Álvarez's best-known films, including *Ciclón* and *Now,* were produced as special issue newsreels, occasionally doubling in length. I specify when discussing these. But when referring to the newsreels of the period, I am referring to films produced on a weekly basis as ICAIC's *Latin American Weekly Newsreel.* To be sure, their integrated structure, varied narration, stylized visuals, rapid editing, use of multimedia objects, contrapuntal audio, and overall reliance on opposition, conflict, and combat distinguish these films in what is often thought to be a formulaic, rote visual and aural form. But, as I will demonstrate, even during this period they sought to shape different aspects of the social imaginary. They made use of the regulated structure (multiple stories and prescribed length) to shape the laboring sensibilities of the Cuban worker. And perhaps surprisingly, in Álvarez's output, they were more likely than the documentaries of the time to attend to personal and domestic matters, even if such items in turn took on a new political valence.

WHICH SIDE ARE YOU ON?

We mean action now!

—LENA HORNE, "NOW" (1965)

In the initial post-revolutionary years (1959–1965), Cuban nonfiction film sought to identify a new national collective by reimagining urban and rural divides and by providing evidence of new international alignments, most notably with the people and governments of the USSR and members of the Eastern Bloc. This effort aimed to confer a sense of legitimacy on the new government, and it reconceived traditional international alignments. The second period (1965–1971) witnessed a transition in the imagination of the national body and Cuba's international alliances. In both newsreels and documentaries, Álvarez increasingly sought to shape a (trans)national imaginary devoted to racial justice and the viability of multiracial harmony. This is evident not only in films that directly address an issue related to Cuba but also in films about the United States and conflict in Southeast Asia—topics that increasingly dominated Álvarez's documentary output as the decade progressed. As a group, these films envision an intensely unified national body with a *conciencia* committed to racial, ethnic, and cultural equality and social justice both within and outside of its national borders.

While *Ciclón* served to announce Álvarez to the international film community, his intense six-minute found footage film on racial discrimination in the United States, *Now,* solidly established him as a creative force who was challenging the relationship between newsreel and documentary in innovative ways. The film is structured around a song by the African American singer, actress, and activist Lena Horne called "Now," a black liberation anthem set to the Jewish dance song "Hava Nagila." The film is rapidly edited and composed of photographs and live-action footage of racial conflict sent to Álvarez clandestinely by friends in the United States. It is a politically confrontational and visceral film, implicating the viewer in its transhistorical argument for a multiracial society.

The film immediately establishes its interest in confrontation by opening with a twenty-five-second sequence of the violent encounter between police and protesters during the Watts riots of 1965. This thematic continues in the title sequence. Breaking a famous photograph of civil rights leaders (including Dr. Martin Luther King Jr.) meeting with President Johnson into fragmented parts by means of shading techniques, Álvarez makes the point that division and confrontation between those seeking justice and those denying it exists at the level of the people and leadership. The film then goes on to provide photographic evidence of the violent confrontations and the physical and emotional impact on the lives of those oppressed.

The main body of the film commences with three matching profile photographs of Lena Horne lined up vertically. The image twice fades into other shots of Horne, culminating in her looking almost directly at the camera (and thus the viewer) in mid-speech as the song begins to play. The film then points to the mistreatment of black youth who are imprisoned and beaten while attempting to peacefully protest racial injustice. Expanding on the theme, the images follow the lyrics of the song as Horne sings about how legendary figures in U.S. history—Washington, Jefferson, and Lincoln—would not approve of such treatment. Two heads of the Lincoln Memorial literally emerge from the eyes of a young black boy, coming together and then returning to the statue. The first pronouncement of the lyric "We mean action now!" concludes with a scratched "now" superimposed over the base of the memorial. In this brief creative sequence, Álvarez unites the "youth" and "roots" of the country with the "youth" of today by bringing together Lincoln and the maltreated black child. He accomplishes this not only by having Lincoln emerge from the eyes of the boy but by writing "now" in a style that connotes graffiti.[6]

The rest of the film follows the emotional trajectory of the music, the editing rhythm speeding up to align with the increasing energy of Horne's voice. Visually, it consists of a combination of still photographs and live-action footage of confrontations between police and protesters and witnesses' reactions to those moments. Multiple eyeline matches draw connections not only across spatial dimensions but also across time, continuing the film's attention to history. Black Americans witness

FIGURE 4.2. Eyeline matches with discontinuity: connecting
racial protest and injustice in *Now*.

and react to contemporary injustices and to lynchings and mob beatings
from the past. The film thus addresses the brutal legacy of racism in the
United States while uniting those in support of racial justice. Whites are
seen not only as oppressors; many are shown to support racial equality
and willing to put their bodies in danger for their beliefs.

Whereas *Now* primarily deals with the history of racism in the
United States, like all of Álvarez's films, its primary address is to Cuban
citizens.[7] Its attention to conflict at the aesthetic and explicitly rhetorical
levels and its establishment of binary oppositions coordinated according
to questions of justice and freedom inevitably locate Cuban society and
its government on the positive side. The film's critique of race relations in
the United States serves as a counter-assertion of racial progress in Cuba.
The film encourages viewers to think about the relationship between race
relations, history, and the state in complex ways. The sequence about
Washington, Jefferson, and Lincoln reveals a disjunction between the

foundations of American democracy and its contemporary government. Although many were and continue to be disappointed with the Cuban state's record on race,[8] the revolutionary leadership proclaimed that both the government and people of Cuba were committed to a racist-free society. *Now* not only distinguished contemporary Cuba from the contemporary United States but, by mobilizing history and celebrating the revolutionary roots of American society, associated contemporary Cuba with the spirit of revolutionary America and differentiated both from the contemporary U.S. government. The reflexive aesthetics of the film, reinforced by its critical historiographic status, worked to allay fears that Cuba would follow a similar path. But more than that, the film's emphasis on confrontation and its attention to visual "witnesses" implicate the viewer, who is confronted by and forced to witness the brutality. The choice that viewer is asked to make is not at all ambiguous.

The solidarity Álvarez urges viewers to have with black Americans in *Now* is realized through different registers in his 1967 film about Vietnamese daily life under American bombing raids. *Hanoi, martes 13* (Hanoi, Tuesday 13th) takes its title from the time and date of one of these attacks—Tuesday, December 13, 1966—and is one of his most poetic, sensitive, texturally rich films.[9]

Hanoi, martes 13 is unique in its effort to capture an enduring spirit of Vietnam and its people—a revolutionary spirit aligned with Cuba's own. This attempt is visible in the rhythm and specific motifs of the film. The sequences of everyday life in Vietnam are slow-moving and peaceful. The film pays particular attention to the hands and feet of the people as they work with and move through an array of materials. We see hands and feet in contact with recently caught fish, hands and feet covered in mud, people walking through and separating vast quantities of rice, people carrying straw and trudging through hayfields, women smoothing textiles and caning furniture, and an isolated hand dancing rhythmically. Extremities are often isolated in close-up and the shot held so that the interaction between texture and flesh becomes indelible. Combining attention to the relationship between the physical environment and the Vietnamese people with a slow and evenly paced editing rhythm not only offered Cubans a glimpse into the daily lives of the Vietnamese but sought to articulate a temporal and textural experience of it.

FIGURE 4.3 AND FIGURE 4.4. Vietnamese labor and war in *Hanoi, martes 13.*

While much of the culture, work, and rhythm of Vietnamese life can be understood to be unique, a comparison with and message for Cubans was embedded in the film and its context. The film makes this fairly explicit in the opening section. It begins with a rare color sequence of paintings and engravings by past Southeast Asian artists. Coincident with the images, a voice-over reads text from José Martí's children's book *La edad de oro* (The golden age), which applauds the people's determination in their ongoing struggle for freedom. This textual emphasis on solidarity between the peoples of each nation combines with an extra-textual emphasis (legible beyond the film in a number of political and cultural examples, including Álvarez's own *Solidaridad Cuba y Vietnam*, 1965) to encourage Cubans to draw comparisons between their daily lives and those of the Vietnamese. The film celebrates the Vietnamese people's strong will and determination, their unity and community, their patience and focus. The Vietnamese workers serve as models whose behavior (consistent, determined effort) and attitude (focused, willful) should be emulated.

In addition to marking the Vietnamese as historical and contemporary comrades and as models for Cuban work ethics, Álvarez visualized them as models for maintaining national unity. The sections of the film explicitly devoted to rural and urban areas have analogous structures. In each, daily life is interrupted by air raids, which cause the people to fight back. After the battles are over, the people in each region return to their original tasks as well as respond to new needs. For example, at the conclusion of the bombing of the fields, the people immediately work to rebuild the trenches that provide protection during the air raids. Similarly, following the bombing of Hanoi, many Vietnamese build small drum bunkers, capable of containing one or two people, and set them into the ground. They are united in their response to the imperialists, and, while each physical context requires a different adaptive strategy, each group recognizes that unity and detailed effort create its only hope for success. Such a message sought to resonate with a Cuban nation-building agenda focused on uniting rural and urban populations and increasing the discipline and productivity of the Cuban worker.

It is in the special issue newsreels (*Now*) and in the longer documentaries (*Hanoi, martes 13; Año 7* [Year 7, 1966]; *La escalada de chantaje*

[Escalation of blackmail, 1967]) of the period that Cubans were encouraged to develop the new multiracial, transhistorical,[10] and transnational imaginaries definitive of the late 1960s. Although attending to different intellectual and emotional registers, these films convey an intensity that speaks to the stakes involved. They do not just envision an intensely unified national body adhering to and performing such values in Cuba but recognize that calling for a *conciencia* committed to racial, ethnic, and cultural equality and social justice depends not only on a national but an international outlook. In the more traditional newsreels of the period, however, international alliances serve a different function.

The weekly newsreels still on occasion celebrated the Soviet Union. An issue from 1966, for example, highlights the role the Soviets played in brokering the India-Pakistan peace treaty. But increasingly, two trends emerge when international solidarity is under consideration. First, when references to international alliances are the subject of newsreels, they are often concerned with establishing comparable historical revolutionary legacies. The French Revolution serves this purpose in an example from 1967. Second, they are more likely to refer to revolutionary movements outside the Soviet Union and Eastern Bloc during this period. They honor a fallen Venezuelan revolutionary fighter in an issue from 1966 and celebrate new Cuban and Korean diplomatic relations in 1966 as well. The newsreels of the period, when attending to international issues, focus on the role these countries played in the development of the Cuban economy. Escaping the confines of underdevelopment, we will see, required both that type of assistance from international allies and, perhaps more important, a Cuban citizen deeply committed to hard work and the spirit of voluntarism.

NEW ETHICS AND INTERNATIONAL REVOLUTION

It is still necessary to deepen conscious participation, individual and collective, in all the structures of management and production, and to link this to the idea of the need for technical and ideological education, so that the individual will realize that these processes are closely interdependent and their advancement is parallel. In this way the individual will reach total consciousness as a social being.

—CHE GUEVARA, "SOCIALISM AND MAN IN CUBA" (1965)

The initial post-revolutionary period of Cuban nonfiction film sought to imagine a new collective and to instill a desire for Cuban subjectivity across that collective. Cuban newsreels and documentaries of the second period aimed to establish unambiguously the identity of those with whom Cubans became aligned. These identifications and allegiances informed not only Cuban citizens' international outlooks but, in part, their understandings of what it meant to be a Cuban national subject. But if, as Che describes, becoming a model communist citizen (and therefore achieving Cuban subjectivity) requires a new understanding of an individual's relation to himself or herself and the world, values need to be established upon which these foundations can be built. This section explores how Álvarez's promotion of a new ethics of labor, a new model of international revolution, and a new call to live a critical, moral life responded to changes in the political-economic landscape of Cuba. The effort to "deepen conscious participation" by linking technical and ideological production aimed to shape a Cuban citizenry that not only approximated the commitment of the revolutionary vanguard but in turn served as a model for other international revolutionary movements.

Economic Mobilization and Personal Life

By 1968, Cuba had adopted a much more decentralized model of economic planning than was commonly practiced in the Soviet Union and Eastern Bloc nations. In place of long-term macroeconomic, integrative planning, Cuba established medium and short-range mini-plans for special sectors or plants such as those producing electricity, textiles, and sugar and "special plans" that tackled a particular problem or developed a concrete project. Supporters of this strategy saw it as a method for dealing with unforeseen contingencies and as recognition of the lack of workers' cadres.[11]

The most important of the special plans was the sugar plan, which Cubans hoped would gradually increase sugar production from six million tons in 1965 to the ultimate goal of a ten-million-ton harvest in 1971. The economic logic of such a program was that it would take advantage of the high price of sugar with the resultant profits enabling the government to invest in other areas of the economy.[12]

Cuba's use of the "unbalanced economic development theory" was heavily criticized at the time.[13] But Castro himself questioned the applicability of these criticisms to the Cuban situation. In 1969, during his annual July 26th speech, he said, "The Revolution aspires to equalize incomes, from the bottom up . . . regardless of the type of work. . . . This principle will surely be given a name by 'learned,' 'experienced' economists . . . who will claim this goes against the laws of economics. The question is which economics?"[14] Castro's comment demonstrates that he believed the special plans functioned according to a different logic or, as he describes, a different "economics." But Castro is not simply distinguishing socialist from capitalist economic models. Like Che, Castro had been insisting that economic issues were indissociable from questions of unity and morality. The unbalanced economic development model built in flexibility for the government to mobilize the population when it saw fit. It was a way of using what it saw as the strength of the revolution—the commitment of the people—and shaping that so as to transform the moral character of the people by altering their relation to work.

Despegue a las 18:00 (Takeoff at 18:00, 1969) is a film about the mobilization of workers in Oriente Province, one meant as a dry run for the large-scale mobilization to take place in the upcoming years. But more than that, Álvarez's film about the conditions of and efforts to eradicate economic underdevelopment affectively integrates the economic with moral responsibility.

Despegue begins by asserting what the viewer is going to see through an array of titles: a DIDACTIC/INFORMATIVE/POLITICAL/PAMPHLETEER-ING film ABOUT A PEOPLE/IN REVOLUTION/ANXIOUS . . . /DESPERATE . . . /TO FIND A WAY OUT OF/AN AGONIZING/HERITAGE . . . /UNDER-DEVELOPMENT. The pre-title section concludes with a question, or perhaps a challenge. The titles read: IF WE WERE BLOCKADED/COMPLETELY/WHAT WOULD WE DO?/STOP PRODUCTION?/FOLD OUR ARMS? The section closes with an old map of the Antilles, which invokes Cuba's colonialist legacy and offers a rationale for their "heritage" of underdevelopment.[15]

The rest of the film is made up of an extended metaphor comparing the mobilization of workers in Oriente Province to the mobilization of the military for an upcoming battle. For example, while those on the "front lines" (in Oriente) fight for the life of the nation, those remaining home—the "rear vanguard"—take care of the local responsibilities. The emotional and agitational direct address of the titles combined with the extended comparison between economic and military mobilization reinforce a sense of urgency and need for collectivity. Moreover, the film does not just make reference to the contingency of war and the energy required for battle. It aims to infuse citizens with the desire to work beyond their normal means by offering a vision of *sustained* effort and imbuing that effort with the urgency of military battle.[16] In the process, it creates a different relation between contingent mobilizations and time.

This metaphor of the population "engaged in combat, not only military but in all spheres" of life was a common one. Tzvi Medin argues that the notion of "existence as confrontation" is in fact one of the three discursive patterns that defined and legitimized revolutionary action in Cuba.[17] Irving Louis Horowitz explains that the mobilizations associated with these "special plans" relied on moral instead of material incentives:

> In some strange way, the Cuban economy has responded to the role of political ideology by noting that the essence of planning is not so much economic growth as it is political mobilization. And, in this sense, the theory of moral incentives has had a binding value on Cuban society far in excess of economic profitability or losses occasioned by the premature disavowal of market incentives to labor. . . . The anomaly is that Cuban leaders, whether they be Guevara or Castro, have in effect spiritualized problems of economic production and allocation.[18]

Rather than highlight political mobilization over economic growth, as Horowitz does, I would argue that Cuba's economic policy relied on what it saw as the greatest strength of the revolution—the will of the people. In such a framework (and taking into account the commercial, economic, and financial embargo in place since February 1962), economic progress was inseparable from political mobilization. Horowitz is correct to emphasize the "binding value" of the special plans. In *Despegue*, Álvarez even expands on this by means of his agitational titles—a strategy that transfers the burden of revolutionary responsibility onto the workers/viewers, urging them to enlist fellow citizens to perform similar efforts on behalf of the mobilization. But that is not to say that this voluntaristic aspect marks the political mobilizations and their nation-building elements as completely irrational or "spiritual." The Cuban leadership needed to be able to adapt to the possibility of increased isolation by the United States and what they feared would be an insufficient counterresponse by the Soviet Union. The lack of centralized planning and its emphasis on contingency contributed to their functioning in continual crisis mode. By avowedly combining economic, ideological, and moral incentives, they aimed to sustain the revolution in a climate of increasing uncertainty. Álvarez's work sought to aid this process.

The newsreels of the period were also committed to transforming the work ethic of the Cuban citizen. However, instead of integrating economic, ideological, and moral incentives, they sought to promote efficiency, attention to detail, and the role of expertise in economic production. Whether it was a detailed description of a successful kidney transplant (1966), the development of water purification and electric plants (1966), new approaches to safety on the factory floor (1971), genetic experimentation to produce more milk (1969), or the use of discarded plants for sugar sacks (1967), these issues continually emphasized the details of production processes. But as in the documentaries, labor was integrated with other spheres of life. In an issue from 1967, for example, modern agricultural equipment is visually and thematically aligned with the spaces and production of modern art.

Two consecutive newsreel issues from 1971, the "Year of Productivity," provide examples of how newsreels addressed their primary concern—that of economic production in the industrial and agricultural sectors. But they also demonstrate the range of thematic integration within and across issues. The second issue of the two is far more aesthetically and conceptually far-reaching, integrating the productive element with other spheres of life. Together, they demonstrate some of the variety of newsreel discourse during this period while reminding how centrally concerned newsreels were with worker productivity.

The first issue, #518, begins with images of camels sauntering through a desert accompanied by exotic Middle Eastern music. As the image returns to Cuba, the voice-over (now Enrique Lopez) describes new agricultural techniques designed to promote efficiency. Lopez's narration gives way to a worker in a field testifying about the process of cutting burnt sugar cane stalks. Following the worker's testimony, a professional scientist in a laboratory office details the research he and his team have done on the effects of this practice. It is clear that workers maintain a fear that cutting burnt cane will cause disease. The three voices hope to dispel those fears. The testimony of worker and scientist overlap significantly.

The second section of the newsreel submits the Australian long-cut technique as an alternative method of cutting the sugar cane. The images provide visible examples while the voice-over depicts the process. Álvarez connects this work with the gathering and clearing performed by newly developed machines. It concludes with the worker in the field imploring other agricultural workers to rid themselves of the old methods and embrace the new. The final image is a title that reads, "The Revolution of Productivity in the Year of Productivity."

The ensuing issue, #519, opens with an introductory sequence of superimposed images of witches flying through the sky on brooms. These images are immediately contextualized as the film announces its title, "Burning Traditions." The second full section, which also looks at the process of burning cane, is much more aesthetically innovative and tonally distinct than the previous issue. It argues that Cubans must burn according to a specific, organized plan, paying close attention to wind speed, wind direction, precipitation, and hour of day. The rhetoric and tone of the film change as the attack on traditionalism referenced in the title becomes more explicit and expansive. On-screen come titles of traditional sayings whose wisdom is questioned in humorous ways. One recounts the phrase THE EGG IS BAD FOR THE LIVER as creatively edited found footage testifies to its absurdity. Animation sequences return to the subject of burning cane, again illustrating how it needs to be done and explaining why it needs to be done in this manner. The final section of the film is also animated. It provides detailed explanation of the Australian long-cut method, glimpsing below the surface to see how roots grow and framing the efforts within an overall process of field cultivation.

The opening sequences from the newsreels highlight regressive modes of transportation or antiquated modes of thought, each of which has no place in a progressive socialist society. Furthermore, each establishes the tone of the issue. The camels are indicative of the slower pacing and the attention to detail of #518; the witches sequence points to the playfulness, humor, and originality of #519.

Whereas each newsreel aims to dispel what it sees as outmoded thoughts or practices, the second issue is more ambitious. The first issue imparts specific information by means of a variety of narrational voices and devices. Each voice reinforces the others and contributes to the argument in ways the others cannot. The worker appears trustworthy and equipped with practical knowledge. The scientist offers expert testimony and evidence of the efforts to which the state has gone to secure this knowledge. The voice-over frames the larger argument and does so efficiently. The intertitles highlight and encapsulate the critical points. The goal of the film is to provide concrete, convincing information from a variety of sources in the hopes of changing agricultural workers' practices. Some viewers may be swayed more by the direct testimony of the people, some by the disembodied authority of the narrator, some by the direct pleas of the titles, most by some combination thereof. In the first three, the effectiveness of the testimony depends largely on the relationship between the narration and the visible evidence. But what is apparent is that Álvarez employs a relatively realist aesthetic with multiple, less hierarchical voices when his goal is to communicate information as efficiently as possible. That is not to say that Álvarez offers a democratic vision through his interactive mode of address. Álvarez's voices are not in conflict, nor do they allow for the potential for disagreement. Rather, Álvarez's mode of address relies on an experientially unified Cuban spectator and aims to construct an ideologically unified subject attendant to detail and committed to productivity even as he assembles a more diffuse authority.

The second issue attempts to reinforce the informational elements while connecting the lesson to other spheres of life. The newsreel insists that traditionalism needs to be defeated not only in the arena of sugar cane production but also with respect to outmoded thinking about issues like gender, race, and even diet, all of which require reconsideration. During this period in Cuba, there was an acknowledgment that while the revolution could and did transform the political register of the Cuban people, there was a difficult battle to be fought in the domain of the personal and the domestic. While such topics receive considerable attention in fiction films, theater, literature, and even in other documentary film-makers' work, Álvarez was far more likely to integrate progressiveness in the personal or domestic sphere with productive labor in newsreels than he was in documentaries.

International Revolution and Models of Leadership

If one's revolutionary zeal is blunted when the most urgent tasks have been accomplished on a local scale and one forgets about proletarian internationalism, the revolution will cease to be a driving force and sink into a comfortable drowsiness that imperialism, our irreconcilable enemy, will utilize to gain ground. Proletarian internationalism is a duty, but it is also a revolutionary necessity. This is the way we educate our people.

—CHE GUEVARA, "SOCIALISM AND MAN IN CUBA" (1965)

The commitment to voluntarism so evident in questions of labor during this period likewise infused Cuban leaders' increasing commitment to international revolution. In January 1964, Castro traveled to Moscow and acknowledged the practicality of the Kremlin's more moderate international policies. He determined that normalizing relations with the United States could reduce Cuba's increasing dependence on the USSR and allow it to become more active internationally. Cuba's commitment to the "evolutionary" line of thinking was evidenced by the 1964 Havana Conference, which assembled the twenty-two Communist Parties in Latin America but excluded the independent revolutionary blocs.[19] This concession to Soviet moderation, however, was short-lived. The electoral defeat of Salvador Allende in Chile in 1964, the CIA-sponsored ouster of Brazil's João Goulart also in 1964, and the U.S. Marines invasion of Santo Domingo in 1965 all forced Cuba to question the efficacy of Soviet policy and the USSR's commitment to the western hemisphere.[20] Instead, two cases—that of its own revolution and that of the Vietnamese in repelling a militarily superior foe—convinced the Cuban government that militant solidarity with (and financial support of) revolutionary causes in nonaligned nations was the route to pursue.

Che Guevara articulated this alternative position in a December 1964 address to the United Nations, where he unabashedly asserted that Cuba's allegiances were to the nonaligned nations of the world involved in the fight against imperialism. This speech played a pivotal role in Álvarez's *Año 7,* an eighteen-minute documentary recounting the events of 1965.[21]

Año 7 integrates the celebrations of the sixth anniversary of the revolution throughout Cuba with a focus on international policy. Following the pre-title sequence, the body of the film opens with a four-frame screen presenting Cuban officials meeting with international leaders attending the First Tricontinental Conference in Cuba in January 1966. It is this conference that founded OSPAAAL (Organización de Solidaridad con los Pueblos de Africa, Asia y America Latina) and served as Castro's call for armed struggle. In effect, the conference functioned as a de facto critique of Soviet policy and publicly reformed Cuba's international agenda. After the title, the film recounts a number of events of the past year such as the Fischer/Spassky chess matches, Cuban cultural events, and the revolutionary parades. The last section of the film returns to the issue of international policy. An abrupt cut interrupts Fidel's reading of a letter from Che (abrupt cuts fill the film and are often prompted by musical changes). The ensuing sequence shows Che delivering his December 1964 speech to the United Nations. Thus, a film purportedly about the events of 1965 (January through December) actually begins with an event from January 1966 and returns to an event from December 1964. Highlighting these events implies not a drastic reformulation of Cuban international policy but a consistent trajectory, one driven by Che's internationalist revolutionary commitment.[22]

What distinguished Che's position, the one that Cuba publicly adopted by 1966, was not just its internationalist policies but its commitment to voluntarism. Both Che and Fidel argued that the intellectual, physical, and moral activity associated with voluntarism was far preferable to what they saw as the passivity many Communist Parties inculcated in their citizens by being overly centralized and directive. Castro's stance was that Cuban voluntarism was necessary to create revolution in the first place, since struggle needed to come before educating people about socialism and Marxism. Thus, their dedication to voluntarism can be understood as integral to their internationalist policies, since revolutionary struggle (avowedly socialist or not) was what needed supporting, not established Communist Parties.

Support for these policies was in part driven by Che's shifting status in Cuba at the time. Following his speech to the United Nations at the end of 1964, Che took a brief tour of the anti-imperialist African states. Interspersed with stops in Algeria, Mali, Guinea, Ghana, Tanzania, and Egypt were a short stint in Peking and a secret excursion into guerrilla-held territory in the Congo (renamed Zaire in 1971 and the Democratic Republic of the Congo in 1998). Che returned to Havana on March 14, 1965, before setting off secretly to aid the rebels fighting in the Congo. Che's specter and image loomed over the Tricontinental Conference in Havana during January 1966 and the Latin American Solidarity Conference, also held in Havana, during the summer of 1967. His whereabouts were not made public until it was announced he had died fighting in Bolivia on October 8, 1967.[23]

Che's death (and life) and his status as a revolutionary leader became the impetus for Álvarez's *Hasta la victoria siempre,* a film that not only insists on the interrelation of voluntarism and international revolution but crystallizes the notion in the figure of Che himself. Álvarez and his team were given two days to prepare a film that was to precede Fidel's eulogy for Che on October 18, 1967. It was shown in the Plaza de la Revolución on a massive screen to a truly mass audience mourning the death of the already legendary revolutionary figure.

Situating the film within that unique, original exhibition context requires analyzing it in relation to Fidel's speech. That is not to say that they were constructed in unison; such close cooperation was unnecessary. Instead, Michael Chanan writes, "it is not that Fidel told Álvarez what he was going to say or what to put in the film—there was no time for that and, in any case, Fidel was not inclined to such artistic collaboration. . . . It was rather that Fidel had seen the closeness of Álvarez' thought to his own."[24] As in *Hanoi, martes 13,* Fidel identifies the Vietnamese and Che as models of revolutionary behavior. In reference to the fallen hero, Fidel declares that "blood was shed for the sake of all the peoples of the Americas and for the people of Vietnam—because while fighting in Bolivia, fighting against the oligarchies and imperialism, he knew that he was offering Vietnam the highest expression of his solidarity."[25] Both Álvarez's film and Fidel's speech end with reference to international revolution and to solidarity with people involved in similar struggles. It is this Che-inspired vision, they assert, that marks the acme of a journey and the height of revolutionary thought.

Hasta la victoria siempre is a biography of Che that symbolically marks his progression as a revolutionary and culminates with his theory of international armed struggle. It consists of an array of found footage material of images of Bolivia and other Latin American and Caribbean nations involved in revolutionary efforts. There are extended clips from two of Che's most notable speeches—the speech at the nonaligned conference in 1965 and his address to the United Nations in December 1964, which concludes the film. The first section of the film focuses on the hardship the people faced in Bolivia. There are a number of close-ups of Bolivian adults and children, whose difficulties, the film argues, are due to the presence of imperialism. But the section also includes a travel motif that harkens back to Che's original journey through Latin America. A number of aerial shots of mountainous landscapes as well as long and medium shots of extended roads drive home this point. The first section can thus be seen to encapsulate the trajectory of Che's life—from his awakening as a revolutionary during his continental journey to his realization that the struggle must be fought in small battles with the larger effort always kept in perspective.

Like the newsreels of the period and *Hanoi, martes 13*, *Hasta la victoria siempre* stresses the role of sacrifice in the achievement of socialism. Whereas the newsreels and *Hanoi, martes 13* emphasize the commitment to work and national defense, this film, more than the others, highlights the moral aspect of such effort. Che is seen volunteering to assist Bolivian guerrillas and working in the fields back in Cuba. In the eulogy, Fidel consistently refers to his exemplary work ethic and his organization of the voluntary work brigades. Che is constructed like many heroes—one to be emulated and yet one whose achievements are practically impossible to duplicate. In contrast to the volunteer labor efforts (which anyone can perform), the magnetism of Che's personality and the uniqueness of his intellect also resonate from the film.[26] An extended excerpt from Fidel's eulogy indicates not only which aspects of Che Fidel celebrated but how, at this moment in history, with the recent defeats of revolutionary struggles in Latin America, Che's model could serve as a guiding principle:

He left us his revolutionary thinking, his revolutionary virtues. He left us his character, his will, his tenacity, his spirit of work. In a word, he left us his example! And Che's example will be the ideal model for our people!

If we wish to express what we expect our revolutionary combatants, our militants, our people to be, we must say, without hesitation: let them be like Che! If we wish to express what we want the people of future generations to be, we must say: let them be like Che! If we wish to say how we want our children to be educated, we must say without hesitation: we want them to be educated in Che's spirit! If we want the model of a person, the model of a human being who does not belong to our time but to the future, I say from the depths of my heart that such a model, without a single stain on his conduct, without a single stain on his action, without a single stain on his behavior, is Che![27]

When combined with Che's address to the United Nations that concludes the film, Fidel's speech creates less of a sense of the imminence of the international revolution than the importance of committing to Che's vision. Such a position put greater stress on voluntarism, with its moral dimension and material impact. In other words, achieving Che's utopian future required a dedication to work, to building socialism in Cuba, so that Cuba could become an even stronger model for the rest of Latin America and the Third World. It required sacrifice and belief. In determining how to act in daily life, the Cuban citizen was to look to the Vietnamese and to the model of Che himself. The film and Fidel's speech together offered a reason to believe in Che's vision of international revolution even as its present prospects appeared bleak. They offered models of revolutionary behavior (Vietnamese and Che himself), spheres of application (domesticity and national defense), and a cause for action (exploitation of poor people by imperialists and oligarchs). They insisted on sacrifice, determination, moral commitment, and solidarity with those in similar conditions. And they did so by celebrating a man who came to the conclusion that unity beyond the bounds of nation or ethnicity was the most moral way to act in the world.

Media Literacy and the Moral Life

If, at the time of his death, Che was the archetypal revolutionary figure, one "without a single stain" on his conduct, action, or behavior, he was part of a revolutionary vanguard constantly presented as heroic. This is true not just in nonfictional and fictionalized representations but in political public spaces as well, be they speeches, congresses, or sporting events. One of the new responsibilities members of the vanguard took up after the revolution was film and media criticism. Hector Amaya provocatively analyzes the role of film criticism in Cuba and the United States from the revolution to the end of the Cold War, arguing for its importance in Cuba as "civic public behavior and a way of performing citizenship."[28] As I maintained in chapter 2, this categorization applies not just to the vanguard but to regular film-viewing citizens' efforts to perform citizenship (modeled after the vanguard's performances) as well. Both examples emphasize the effort to create subjects capable of critically and intellectually responding to changing discursive and material conditions.

ICAIC was actively involved in this process from the outset. In addition to publishing critical writings in newspapers and journals, ICAIC developed a television program called *Twenty-Four Times a Second* that demonstrated a Marxist politically and aesthetically informed film criticism.[29] Instead of reviewing and recommending films in the Western journalistic manner, the program analyzed popular films from the United States, Europe, Latin America, and Cuba and exposed their ideological forms and messages. Enrique Colina, the popular film critic and filmmaker who appeared on the show, saw its intervention as part of a larger effort that "stresses the importance of decolonizing our country's movie screens... which would contribute, along with national film production, to the intellectual and cinematic development of our people."[30] ICAIC also ran discussions of films after large-event screenings and after *cines moviles* screenings. These efforts demonstrate ICAIC's commitment to ensuring that viewers not only understood the politics of the films circulating in Cuba at the time but also were given an opportunity to publicly rehearse film criticism themselves.

Instruction in film criticism, of course, took place on the screen as well. For Cuban filmmakers and critics, decolonizing vision required a distanced perspective and recognition of the political nature of all media. Underlying almost all post-revolutionary Cuban cinema (nonfiction and fiction) was a desire to lay bare the filmmaker's craft by exposing the machinations of technique and form. But Cuban reflexivity took a unique direction. Filmmakers chose to combine and appropriate a variety of Western forms, strategies, and subjects within particular films and over time.[31] The practice of modifying, appropriating, and combining a variety of established aesthetic traditions and genres sought to decolonize the vision of Cuban audiences by engaging with audiences on viewers' terms—even if the filmmakers' intention was to expose and transform those conventions.

Álvarez's films of the second period offer numerous examples of reflexive commentary on the aesthetics and techniques of dominant Western filmmaking. In *Now*, for example, Álvarez used eyeline matches to connect viewers from different times and spaces. Eyeline matches were part a Hollywood system of continuity editing that sought to focus, with maximum efficiency, viewer's attention on the narrative and not on the construction of the narrative. Eyeline matches became one aspect of a system designed to establish a coherent pro-filmic space within which narrative action could proceed. If, in the Hollywood system, eyeline matches served to overcome spatial distance by denying filmic construction and asserting spatial congruity, *Now* had alternative goals. As in the Hollywood system, eyeline matches align people in different spaces and times. But in *Now* they do so avowedly. Álvarez shows the edges of the frames and marks the different photographic qualities of each representation, testifying to the integrity of each time and space. In so doing, the connection between the discrepant times and spaces remains even though their spatiotemporal incongruity is established. His editing and framing choices bring together those fighting for racial justice across time and space by making it seem like people in the present (or just in different locations) were reacting to injustices occurring at another time or place. Álvarez thus reworks the value of the eyeline *connection*, emphasizing the principal of racial justice across time and space over the desire to maintain narrative intensity. By avowedly citing and reworking this formal strategy, Álvarez not only distinguishes his cinematic political priorities from those of Hollywood but also provides viewers tools to apply to other films.

Álvarez's commitment to decolonizing, as Colina describes, the vision of Cuban citizens extends from film criticism to media culture more broadly in perhaps his most difficult film of the period, *LBJ* (1968).

If *Hanoi, martes 13* argues for discipline and determination within an internationalist political framework and *Hasta la victoria siempre* insists on sacrifice for both moral and materialist ends, *LBJ* asserts that an acute critical and intellectual engagement with media is required for Cubans to avoid the immoral path their neighbors to the North have taken.

The assassinations of Martin Luther King Jr. and Robert F. Kennedy in 1968 (the year the film was made), combined with memory of the assassination of John F. Kennedy in 1963, served as the impetus for the film. Álvarez insinuates that it is no coincidence that the death of all three resulted in an increase in power for Johnson.[32] As in many of Álvarez's documentaries, the pre-title section offers insight into the work's broader argument.[33] The first sequence is a series of photographs of Johnson's daughter's wedding, from a long shot of the church to a close-up of the kiss between the bride and groom. A highly colorized image (in red) of Johnson and the groom concludes the sequence. The next sequence is a series of photographs and cartoons from *Playboy* magazine intercut with a tight shot of Johnson staring at the camera (the cut makes it appear as if he is staring at the magazine's naked women) and more images of the wedding festivities. Álvarez again red-colorizes the shot of Johnson and a few of the wedding photographs. He closes with a five-shot sequence that clarifies his position. The first is of the bride and groom cutting their wedding cake—the last image from the wedding. The subsequent shot is an anamorphically squeezed and red-colorized image of the famous scene from Howard Hawks's 1932 film *Scarface* in which Paul Muni emerges from a cake firing rounds with his machine gun. The third, fourth, and fifth are rapidly cut images of magazine advertisements for Winchester guns and bullets.

The decadence of Johnson's daughter's church wedding is associated with the immorality and hypocrisy of American society. Johnson is seen as wholly removed from the wedding and the attendees and yet a product of a society that is at its heart pornographic and violent. The United States celebrates and exports exploitative images of nude women, guns, and, of course, movies (one of the prime vehicles for the exportation of the previous two). The audience is prompted to understand this relation between the sequences not just as an effect of the montage but through Álvarez's highly colorized images. The intensity of the reds, a color theme that pervades the section, aims to evoke emotion while sparking intellectual and critical associations.

In the post-title sequences that complete the introductory section, Álvarez expands the movie reference and comically deconstructs the idea of Johnson as a heroic cowboy. The sequence centers on a comparable photograph and cartoon image of Johnson atop a bucking bronco holding the horse's reins (*"Il bravo cow-boy"*). Both shots get repeated to drive home the iconography of the image. Álvarez then expands the argument of the first section with an extended violent sequence from a Hollywood Western. Similar to the effects used in the first section, here the clip is colorized and squeezed while the pace is intermittently slowed. The effect is again a defamiliarization of a recognizable reference and a critique of its politics.[34] Through newspaper and magazine images, Álvarez showcases the attempt by Johnson and by those connected to him to associate the president with the iconic rugged cowboy. Álvarez isolates and critiques these images, pointing to their absurdity. In their place, Álvarez offers a new association for Johnson (and even Eisenhower) when he visually matches Johnson's facial features and expressions with a long-faced dog.

Each of the three main sections of the film corresponds to one of LBJ's initials. The *J* ("Jack") and the *B* ("Bobby") stand for the Kennedy brothers, while the *L* stands for the "Luther" in Martin Luther King Jr.'s name. In the *J* section, Álvarez again exposes and extends a familiar fiction filmmaking strategy, here addressing the assassination of JFK by employing the "Kuleshov effect" for both humorous and chilling ends.[35] The first shot is of a medieval man (a character from a film) with a crossbow standing clandestinely behind a tree. As he holds up his bow, the film cuts to the view of a scope aimed at the back of Kennedy's head. The third shot cuts back to the hunter as he shoots the arrow. Screams heard from the opera music on the soundtrack mark Kennedy's death. Quick cuts ensue (matched to the beat) of people and an owl apparently reacting to the assassination. As in the example of the eyeline matches, it is abundantly clear that the viewer is not supposed to literally link these spaces. We are not, of course, to understand the film character as the assassin of JFK. Rather, the initial absurdity of this use of the "Kuleshov effect" becomes generative when the sequence is conceived in relation to the arguments about American politics and visual culture established at the beginning of the film. Álvarez asserts that cinematic violence and violence in the political sphere are not only mutually reinforcing but an integral part of American visual culture. For Cubans to critically engage the visual politics of Hollywood/Washington/Madison Avenue requires attending to iconography, film construction, and the political principles according to which they operate. Through this critical process, Álvarez hopes, the Cuban individual and society itself will progress intellectually and will avoid producing a figure like LBJ.

Throughout his work of the period, Álvarez draws sharp distinctions between the ideas and communities he is endorsing and those he is condemning. This remains the case in his efforts to model and teach media literacy. His appropriation of cinematic conventions in *Now* and *LBJ* aims to reveal how cinema works. By exposing such conventions, he is not only providing viewers a valuable set of tools with which they can work but also asserting the honesty of his practice in contrast to Hollywood cinema, which conceals its conventions. This discourse is likewise prevalent in the newsreels of the period, where Cuban journalistic practices are consistently contrasted with those of the Americans.

We can see this in issue #394 (1968), which centers on spying and the betrayal of revolutionary values. The issue begins by reporting on the capture of an American spy boat in North Korea. It provides a detailed explanation of the event and offers images from the North Korean press conference where the story was revealed. The issue takes shape when the images return to Cuba. Rapid shots of *Granma* (the newspaper of the Communist Party) being printed precede a revelation that the Cuban government has discovered counterrevolutionaries in Cuba by seizing their newspapers. As the issue moves to a Central Committee meeting on newspapers, it becomes clear that Álvarez is linking the honesty and openness of Cuban journalism—its practices and institutions (both newspaper and the newsreel being watched, #394)—to revolutionary commitment. And he is distinguishing both from the dishonesty associated with American covert operations and counterrevolutionaries within Cuba's borders.

Álvarez's efforts to identify newspaper and newsreel as similarly committed to open, honest discourse extends its media scope to include television in an issue from 1970. (This was in fact the only issue that dealt in detail with the ten-million-ton sugar harvest of 1971 that ICAIC granted me permission to view. I was not given an issue number.) The entire newsreel takes place in a television studio, as Fidel outlines on national television the plan for the sugar harvest. In addition to the fact that an entire television show was devoted to Fidel's explanation of the sugar harvest, the issue is significant for two reasons. First is the decision ICAIC made to cover the broadcast in an issue at all. To be sure, it is possible that the explanation and Fidel's performance of it was deemed so important that the government wanted it distributed in numerous forms. But the issue does not come across as a staged event. Rather, there are differences between the presumed television broadcast and the newsreel issue. In the newsreel, we are offered glimpses behind the scenes of the studio. We see Fidel preparing, speaking, and concluding. We see the entire process of production. As such, the issue seeks to assert the honesty and openness of newsreel discourse while edifying Cuban citizens on the process of modern media production. Second, the issue again demonstrates the distinctive yet related goals of newsreel and documentary/special issue newsreel practice. Whereas in the documentaries teaching media literacy aims to create a viewer attendant to the sophisticated and shifting strategies mainstream media producers employ to shape viewers' social and political imaginaries, in the newsreels exposing the process of media production aligns the work of media with the work of the industrial and the agricultural sectors. This is realized not just through the content itself (here media and sugar production) but through the means by which it is communicated. The effort to transform the work ethic of the Cuban citizen by means of efficiency and attention to detail that I discuss above remains cogent here. We see detailed exposition of production processes, insisting that attention be paid, whether it is producing sugar at a rate heretofore unimaginable or producing media efficiently, honestly, and openly.

So far, the effort to teach media literacy and expose the process of media production in both documentaries and newsreels on which I have focused attends primarily to questions of media epistemology. That is, they address concerns with how knowledge is communicated in and through media. But Álvarez is also attendant to issues of media ontology.

Fittingly, his reflexive references to the ontology of film and photography speak to larger concerns about what it means to live a moral life. I want to conclude this section on the new revolutionary values and practices Álvarez sought to project, model, and instill in the Cuban citizen during the second period by considering his answer to a question central to the *conciencia* of the new man, namely, "What does it mean to live a moral life?"

The first image of Ho Chi Minh in *79 primaveras* follows a juxtaposition between a time-lapse image of a blooming flower symbolizing Vietnam and its people (natural beauty and growth, accelerated development) and visually matched bombs exploding over the landscape symbolizing American efforts in the region (destruction of the natural and human environment). A negative image of a young Ho promptly dissolves into a positive image of the same shot. Álvarez then slowly fades a close-up of the same image over the medium close-up that was on-screen. He repeats the action again, moving to an extreme close-up. The ensuing images are continuous dissolves into extreme close-ups of Ho Chi Minh as he ages. When the last shot of Ho as an old man wearing glasses appears, the film cuts to a medium close-up before dissolving the image to negative. The graininess of the extreme close-ups of the photographic image calls attention to the nature of the photographic image itself, an issue to which Álvarez returns later in the film. The negative images and the process of aging link ontological questions about photography with one of the dominant themes of the first two-thirds of the film—that of living a politically committed and moral life. The negative images that frame the aging process (the life Ho lived) visually mark the contours and structures of his face, glasses, hair, and eyes in ways that a positive image cannot. Returning to the negative image at the end of the sequence creates symmetry not just of the scene but of his life. His face has become a socially inscribed landscape. The image registers the *traces* of his roots in his maturity. And the constantly dissolving intervening images prompt a projection of continuity into his life.

At the subsequent funeral, Álvarez dissolves from one leader to another, emphasizing the interconnectedness of the international socialist community. We are then struck by a jarring cut to a popular Cuban woman artist singing about pain and suffering in the world, again linking Cuban and Vietnamese experiences. The song continues as the film cuts to young Vietnamese children dancing, clapping, and singing in a schoolyard as Ho Chi Minh leads the fun. We then witness the first dramatic and disjunctive tone change in the film. Following a bomb explosion, absolutely horrific still images of children disfigured by napalm are visible on-screen as the music becomes discordant. Gruesome shots occasionally share the screen with each other and move into and out of the frame. The edges of the photographs are often in view, and the camera cuts or zooms into extreme close-ups of wild eyes, cracked mouths, and torn limbs. As with *Now*, photographic images are exposed as a particular view, situated within a specific frame. Here, however, they initially provoke a visceral response rather than prompt analytic reflection.

The second major tone shift in the film is generated by a transition from an ironic use of patriotic American music to a gentle guitar playing over an intertitled poem written by Ho Chi Minh. In the passage inspiring the film's title, Ho writes:

Without the glacial winter, without grief and death,
Who can appreciate your glory, Spring?
The pains which temper my spirit are a crucible
And they forge my heart in pure steel.

Such determination and moral and political commitment are shown to be the legacy Ho leaves to his people, who mourn his death with great emotion in the subsequent section. Foreign diplomats as well as Vietnamese children, adults, and seniors are visibly overwhelmed by the loss. As a funeral speech is read (not subtitled into Spanish), accompanied by the non-diegetic drumbeats and electric keyboard of Iron Butterfly (which shortly thereafter take over for the speech), an array of people walk past to pay their respects. Each group is presented in slow motion. In one example, people's movements superimpose and eventually dissolve into that of another group's. In another, ambulating feet gradually dissolve into a negative image, recalling the sequence in which Ho Chi Minh is seen aging. In one other, Álvarez and his special effects coordinator Pepin Rodriguez construct a shot in which it appears that people walk with their own ghosts slightly behind them. The effect is achieved by the superimposition of two shots. The first is an image of visibly distraught students descending a staircase in slow motion.

The second consists of the same shot as the first, only captured after a one- to two-second lag time. When these images are superimposed, the students appear to be walking along with their own transparent traces. It is a remarkable effect that, along with the other aesthetic choices in the sequence, articulates a sense of collective unity and historicity. The superimpositions reinforce the idea of a populace united behind a leader. The negative images and trace effect capture a shared history—shared between Ho and his people and shared among the people. In this case, it is not just the photographic nature of the image but what distinguishes cinema from photography—its existence in time—that is critical. Álvarez's effects in this sequence rely on motion to construct a sense not of embalmed history but of historical progress. It is movement in time and through time. The point, and this is reiterated at the end of the film, is that the funeral is not the culmination of a struggle. The film is not a wholly historical document of Ho's life. It is a statement and an attempt to realize historical movement. The people, both Vietnamese and Cuban, are in the midst of a battle that must continue until "an everlasting Spring"—the realization of both Ho's and Che's visions—is finally reached.

The section concludes with another intertitle, this one from José Martí. He writes, DEATH ISN'T REAL WHEN A LIFE'S WORK HAS BEEN WELL FULFILLED. The quote reinforces this section's connections with the first section of the film about Ho's life and contrasts it with those that focus on the war. Both the funeral and the biographical sections urge citizens to think about what is involved in living a meaningful life (and therefore leaving a lasting legacy). They are emotionally and intellectually reflective as opposed to viscerally jarring. They are about steeling the heart for action and preparing to engage a battle without fear, no matter the consequences.

MOBILIZEABILITY

In this chapter, I have identified Álvarez's political, artistic, and ethical commitments of the second period. I have situated the new transnational, transhistorical, and multiracial alignments—and the principles on which those foundations depended (a new ethics of labor, a new model of international revolution, and a new call to live a critical, moral life)—in relation to Cuba's shifting political, social, and economic climate. I have marked the closeness of Álvarez's vision to that of the revolutionary leadership, highlighting Che Guevara's dream of the new man. And I have done so by carefully describing the distinctive techniques by which Álvarez sought to shape Cuban social imaginaries, recognizing, as Charles Taylor maintains, that "if the understanding makes the practice possible, it is also true that the practice carries the understanding."[36]

The newsreels of the second period are predominantly (though not exclusively) focused on Cuban industrial and agricultural productivity. They provide detailed information on all aspects of production processes through narrative exegesis as well as through audiovisual attention. Over the course of the period, they increasingly and persistently take advantage of the regulated structure of the newsreel to enact a rhythmically consistent, at times machine-like pattern of editing and framing. This is especially true when the focus is on industrial production and new efforts to mechanize agricultural production.

This mechanistic element is balanced both within the newsreels themselves and, more frequently, by a persistent and varied juxtapositionality evident throughout Álvarez's documentaries from 1965 to 1971. Juxtapositions occur at the level of the singular image through the use of collage in, for example, *Now.* They occur between sound and image in almost all of the films, perhaps most notably in *Hanoi, martes 13.* They occur across sequence, as I have described, in *79 primaveras.* They occur across section or reel in *LBJ.* And they occur across films, whether it is across documentaries from multiple years or across newsreels and documentaries of the same period.[37]

Together, this dynamic is at the heart of the interrelationship between what I want to call Cuban productivism and nonfiction film during this period.[38] It is a combination that aims to shape a subjectivity responsive to the need for efficient, focused productivity and is flexible enough to respond to the requirements of industrial and agricultural mobilization, a result of the unbalanced economic approach. To explain, the range of juxtapositions, their effort to jar, and their intensity combined with the films' declared focus on productivity and collective effort aim to create a subject uniquely responsive to the shifting conditions of existence facing Cuban citizens. Such a model of revolutionary behavior and thought is subtended by the newsreels' celebration of the mechanistic, with its displays and projections of consistent, efficient laboring processes. Combined, the aesthetics of the films themselves require a level of attentiveness and adaptability consonant with that of government efforts to mobilize the citizenry for urgent operations, be they economic, social, educational, national defense, or international in nature. During the second period of the post-revolutionary nonfiction film project—the period often considered the height of Cuban cinema—Álvarez worked to critically and sensorially prepare citizens for the likelihood of mobilization while always reminding them of the public nature of such performances.

PART THREE

FIVE

Esfir Shub, Factography, and the New Documentary Historiography

Today it's utterly inconceivable how we could get by without the photographer who takes pictures of the Five-Year Plan, who takes pictures of the launch and growth of our industrial giants, and thereby carries out a great and authentic agitation through display. The juxtaposition, for example, of a photograph of a tiny village on a putrid little river with one taken a year later in which a glass building has replaced the village—such stunning juxtapositions force you to radically reconsider the obsolete notion of a "human lifetime," for our century equals a millennium in earlier times.

—SERGEI TRET'IAKOV, "FROM THE PHOTO-SERIES TO EXTENDED PHOTO-OBSERVATION" (1931)

The "play" side of art shouldn't be exaggerated. The phenomenon of "play" is inherent in art, but art itself periodically reorientates itself towards the material.

—VIKTOR SHKLOVSKY, "*LEF* AND FILM" (1927)

THE KALEIDOSCOPIC AND COLLECTIVE KNOWLEDGE

Title: BUSES ASSEMBLE AT THE SOVIET. Tight shot of a truck bearing down on us. Trams hastily leave their station. Title: IN PLACE OF PUBLIC

SPEAKERS. A low-angle image of a loudspeaker. Title: IN PLACE OF AP-PLAUSE. Increasingly rapid close-ups of a hand squeezing a horn, a finger pushing a horn button, a pulsing cone-shaped amplifier, and the loudspeaker. Title: WELCOMING YOU. Six shots of circular automotive parts. Loudspeaker. Title: IN THE NAME OF THE SOVIET. Loudspeaker. The Moscow Soviet symbol appears. It becomes superimposed over a wheel. It reemerges on its own. Superimposed again, this time over steps on a bus. Loudspeaker.

In 1925, the Moscow Soviet, faced with an election in 1926, decided to commission a documentary film that would portray its numerous accomplishments during the past year. This resulting film was Dziga Vertov's *Stride, Soviet!*, and the sequence I describe above is Vertov's way of "covering" the election rally of 1925 held in front of the Mossoviet building. There are no people present at this rally. Machines speak to machines, which listen (cone motif), watch (circular motif), and applaud (horns and pulsing). For Vertov, the replacement and combination (via superimposition) of the human with the mechanical points to the possibility of what he called "the perfect electric man."[1] Not surpris-

FIGURE 5.1-FIGURE 5.3. (*left and above*) Attentive automobiles at
the Moscow Soviet election rally of 1925 in *Stride, Soviet!*

ingly, members of the Mossoviet Presidium were dumbfounded to see their well-attended election rally devoid of people. Various members described the film as "too kaleidoscopic," "incomprehensible to peasants," and just simply "too fast."[2] And they were keenly aware that machines could not vote.

When one recalls the critical response to Vertov's *A Sixth Part of the World* discussed at the end of chapter 3, the reaction by the Presidium should not come as a surprise. But additionally, these reactions point to a larger concern about Vertov's and other 1920s experimental artists' aesthetic and methodological choices. Many critics and political leaders felt that avant-garde art had become incomprehensible to the masses, and they sought a new dialogue between cultural producers and audiences that would result in the achievement of the contemporary watchword—intelligibility. In the pages of the journal *Novyi Lef*, critics encouraged the correction of what they saw as an inherent problem with the production art of the 1920s, which, they felt, had deemphasized the symbolic and ideological components of objects. They believed that many Constructivist artists (including Vertov), in their efforts to transform the intellectual and perceptual lives of their audiences, had created an uneven relationship with audiences. The conversation had become too one-sided, critics contended, recognizing "only the sensuous and somatic features of objects." To rectify the situation, artists had to engage "not just with physical and dimensional bodies, but also with bodies of collective social knowledge and the networks of communication."[3] In order for work to perform a "great and authentic agitation through display," as Sergei Tret'iakov writes,[4] they had to return the compositional aspect to the work. They had to find a place for the informational and discursive components of language if they were to generate productive conversations and productive citizens.

This was especially true for discussions of nonfiction film, which was presumed to possess a unique capacity to aid in generating productive citizens. Shortly after Vertov was dismissed from Sovkino, many political officials, film industrial leaders, and cultural critics came to see Esfir Shub's historical compilation method of documentary filmmaking as preferable. They saw her model of making films in an archive, with a plan in mind, as more efficient and appropriate for the shifting sociopolitical climate—one that privileged organization and centralization over inspiration and fragmentation. Shub's method and aesthetics did not threaten the political message; it communicated it more clearly. It produced the dialogue between film and viewer that critics and political leaders sought. And it was thought to do so in an efficient economic and linguistic manner.

This chapter examines what Mikhail Iampol'skii describes as the break from the Dziga Vertov–dominated phase to one in which Shub's historical compilation method serves as the model.[5] I locate this shift in relation to larger artistic and political-economic currents in the Soviet Union at the time, in particular the relationship between culture and the establishment of the First Five-Year Plan (1928–1932). During this period, policy makers began to insert themselves into cultural affairs in ways they had not in the early 1920s. Criticism, in turn, came to play an increasingly significant role in the direction nonfiction film took by identifying the methodological and aesthetic features that, critics argued, best served the needs of the nation-state. I focus my attention on criticism associated with the journal *Novyi Lef* and the factography movement. Factography was an interdisciplinary movement that sought to align with the First Five-Year Plan by eliminating the opposition between signification and production, transforming the relationship between language and work. Shub's films were consistently held up as models of factographic work, despite the fact that her use of historical materials ran counter to factographers' promotion of a "presentist" practice that privileged newspaper reports, diaries, and *ocherks* (essays or short sketches) of contemporary life.

Whereas the previous two chapters on the USSR focus on both documentary and newsreel, this chapter locates changes in documentary practice in relation to the photo-essay. There are two primary reasons for this. First, by 1926 (the year Vertov was fired from Sovkino), newsreels had fallen out of favor significantly. They became associated with poor-quality nonfiction filmmaking and were seen by both leaders and distributors as poor investments. Production had fallen over 66 percent since the civil war period. They reached a new low in 1926, demonstrating their decreased role in communicating the vision of the nation-state and its political leaders.[6] Second, examining Shub's documentaries and a photo-essay in light of the critical responses to them reveals the set of beliefs these practitioners, critics, and audiences held about the meanings these mediums convey—disclosing what Ilana Gershon describes as their media ideologies.[7] In other words, the responses to documentary and the direction it was urged to take was conceived and articulated in relation to other media. Moreover, because factography was an interdisciplinary, transmedia movement, this approach accounts for the original concerns of the critics themselves. Overall, this approach allows me both to explicate a nuanced shift in documentary discourse (one important to documentary history) and to elucidate a set of critical and theoretical issues that remain relevant to discussions of documentary today. These involve the relationship between documentary form and politics, between the image and its rootedness in time and space, and between expectations of viewers' engagements with the nonfiction film image. In doing this analytical work, I am able to point to the assumptions factographers make about the Soviet citizenry, how these beliefs lead to photographic and cinematic projections designed to reveal their goals for that citizenry, and the disjunctions that arise between the documentary (still-image and moving-image) practices and critical statements. Put another way, this effort not only allows me to understand why the Shubian model was seen as the appropriate vehicle for shaping citizens' social imaginaries in the late 1920s in the USSR but also raises core concerns about documentary's role in communicating social and political transformation itself.

THE TERRITORY OF REALISM

The Soviet Union of the early 1920s was a site of considerable artistic contestation as various groups angled to become the privileged means by which to communicate revolutionary political and social change. In the first half of the decade, the Communist Party was reluctant to officially favor one group or another. The 1925 Party Resolution on Literature set a new precedent for the party's involvement in cultural affairs. Written by Nikolai Bukharin, the document urged that material and ideological support be given to the proletarian groups calling for a conservative realist form with revolutionary characters and themes. Whereas the resolution explicitly addressed only literature (the All-Russian Association of Proletarian Writers [VAPP] was the greatest beneficiary), its applicability to the other arts became evident in the rise to prominence of the proletarian Association of Artists of Revolutionary Russia (AKhRR).

The Constructivists, notably members of the avant-garde experimental group Lef, became somewhat marginalized as many officials saw their production work as unintelligible to the masses. But Lef did not abandon its belief that form and content were dialectically intertwined. It challenged the idea that combining conservative "form" with revolutionary "content" would produce a legible, revolutionary culture. At the end of 1926, the party granted Lef members the right to follow up their previous eponymous journal, *Lef,* with a new journal, *Novyi Lef* (New Lef). It was primarily in the pages of *Novyi Lef* that critics and artists such as Tret'iakov, Nikolai Chuzhak, Viktor Shklovsky, Osip Brik, Esfir Shub, Aleksandr Rodchenko, Viktor Pertsov, Boris Arvatov, Dziga Vertov, and others articulated a counter-model of realism centered on the fixation of facts. As Leah Dickerman summarizes, "At stake for Lef was a claim to defining the territory of realism."[8] Doing so required situating its project both in relation to earlier production art as well as in relation to the newly privileged proletarian realism.

Tret'iakov, arguably the foremost leader of the factography movement, began the inaugural issue by attacking what he saw as the erroneous assumptions of those proletarian realists dreaming of "New Red Tolstoys."[9] Works of art, he maintained, are objects that process human emotions and that serve a social function. Producers that separate form from content deny the social nature of the art object. It is only in recognizing form and content's interrelation, Tret'iakov argued, that new ways of apprehending and processing social phenomena are communicable. He wrote that movie directors who seek to change the material without changing the form "are terrifying meat grinders for all the fresh material that falls into their hands." These films do not respect the quality of the individual materiality but transform "an everyday life that is close to us into a strange and unreal world, a world into which the spectator flees from such reality."[10] Tret'iakov pointed to three ways in which the form of belles lettres served to disempower people and proposed three solutions that would serve to bring the citizenry into closer contact with the changing physical and social landscape. These principles informed the methodological and formal choices made by the new fact-producers (sometimes called *factoviki*, literally "factists").

Tret'iakov's first contention was that belles lettres' celebration of isolated, inspired, individual artists (and the authority that gets reinforced by imagining them as such) ran counter to socialist belief in collective social action. In its place, he proposed a mass movement of de-professionalized, yet skilled and trained, worker-correspondents capable of communicating the truth of everyday life, whether in words or images.[11] Second, he argued that the narrative structure of realist Russian literature (and its translation into cinema), with its sense of closure and concomitant fatalism, worked to placate citizens rather than to inspire them to act on behalf of the revolution. The alternative, he proposed, was more open-ended narratives that emphasized the accumulation and collection of thematically related facts.[12] Third, he decried the prominence of the individual psychologized hero of the narrative or the sole emphasis on an individual figure in the photographic portrait as likewise inconsonant with socialist belief. Instead, he proposed a practice focused on communicating collective deeds or biographies centered not on people but on raw material that gets "transformed into a useful product through human effort."[13] Tret'iakov believed that emphasis on a collectivity as makers and communicators of deeds combined revolutionary form and content into a socialist practice.

Tret'iakov's emphasis on the collectivity as not just "makers" but "communicators" of deeds thus aligns with critiques of Vertov that saw his work as excessively personal, as unrestrained in its ambition, and as a move away from reality. Boris Groys sees this as part of a larger trajectory, writing, "The evolution of the avant-garde from Malevich to Constructivism and, later, to *Lef* proceeds by way of increasingly radical demands for the rejection of traditional artistic individualism and the adoption of new tasks."[14] The artist was obliged to relinquish his or her position as an observer of life and become part of a collective imagining a better future.

But factographers did not see their proposed formal and methodological changes as timeless solutions to age-old problems. "Every epoch has its own written forms," Tret'iakov wrote.[15] Because the sociopolitical sphere and the cultural sphere are mutually dependent, the factographers argued, the revolution in industrial production required a concurrent revolution in signification.[16] For factographic principles to become culturally dominant during the period of the First Five-Year Plan, its mode of communicative production had to align with new socialist industrial production. Newspapers, photo-essays, *ocherks,* and documentaries (both films and photo-essays) were to become the forms of contemporary industrial and social change.

NEW METHODS

Tret'iakov's emphasis on worker-correspondents was intended to apply, among other practices, to nonfiction film production. He claimed that this cadre of trained and untrained workers could supply the archive with sufficient material and that the film documents would not be too subjective. He writes, "The masses of amateur photographers, and the thousands of reporters and worker-correspondents, are potential factists. . . . They will become more valuable for a genuine socialization of art than any of the highly qualified masters from the ranks of artists or belletrists."[17] Tret'iakov and others assumed that since these fact-makers (facts are not found, they have to be processed and constructed) had little aesthetic experience, they could produce more objective documents. Even if a little subjectivity seeped into some of the facts, the implication was that such an assortment and multitude of collectors would cleanse the document, restoring its authenticity and facticity while making the document more likely to connect with a variety of viewers. He saw this process as increasing the authority of the document and enabling greater communicability.

If, for the critics in *Novyi Lef,* the first step was to send a number of people into the country to collect visual material that would then be gathered and catalogued in the archives, the second step required the editing of what Iampol'skii refers to as the "second-hand" material in the film factory-archive by a director-editor, the author of the film.[18] Late in 1926, Shub received a commission from Sovkino to make a historical film for the tenth anniversary of the Bolshevik Revolution. Assembled and released in 1927, Shub's *The Fall of the Romanov Dynasty* was the first of three compilation films she made during 1927–1928 (*The Great*

Way, 1927, and *The Russia of Nicholas II and Lev Tolstoy,* 1928, were the others).[19] Shub researched the film at the Museum of the Revolution in Leningrad, where for two months she pored over 60,000 meters of film. Her major difficulties were locating and organizing existing film material. Much of the footage had been taken out of the country, sold to foreign producers, or destroyed by terrible archive conditions. She persuaded the government to buy 2,000 feet of negative about the February Revolution (including famous shots of Lenin) from the United States. Eventually, however, she had to shoot 1,000 of the total 6,000 feet of the film. The film was an unequivocal success, drawing critical praise and substantial box office earnings.[20]

The fact that Shub worked in an archive with material others had shot was seen as indispensable to her success. But she was also seen to approach the archival material *properly.* In his critique of Vertov's *The Eleventh Year* (1928), Osip Brik argues that one of the reasons Shub's work is preferable to Vertov's is that she enters the archive with a plan in mind. It is this already imagined framework for the material that, paradoxically, allows an individual image to be properly situated within its context and, as such, retain authenticity and depth. Since Vertov worked without a plan, his cameraman Mikhail Kaufman captured material that "could almost be included in any film. The reportage element is completely lacking and what emerges is essentially beautiful 'natural' shots . . . his material is filmed from an aesthetic, not a documentary, position."[21] In effect, Brik is proposing that Vertov approach the historical world the way Shub approaches an archive: he ought to have a plan in mind, research, shoot, and select accordingly.[22]

Shub's combination of assembling films in an archive with material others had shot and approaching that material with a plan in mind prompted Brik, Tret'iakov, Shklovsky, and others to see her method as more efficient, organized, and objective than Vertov's. But that is not to say that Shub or the critics were being naive about the process of image making. (As mentioned above, Tret'iakov insisted that facts were made, not found.) Rather, what is striking about the nonfiction cinema debates, specifically concerning *The Fall of the Romanov Dynasty* and *The Great Way,* is that while refusing the naïveté of a pure "objectivism," each demonstrates a commitment to directorial restraint in both

method and aesthetic—a restraint that aligns with new conceptions of
the (objective) scientific self embraced by so many Soviet cultural workers.[23] What emerges is a shift in emphasis from rhetorical and visual
complexity to communicability. This modification was informed by a
new understanding of the Soviet audience. Scientific studies of peasant
audiences conducted in the mid-1920s found that they did not enjoy
films with long intertitles, which they could not read, nor did they care
for artistic experimentation in the form of quick cutting and unusual
juxtapositions in montage.[24] The cinema establishment aimed to counter
this problem in two ways. The first was the formation of an organization
called the ODSK (Society of Friends of the Soviet Cinema), which aimed
to "bridge the gap between film producers, directors, and audiences" by
training and educating common people "to introduce films, explain difficult parts and lead post-film discussion."[25] The second was to support
not just a shift in methods but a shift in documentary aesthetics so as to
differently engage the vast Soviet audience.

DOCUMENTARY AND FACTOGRAPHIC AESTHETICS:
ROOTEDNESS AND MOBILITY

Tret'iakov elaborates on the relationship between the personal (or subjective) and the aesthetic in his concern over the "deformation" of nonfiction material. For Tret'iakov, deformation is the "random *personal*
factor in any given film" realized through "the arbitrary distortion and
displacement of 'raw' elements."[26] One of the central ways this issue
gets negotiated in factographic criticism concerns the rootedness in a
particular time and space of the object in a photograph. Shklovsky[27]
and Tret'iakov[28] each have argued that a work's "documentary value" is
dependent upon audiences' ability to locate the event covered in a specific time and space. But that concern with rootedness intersects with
what many politicians and cultural producers consider its requirement
to travel across contexts. For facts to speak agitationally to the vast and
multinational Soviet citizenry—and thus to do their propagandistic and
agitational work—they needed to exceed their particularity. Peasants
in Kazakhstan, factory workers in Ukraine, and intellectuals in Leningrad had to be able to see the events and social actors portrayed as

typical—as evidence of something else—and yet still applicable to their particular situation. If the communicated facts were too deeply rooted in how an individual person acted in a specific context, the facts could not do the required agitational work. There was a risk that the facts would become about a particular context or about a particular person, not inspirational articulations of the process or deed. For factographers, these works had to signal the context and register the detail but speak to the whole Union (and sometimes beyond its borders) about the industrially and socially transformative processes taking place. Arguments about the way in which these media forms resolve the issue of material and symbolic location depend, to a large degree, on the ideological beliefs people maintain about these forms.

Recent work on language ideologies provides a set of tools for understanding how people negotiate this relationship between text and context so as to encourage (and affix) meanings that can create a shared, transmissible culture. And, as we will see, it has particular applicability to the historical compilation method of documentary production. The simultaneous processes that Richard Bauman and Charles Briggs describe as "entextualization," "decontextualization," and "recontextualization" are, I want to argue, in many ways at the heart of this critical and artistic project.[29] Factographers generally supported the state's position on industrialization and saw its new linguistic dictates as a means of building national support for the revolutionary efforts. But they were also well aware of the theoretical problems with conceiving of textuality in a deprocessualized manner and saw a new relationship to language as the way forward. Thus, exploring strategies of entextualization helped break down the various ways factographers answered the key question: How do cultural producers simultaneously ensure the mobility and stability of this material? The process of bounding (entextualizing), separating (decontextualizing), and integrating (recontextualizing) utterances, texts, and interactions into legible chunks of text requires a metapragmatics of utterances—a force dependent upon language (in this case, media) ideologies. But examining entextualization practices when the goal is the achievement of visual texts requires a modification of certain linguistic concepts to account for its specific *cinematic* or *photographic* dimensions.

Bauman and Briggs note that while entextualization is "the process of rendering discourses extractable" such that a unit "can be lifted out of its interactional setting," it "may well incorporate aspects of context, such that the resultant text carries elements of its history of use within it."[30] Carrying that history is a core requirement of factographic assumptions about film's potential for effective communication, a potentiality Shub and Tret'iakov inscribe in the mechanics of their practices. Thus, when Bauman and Briggs focus on the "factors [that] loosen the ties between performed discourse and its context," despite the apparent inseparability of the performer to the audience, scholars of photographic-based media have to amend the questions so as to account for the mediums' unique temporalities.[31] Any analysis of cinematic or photographic entextualization, therefore, must account for the relation between the viewer and the text at the moment of projection as well as the relation between the text and the historical context it "carries." Film theorists have turned to C. S. Peirce's concept of indexicality as a trace of a past event to explain the unique, and often implicit, historical claims that accompany photographic-based media, what Roland Barthes describes as the "that has been."[32] The idea is that the photograph has an existential bond with an object that leaves its imprint on light-sensitive material ("they are in certain respects exactly like the objects they represent").[33] Photographs also merge index with icon (and often symbol), their images resembling the objects themselves. But in so doing, the image's iconicity relies on the index, depending upon the fact that it was "physically forced to correspond point by point to nature," in this case, the object photographed.[34] Cinema's basis in photography and projection sustains and even extends this claim; light carries the embedded information directly to a screen (which viewers then engage), thus maintaining this physical connection.

If the index as trace upholds an alignment with iconicity, deictics (indexical denotationals, words like "this," "here," "now," "I," or "you") also partake of the symbolic order, which allows their enunciation to transcend the token-specific historical uniqueness marked by the index as trace and creatively transform their context of enunciation. This performative power of deictics to creatively direct or align the attention of participants within a multidimensional "deictic field"[35] speaks to the direction of attentivity so central to the management of the cinematic gaze. Christian Metz describes how the image *actualizes* a real for the viewer, a quality he identifies as an "index of actualization." For example, "a close-up of a revolver does not mean 'revolver' (a purely lexical unit), but . . . 'Here is a revolver!'" For Metz, even a straightforward cinematic image corresponds to a sentence rather than a word. It does so less by the "quantity of its meaning . . . than by its *assertive* status."[36] Whereas Metz's conception emphasizes the present moment and the index's power as a cultural and semiotic force, it is interesting to note that Metz uses precisely a presentational sentence containing a deictic ("Here is . . .") to illustrate this "assertive" status.[37] If the index as trace speaks to the historicity of the photographic image, the index as deixis marks the enunciative moment itself as critical to the establishment of spatial and temporal context.[38]

A conception of indexicality as trace and as deixis opens to analysis the entextualizing processes and thus makes more salient the overlapping and contrasting photographic media ideologies embedded in factographic principles. This architecture allows us to access a more nuanced notion of factographic temporality—its emphasis on presentness, its reliance on pastness, and its recognition of the inherent instability of its own entextualizing practices. I explore such concerns by paying attention to a specific set of aesthetic strategies or what Bauman and Briggs would identify as "keys to performance" that "may be seen as indices of entextualization."[39] I take my cue from the factographic critical interventions themselves and focus on narrative structure and image composition.

UNITY IN ACCUMULATION (PRINCIPLES)

In "Our Cinema," Tret'iakov argues that the material itself (here, documentary or nonfiction photographic images), the construction of material (compositional manner), and the social purpose (agitation) are the legitimate questions researchers and audience members should ask of a work of art. Shub's documentaries *The Fall of the Romanov Dynasty* and *The Great Way* and Max Al'pert's and Arkadii Shaikhet's photoessay *A Day in the Life of a Moscow Working-Class Family* (1931) begin with the premise that documentary or nonfictional material should be the building block of their pieces. In addition, these artists all chose to work with a photographic-based (mechanistic) medium of inscription. Shub selected moving images (this was a few years before the Soviets obtained sound cinema capability), and Al'pert and Shaikhet selected still images. The social purpose, according to Tret'iakov, is revealed by the combination of the initial material choice, the composition/construction of material, the distribution and exhibition of the material, and the larger sociopolitical and cultural contexts. Mobilizing the concepts of entextualization, decontextualization, and recontextualization allows us to reformulate slightly Tret'iakov's perspectives by breaking down these laborious processes.

Through her found footage method, Shub worked with material that had already been entextualized by other filmmakers and historical social actors. Her initial process of selection was thus different from Al'pert and Shaikhet's, who began by selecting a photographic subject from the real world, imaginatively removing it from its larger surround, and only then inscribing the image onto a piece of celluloid. Shub's initial selection occurred at the Museum of the Revolution, where she isolated moving-image material that had already been prepared for circulation by someone else and rebound the frames into new, discrete chunks of cinematic text. Before organizing the material into larger texts, the photographers had intermediate steps: they had to process and print the image, actively transforming the tone, brightness, and clarity of the negative image into a positive one prior to printing it on photographic paper. The process of recontextualizing the previously decontextualized and entextualized material was of considerable interest to factographers (though, of course, they did not use such language), who sought a new textual unity outside the strictures of traditional narrative organization.

The narrative organizational approach to which factographers turned was informed by their alignment with an empirical scientific mode of inductive thought.[40] Emphasizing an abundance of detail over broad synthesizing strokes, factographers promoted a principle of accumulation that allowed for, and often celebrated, loose connections between objects. They privileged a descriptive mode rather than narrative exegesis, or what Brik calls *protokol* (report) over *proklamatsiia* (proclamation). Brik outlines the distinction between this new approach and the one upholding the conservative realist approach taken by his aesthetic enemies. Addressing film, he writes: "In place of unity of action, unity of intrigue, we have a succession of separate scenes often barely connected with each other. . . . But how is this breakdown in structure . . . to be explained? It is explained by the interest in individual facts, individual details, which create a necessary *unity in their accumulation*."[41] Calls for accumulation, collection, and aggregation of details were commonplace in the pages of *Novyi Lef.* This de-emphasis on narrational authority and promotion of "a certain directorial restraint" guided Shub as well as Al'pert and Shaikhet as they endeavored to provide Soviet citizens with a survey of their new world. But how does one accumulate details in moving- and still-image documentaries? And how does this organizational strategy serve a social function? In other words, if we are to assume a certain audience *activity* is needed to ensure the legibility of this unity, what aesthetic strategies were thought to make that happen?

UNITY IN ACCUMULATION (DOCUMENTARY FILM)

The crucial conflict in both *The Fall of the Romanov Dynasty* and *The Great Way* is between the new (or coming) socialist way of life and the forces that oppose it. Whereas *The Fall of the Romanov Dynasty* focuses on the years leading up to the Bolshevik Revolution (1912–1917), *The Great Way* looks at the battle for revolutionary progress waged in the years since the February Revolution. The first part of *The Fall of the Romanov Dynasty* unequivocally establishes the argument by presenting images of a doomed regime, opening with the title TSARIST RUSSIA IN THE YEARS OF THE BLACK REACTION. The slow, even pace recalls a rural atmosphere, while the images of State Duma politicians casually conversing and wealthy landowners enjoying leisure time contrast sharply with shots of industrial workers and peasants laboring in the fields. Shub's use of titles and editing patterns function ironically to juxtapose the two social and economic spheres. The first part concludes with images of the Romanovs and other Russian nobility parading above a crowd. Whereas this procession is rhetorically, if not formally, contrasted with the marching of needy peasants, the parade scenes also anticipate the forthcoming images of the Bolsheviks. While the images

FIGURE 5.4 AND FIGURE 5.5. Like Vertov's meat, all perspiration is not equal. Nobles and workers sweating in *The Fall of the Romanov Dynasty*.

FIGURE 5.6. The mass as force of revolutionary change in *The Great Way*.

of the nobility emphasize inactivity and distance from the crowd, shots of the revolution articulate dynamism and an organic connection with the people—one of the central themes of the film. This argument is communicated via contrasting spatiotemporal logics. The old order is presented through images and sequences with longer duration and with less velocity than those pointing to revolutionary change.

The Great Way picks up on and deepens this relationship between the rhetoric of "the old and new" and contrasting ways of presenting these messages. Like *The Fall of the Romanov Dynasty*, *The Great Way* conveys the gap between the people and the forces opposing revolutionary change through an immobile (or slightly mobile), distanced, observational look with extended duration. But in addition, Shub increases editing rhythms to demonstrate rising historical momentum across the film—the thematics are echoed at the formal level. The film as a whole accelerates as the average shot length decreases by almost 50 percent in the second half of the film.[42] While the shots of opposing forces remain long in duration, distanced, and static, the images of new tractor factories and the building of model houses increase in number and velocity and shorten in duration.

The aesthetics as a whole, even the more rapidly edited sequences of images of modernization, are comparably more visually stable, with less camera movement and less jarring cinematography, than those common to Vertov. This aspect of Shub's films was lauded as providing "authenticity" to the film document, doing the work Shklovsky and Tret'iakov required, by locating things in their times and places. But there is a puzzle here: How does accumulation work as one of the organizational principles of a chronological film with a narrative drive centered on the historical clash of good and bad forces? In other words, if accumulation, collection, and aggregation are the crucial elements of this "presentist" practice, does not Shub's choice of historical narrative undermine her inclusion in the factographic project? The chronotopic logics themselves—Shub's work around time and space—provide the first key to answering this question and begin to open up ideological distinctions between moving- and still-image documentary projects.

Accumulation through lists, inventories, and oppositions of an array of loosely related phenomena draws attention to the intervals that hold them together. Gilles Deleuze, theorizing on cinema through the work of Jean-Luc Godard, describes this as a "conjunctive 'and' [that] can assume an isolated and magnified value."[43] The looseness of the connection and the lack of a totalizing determinacy create spaces of thought for viewers. These spaces are open, non-teleological, and always shifting—each new and different example has the possibility of radically transforming how one imagines the connections between objects. "They create continual movement," Timothy Corrigan writes, "a recollection and anticipation as a serial activity whose accumulations are endlessly generative."[44] By not fully creating but prompting thought, accumulation reduces narrational authority.

Both *The Fall of the Romanov Dynasty* and *The Great Way* approach a cumulative logic through their use of an aesthetics of spatiotemporal restraint. By means of increased duration, stable visual perspectives, and thematic repetition, the films' found footage sequences constantly exceed their narrative dimensions. For example, when watching the fourth thirty-second clip of a parade of a counterrevolutionary power in *The Great Way*, viewers need not focus on the narrative work the shot or sequence is doing. They are free to roam visually and imaginatively, finding facts in events and figures and making connections not fully articulated by Shub herself. And this occurs throughout the film, even as the shots' durations speed up slightly in the last two reels. Shub herself described as the goal of her montage that "emphasis on the fact is an emphasis not only to show the fact, but to enable it to be examined and, having examined it, to be kept in mind."[45] Beyond encouraging viewers to keep the facts in mind, these strategies offer viewers the potential to create facts themselves. The visual density of the moving photographic image allows for such possibilities, while Shub's formal strategies exploit that potential.

Tret'iakov points to this disjunctive and conjunctive quality in Shub's work. He celebrates her ingenuity by noting that she "does not stage and film the things she needs to realize her montage, but instead works under the hard conditions of incomplete material. She is forced to invent the wildest things so that she can fill the gaps, and so that she can bring together bits of photography whose material and quality are fundamentally different from one another."[46]

In this essay, Tret'iakov is himself operating according to a conjunctive logic. He praises Shub's skill in negotiating challenging working conditions, contending that it is better to effectively manage "incomplete material" than to invent new material.[47] In the process, she manages to create a "new *compound* to ignite and elucidate the social meaning."[48] But for Tret'iakov and other viewers *to recognize* Shub's skill, the material needs to be *identifiable* as incomplete. In bringing together the disparate textual chunks, Shub needs to make their disparateness legible. It is only then that their combination produces the desired social effect. The disjunctive must precede the conjunctive but be sensible therein.

Shub attains such a dialectic by making the processes of entextualization legible on the surface of the film. One way to understand how she does so is by turning to the conception of figure-ground relations that William Hanks developed for the analysis of deixis. Hanks argues that only a conception of deixis that accounts for the relation between the referent (figure) and its indexical origo (the ground, "zero," or "pivot-point" relative to which the referent is identified) can account for the dynamism, subtlety, and productivity of deixis. People do not "choose between an indexical and a referential object. Rather, they identify the referential in relation to the indexical," in the process encoding a relation between the speaker, the addressee, and the time and place of enunciation.[49] The point, then, is not simply that Shub establishes a stable primary-secondary division among parts of the screen, allowing viewers an ease of comprehension through "relative referencing." Rather, she employs stable figure-ground relations throughout the film, establishing legibility for the terms of her comparisons (between "old" and "new," for example). This strategy establishes the cumulative structure ("listifying" the list, so to speak). The stability of figure-ground relations is what allows the disparateness of the film material and even the apparent looseness of the topical connections to exist while maintaining legibility and contextual specificity. Or put differently, the stability of the internal semantic structure combines with the disparateness of the texturally and thematically visual material to produce the desired combination of exhortatory tone and historical context.

This explanation, however, does not fully account for the narrative drive that is clearly in operation in both films. The spatiotemporal logics and use of repetition allow viewers to access and exceed the narrative dimension. But the chronological structure, driven by the clash of oppositional forces, infuses the film with a kind of connective tissue that appears incongruous with Brik's notion of the "barely connected."[50] Accounting for this aspect requires accounting for the knowledge the Soviet citizenry brought to the theater.

Soviet citizens already knew both of Shub's "stories." The Marxist argument that the Great War was between imperial powers and the notion that Aleksandr Kerensky was a member of the bourgeoisie, striving to use the revolution for its own purposes (the argument of *The Fall of the Romanov Dynasty*), were familiar to Soviet audiences. Similarly, the political capitulation of the Provisional Government, the civil war struggle against counterrevolutionary forces, and the campaign to "electrify" the countryside—major subjects of *The Great Way*—were all fairly common historical fodder. Because viewers had this knowledge did not eliminate the role that narrative momentum has in the film; knowing the story neither destroys narrative pleasure nor necessarily reduces the narrative power. But combining acquaintance with the story with Shub's aesthetic strategies tempered the dominant role such narrative dimensions may otherwise have had. Viewers were freed from what factographers would consider overly authoritative narrational control and at liberty to pursue new connections. They were learning about history but doing so differently than they did through more didactic texts. Instead of sweeping, synthesizing proclamations, individual facts inductively drove the viewer's understanding of historical chronology. A film and a practice rooted in twin concerns with the present and with presence are embroiled in historical questions. Shub's goal was to spark new historical imaginations by prompting viewers to see historical processes in objects and events. But they had to do so by vigilantly remembering that history comes to us textualized. Thus, for Shub, the achievement of textuality was required for audiences to begin to think historically, but the mode of historical thought she projected was not at all deprocessualized.[51]

It becomes clear, then, that the structural looseness for which Brik calls is not entirely acceptable for an industrial art–like cinema. At the 1928 Party Conference, Nikolai Bukharin chastised the film industry, noting that foreign industries "know how to win where we are losing, that here they make enormous profits while we make a loss."[52] For the cinema to fulfill its social function, it must both be "intelligible," the current watchword, and "stimulate the public appetite."[53] The considerably positive critical and popular response to Shub demonstrates that, for documentaries of the time, narrative connections must be sufficiently strong and exhortatory if they were to fulfill the requisite social and economic function. It is within that framework that the other factographic elements must be negotiated.

UNITY IN ACCUMULATION (PHOTO-ESSAY)

If Brik's call for organization around loosely related photographic phenomena was rarely fully realized in moving-image documentary production, he found aesthetic compatriots in the field of the photo-essay. Varvara Stepanova, photographer and collaborator of Aleksandr Rodchenko's, distinguishes the shift between former practices and those

guided by factographic principles. She argues that "the value of the photograph itself came to assume primary importance" and that it "now
has become an independent and complete totality."[54] For Stepanova,
photographs have to exist on their own terms. They must neither be
entirely beholden to their place in a montage nor inauthentic syntheses
of a broader idea. But this idea "poses another problem—the need for
a technique to express reality in characteristic and explicit terms."[55]
Rodchenko expands on Stepanova's notion of the individual image as autonomous and poses an answer to her call for a new technique of photographic expression. Rodchenko critiques the tradition of the "illustrated
composition" as a synthetic portrait of an already conceived idea and
instead asserts "the snapshot," a photographic mode that highlights the
fleeting moment in all its uniqueness. In place of the *foto-kartiny* (photo-
pictures), with their emphasis on totality and organic unity, Rodchenko
celebrates the *foto-kadry* (photo-stills), with their emphasis on autonomy
and fragmentation.[56] Rodchenko argues that "small truths" are productive.[57] They correspond to revolutionary time and its presumptive rate
of change by unequivocally choosing the latter in the "battle between
eternity and the moment."[58]

   Stepanova and Rodchenko remain focused on the individual or isolated fact when they shift to consider the photo-essay or photomontage.
Stepanova and Rodchenko are not denying the value of the photomontage but insist that its value is cumulative—that the overall message
of the essay does not subsume the individual images. Once again, the
intervals, the spaces between images, are seen to be both requisite and
generative spaces of thought. For Stepanova, these constructive gaps are
what drive audience *activity,* challenging the passive contemplation that
results from traditional composition. She aims to move, as she wrote
earlier in the decade, from the model of a museum "to [the model of]
an archive."[59] Archival projects are by necessity fragmented—emerging
from various imaginations and spaces, containing disparate forms and
material. And in the factographic imagination, they require a double
reading of both past and present. Once again, implicit in this position is
the notion that for archival projects to be *constructive,* they must articulate difference—that is, their initial entextualization must be legible and
distinct from its present use. In other words, it is the recognition by the

viewer that these photographs have been shot for another purpose, or at least exist outside of the bounds of their role within the photomontage, that creates the activity-driving aporias.

The intervals of the photo-essay, however, are not the same as cinematic intervals. It is here that we see divergence within the factography movement about how photography functions as a medium, as well as discrepant viewpoints across media. In 1931, Max Al'pert and Arkadii Shaikhet produced a photo-essay titled *A Day in the Life of a Moscow Working-Class Family*. The essay was commissioned by the Austrian photography journal *Arbeiter Illustrierte Zeitung*, where it originally ran. Having been well received abroad, it was then picked up by the Soviet photography journal *Proletarskoe Kino* later that year. Framing the piece in the Soviet journal is an essay by Tret'iakov, who critiques it while offering a new direction for photo-essays.

A Day in the Life is organized around the daily routine of what is supposed to be thought of as a "typical" Moscow working-class family. It consists of forty-four pictures (a few of which contain multiple images) of the Filippovs in their new home, having breakfast together, going to work, going to school, working, studying, shopping, socializing, and taking part in cultural and leisure activities. Each picture is accompanied by a caption, which ranges from a brief explanatory note ("After lunch and nap—games" complementing #26, a picture of Vitya at kindergarten) to five-sentence descriptions that provide detailed contextual information on the event taking place. The caption to picture #20, for example, says:

> Yesterday the three [father Nikolai Fedotovich, mother Anna Ivanovna, and eldest son Kostya] walked together to the ZRK to pick up the dress order that was ready, and they also bought Kostya a suit for 44 rubles. Thanks to the decent earnings of the family (over 500 rubles a month), and what they had put aside, there is quite enough to live on. Three of them have savings books. Comparatively the large payment for the apartment, lights, and gas (up to 45 rubles/month), they can easily handle it; it's less than 10 percent of the budget. They've put 700 rubles aside in the state common fund.

The primary image of the threesome walking to the store takes up almost half of the page, while three images of documents that testify to the validity of the caption's claims sit in the bottom right of the page. It is this combination that makes up the picture. For the most part, however, the pictures consist of only one image, but in a few instances, they are supported by close-ups of official documents that testify to the claim of the caption (#20 is an example of this approach). The image composition is for the most part conventional, with only a few images reminiscent of Rodchenko's more jarring style. The composition works to reinforce the parallels between family members' lives, a correspondence evident at the structural level as well.

In his essay framing the piece, Tret'iakov demonstrates his support for Al'pert and Shaikhet's overall approach.[60] At the level of medium, Tret'iakov echoes Brik's arguments about the value of photography over painting by claiming that photography is "immeasurably simpler and more comprehensive than painting."[61] It is more direct in registering the detail of the material world, more efficient in its capture, and yet it maintains a depth required for a dialectical-materialist understanding of the world. He also commends the photo-series as a photographic genre, contending that it represents "the next step beyond the isolated snapshot."[62] The snapshot here retains the dynamism that accrues from spontaneously isolating individual moments of movement, but it also provides that extraction with significance by locating it within a series.

This dialectic between the contingent image and its location within a montage series is what Tret'iakov deems to be the value of the approach. It is achieved by providing the necessary balance between openness and organization. If in Shub's film the sense of rootedness is driven by the film's chronotopic logics, in Al'pert's and Shaikhet's photo-essay the rootedness emanates from the town itself and the Filippovs as a family. To explain, the historical/contextual specificity in both *The Fall of the Romanov Dynasty* and *The Great Way* emerges from a stable figure-ground relation, which is established by means of long takes and stable perspectives. But in *A Day in the Life*, the stability of the location of the family and the topic of the Filippovs themselves provide the legibility of the ground—a legibility unattainable through extended time due to the photo-essay's and cinema's different ontological statuses. As Tret'iakov writes, the Filippov piece is substantive because it locates the family "as a particle in our active social tissue," finding a place for them in the "cross-section of the flux."[63] On the other hand, if in *The Great Way* openness or mobility derives from the various filmic textures, materials, and apparent range of topics of the sequences, in *A Day in the Life* the openness or mobility emerges from the contingency of the snapshots. In both, the figure-ground relations combine to offer a legible framework for viewers while maintaining an apparent limitation on narrational authority. In the case of the photo-essay, its scope (industrial production, sociopolitical activity, and familial life) and its serial structure allow the contingent photograph to maintain its dynamism while imbuing it with a more generalized significance—realizing proper proportions between rootedness and mobility. Like Geertz's "thick description," the photo-series "lets us feel the true weight of one of reality's dense layers," overcoming the "thin scale" of the snapshot.[64]

Whereas Tret'iakov celebrates the synchronic depth and social breadth of the Filippov "series," he argues that its limitations result from its narrow diachronic scope. The next step is the "extended photo-observation, noting every moment of growth and change" in the family's condition.[65] Tret'iakov calls for a model akin to what has come to be called the longitudinal documentary, a documentary subgenre that examines its subjects (often through multiple, semi-discrete films and videos) over an extended period of time.[66] For Tret'iakov, the Filippov piece fails to communicate the reality of social change in a revolutionary context. Calling attention to the momentous growth of the Soviet proletariat would allow the broad citizenry to better understand itself as a unified body and provide invaluable evidence about the laws governing and obstacles challenging socialist production and everyday life in the USSR.

In place of this historical and contextual seclusion, Tret'iakov proposes a photographic form that will emphasize the *process* of social and industrial change in a qualitative manner. This open-endedness at the level of subject matter recurs at the level of genre. Nikolai Chuzhak argues that, ideally, factography would never generically stabilize. It would be a "literature of becoming," an aesthetic and methodological approach that would echo the dynamism of industrial change by constantly innovating. For Chuzhak, the enemy was not those who criticized factography but those who tried to ossify its devices into a stable generic category.[67] In this way, the extended photo-observation becomes a potential realization of this principle. Its indeterminacy served to support the claim that only a truly dynamic cultural practice—one with built-in aesthetic and methodological flexibility—could be revolutionary.

This generic openness, however, butts up against the requirement cultural producers have for inscribing meaning into a photograph. Tom Gunning challenges the idea that faking photographs undermines the promise of the indexical relation (as trace) between an image and its referent. Rather than destroying our faith in the ability of images to reference the real world in a meaningful way, fake photographs work to ensure meaningfulness. They work as *fake* photographs, Gunning argues, only if they can be understood in relation to photographs that are not fake.[68] It is a double-consciousness, a recognition that this transformation is meaningful because people understand it as a transformation. It is precisely this photographic "game" that factographers implicitly acknowledge in their celebration of Shub and in Tret'iakov's calling for an extended photo-observation. They recognize that the potential for reuse is endemic to the photographic "game" (that is, of the power play of what a photograph means and who gets to define it). And it is this reuse, this necessary potential for recontextualization, that makes it so valuable for a generic practice and a world continually open to new imaginations and shifting alignments. It is the threat and possibility of reuse that makes the stakes so high but also the payoffs so great. Photographs and photographic-based media, in the factographic framework, become performatives in their "great and authentic agitation through display," highlighting the reflexive capacity of language.

But more than that, by noting the centrality of the entextualizing process to the factographic imagination and its legibility through a combination of indexical trace and deixis, it becomes clear how dynamic the relation between the entextualizing moments and the present moment of reception is to this "presentist" project. Embedded in the factographic imagination is not just a sense of the Barthesian "that has been" or even the "once now" (this was "once" the present moment) that Mary Ann Doane insightfully coins to nuance the experience of cinematic time.[69] There is an additional step. The audience is charged with recognizing that at one point, *someone* entextualized in this way, with these markers of cohesion and in this manner of speaking. Both of these historical temporalities must accompany the performative moment of actualization—

that is, what is being indexed, not just the trace of the historical moment but the trace of the entextualizing moment(s). That combination creates the possibility for an informed presentist practice, a performance that emphasizes the singularity of the present actualization and its reliance on the original entextualizing moment(s). In this way, entextualization processes not only point to the labor involved in producing texts but also serve to reveal the ideologies subtending such articulations. In other words, by celebrating the historical in Shub's found footage films and by calling for the extended photo-observation model, factographers insist not on the value of historical information as self-evident but on the ways in which strategies of historical photographic inscription are ideologically revealing. And by maintaining aesthetic flexibility, photographic-based factographic works are always able to distinguish their contemporary approach in relation to those past enunciations. Thus, any claim they make on the present depends upon viewers' simultaneous or oscillating engagement with the past. The achievement of textuality is necessary to promote this historical imagination, but it is not an ossified time and space that sustains it.

THE DETAIL IN THE NOISE

To this point, I have focused my argument on the way in which narrative structures of accumulation function in Shub's films *The Fall of the Romanov Dynasty* and *The Great Way* as well as in Al'pert and Shaikhet's *A Day in the Life*. I have discussed the implications of such choices for an understanding of media ideologies, noting how the challenges of its full realization in documentary film (due to its position as an industrial art) and its greater applicability to the photo-series demonstrate factographic notions of how moving- and still-image photographic practices should work. And I have tried to demonstrate how factographers' ideas of effective photographic-based media practice in general came to depend upon a specific mobilization of historical meaning—delineating these practices by calling attention to the specific entextualizing strategies upon which they rely. This relationship between the past and the present thus becomes part of the key to understanding documentary's rootedness in and travel through time and space. For the image to travel productively in a factographic sense, it must remain rooted in the past and be legible as such. It is the dialectical relationship between these past images and other, more contemporary images and words that sparks the cultural conversation for which factographers call.

Whereas my emphasis has largely concerned broader structural questions related to documentary and the implications of factographers' answers to those questions, I now want to turn to the issue of the quality and meaning of the photographic still or moving image in the factographic framework. For it is not just a change in organizational structure of documentary but a shift in notions of image composition that illustrate how factographers sought to mark their documentary praxis against both the proletarian realists and the more aesthetically experimental production art projects of the early to mid-1920s.

In addition to mobilizing his discussion of the index, many art historians and film scholars have turned to Peirce for an understanding of how the photographic image functions as a meaning-making sign. Benjamin Buchloh has argued that factography enacted a shift in emphasis from the indexical quality of the image to its iconicity. Buchloh turns to El Lissitzky's photomontage work of 1927 to demonstrate how the "gradual return to the iconic" is evident not only in the composition of the individual photographs but in the photomontage itself. There, in earlier work, "the network of cuts and lines and jutting edges and unmediated transitions from fragment to fragment was as important, if not more so, as the actual iconic representation contained in the fragment itself."[70] The shift at the compositional level thus echoed the shift at the structural level. In the way I described the structural shift from photomontage to photo-essay or photo-series, here Buchloh notes how the original driving force behind the photomontage (a practice Rodchenko and others popularized that emphasized the interrelationships between the material and pictorial aspects of the image) is replaced by an increased emphasis on the discursive legibility of the image. Whereas earlier production art sought to communicate the sensuous qualities of objects by emphasizing their interrelationships, factography returned to an earlier focus on the informational and discursive components of objects. They emphasized iconicity through structural change and through compositional change. In so doing, they sought to rectify what they saw as the one-sidedness of the cultural conversation by moving toward a more realist photographic aesthetic.

Photographic realism, however, depends not only on semiotic but on experiential ways of knowing. Since its inception, commentators have celebrated photography's visual density, noting that its power lies, in part, in its excessive detail. Its visual density, they claim, shares the complexity of the photographed subject and provides a perceptual richness that stimulates and overwhelms the senses but also creates a certain resistance to precise signification. People experience the polysemy of the image as pleasurable, as uncanny, and, depending upon the function one has in mind for the image, as potentially frustrating. This is certainly true for some of the most vocal critics within the factography movement, who became frustrated with what they understood to be the illegibility of earlier production art.[71] If factographers understood photography's visual density as one of its defining features, cinema's existence in time exacerbates that quality. And it is around the issue of time that we can understand factographers' distinctions between the potential facticity of the moving versus the still photographic image.

Viktor Shklovsky addresses this concern with the facticity of the object when critiquing Dziga Vertov's 1926 film *A Sixth Part of the World* while at the same time lauding Shub's found footage trilogy. Although committed to nonfiction work, Vertov, according to Shklovsky, had begun to film objects as "a curiosity, an anecdote, and not as a fact." In *A Sixth Part of the World,* "the object has lost its substance and become transparent."[72] Vertov's objects are not located in their surround, they are "geographically insecure and enfeebled by their juxtaposition." For Shklovsky, Vertov's increasing overemphasis on the visual and emotional relationship between facts had prompted him to sever the key relationship for the establishment of documentary cinematic facticity: that between the image and the real world. And the establishment of such facticity relies on an indexical relation that provides suitable "security" of figure-ground relations. While Shklovsky admires Vertov's innovation and inspiration, he finds this approach out of step with the contemporary moment. Instead of sparking emotional connections via lyric composition and parallelism, filmmakers need to establish geographical security by indicating the "length and breadth of a place and the day of shooting."[73] One can do this within or across shots, but the security of relation remains essential. Shub does precisely this in her trilogy. But beyond offering stable visual perspectives and longer takes, which allow viewers to recognize the detail and "keep it in mind," the materiality of Shub's found footage method, with its entextualizing processes ever visible, also serves to locate the object in its time and place. These historical artifacts counter the dangers of excessive "artistry" by continually reiterating or even "wearing" their differences on their surfaces.

Shklovsky points to an example in Vertov's film of sheep being dipped into different bodies of water to demonstrate the cognitive confusion Vertov generates. He notes that in one sequence they appear to be dipped into a river, yet shortly thereafter the sheep appear to be dipped into the sea.[74] These choices either lead to confusion or serve to demonstrate to audiences that when and where the sheep are dipped is not of much concern—an attitude in opposition to factography's commitment to the rigorous communication of details. So, again, the key is not simply to locate the image in time and space but to *signal* to viewers the centrality of the space within which figures *act*. Shubian deictics, Shklovsky demonstrates, more effectively signal to viewers objects' relational significance and organize time in such a way that they recognize what is important and what must be retained.

Tret'iakov levels a comparable critique at Al'pert and Shaikhet, though for a somewhat different purpose. He writes that while the "method [approach and composition] for taking pictures is correct . . . it should have been realized more consistently in its details and more meticulously." Tret'iakov questions the photographers' attention to detail in *A Day in the Life*. He notes that their narrative has Filippov riding the streetcar to work when in fact he did not. Moreover, the photoessay claims that a photograph of a half-empty Moscow streetcar was taken in the afternoon, when everyone knows it is "stuffed to capacity at that hour."[75] And Tret'iakov insists that the photographers should have caught the discrepancy between the numbers in the caption below the photograph of a coop purchase and the document also in the photograph meant to confirm the purchase. Through all of these examples, Tret'iakov communicates to viewers of the photo-essay the centrality of detail and the rigor required to ensure productive work (remember,

Tret'iakov's piece accompanied the essay for the Soviet audience—our audience of concern).

Factographers, as I outline above, contend that facts are established through a dialogue between the factographic worker and the audience. Establishing and sustaining facticity requires responding to perceived challenges that moving- and still-image photographic media pose. For cinema, temporality and spatial stability challenge the potential articulation of facts. Factographers in Shub's time responded by celebrating a fairly traditional compositional style, an aesthetic of long takes, and a found footage method. In this way, citizens could identify individual facts, keep them in mind, and locate them in relation to other moments. For still-image photographs located in a photo-series, the challenge was different. Since viewers have control over time when engaging a photograph in ways they do not when watching a film, the excessiveness or noise of the image becomes less of a communicative threat. It remains a perceptual and epistemological pleasure, but it serves less to challenge the communicability of the photographic fact. What remains a challenge, however, is the security and precision of the fact, and this is where the producer must labor to ensure the most precise communication possible.

Buchloh argues that one of the key shifts from earlier production art to factography can be understood as a transition from contingency to stringency. For Buchloh, the discipline and precision evident in factography's commitment to locating photographed objects in the real world works to counter the emphasis on the openness and the divergence of fragments characteristic of earlier photomontage and collage. But I want to argue that this shift, while certainly palpable, is far from totalizing and that it functions differently for moving and still images.[76] I have outlined the factographic commitment to locating the object of the image in its surround while making that image legible and articulable as a fact. Doing so *requires* the noise, the excess, and the visual density to be sensible. It is the realism of the image, or perhaps the indexical force sustaining it, that serves to guarantee that location (its objectness and factness instead of its transparency) and yet at the same challenges the precision of its signification. Shubian strategies aimed to account for such a paradox by means of stable visual perspectives, long takes, and

found footage material, all of which helped the viewer to locate and identify the fact of the image. But the limitations of such an approach also
became possibilities, for its long takes in particular created a density and
undecidability that reasserted, albeit in slightly different terms, the contingency that Buchloh argues has been removed. And yet a stringency
remains as viewers are implicitly instructed to locate the detail while
thinking in rigorous historical terms. The photo-series, on the other
hand, falls more cleanly within Buchloh's framework. The density of the
image and the concern over legible, visible facts is countered not only
by a more traditional compositional style but by the more continuous
framing of the image by the captions themselves.

PROJECTING SUBJECTIVITIES

This dialectic that I have just described—that between the object's rootedness in the visual density of the photographic space and its isolabil-
ity and applicability to other contexts—serves as the key pedagogical
imperative for documentary in general and for these projects in the
late 1920s. But what is so innovative about the factographic aesthetic is
the way in which it depends upon a specific yet variable set of dynamics between the photographed moments; the capture, extraction, and
insertion of those moments within an essay; and the legibility of those
processes at the time of reception. Turning to strategies of entextualization, illuminated in part through a concept of indexicality as trace and
as deixis, allows us not only to explicate the specifics of those dynamics
and to describe how they function differently for moving- and still-
image productions but to point to the implications of these principles
for an understanding of factographic and, in turn, the newly privileged
Shubian temporality. Both the "presentist" practice and the historical
compilation method structure and depend upon individual facts inductively driving the viewer's understanding of historical chronology. How
the indexicals are stabilized and mobilized depends upon the precise
and shifting media ideologies subtending them.

In the process, these principles reveal factographers' larger goals
for the Soviet citizenry. As the self-described cultural work of the First
Five-Year Plan, factography sought to spark new relationships between

industrial work and cultural work. While recognizing that industrial work *determined* the appropriateness of certain journalistic, linguistic, and photographic ways of speaking, factographers saw in photographic-based media unique potential for transforming the subjectivities and social imaginaries of Soviet citizens. They sought to do so through their attention to process, multimediality, and immediacy. By projecting still and moving images on-screen, they projected new ways of being in the world and presented an image of a new Soviet future. Through their embrace of cumulative structures, traditional compositions, and legible frameworks, factographers sought to project a citizenry attentive to detail and attentive to political, social, and industrial change. But rather than promoting revolutionary inspiration as the appropriate response, they taught citizens how to recognize the noise and yet manage within it. They were to focus on the task at hand with rigor, with organization, and with efficiency and yet be able to locate their efforts in relation to larger Soviet schemes. It is in this way that the Five-Year Plan would be (over)fulfilled, with workers and peasants producing industrial goods and agricultural yields at the levels needed and yet never forgetting their role in the current national project.

SIX

The Object of Revolutionary History: Santiago Álvarez's Commemorative Newsreels and Chronicle Documentaries, 1972–1974

The stakes had been raised. What was at stake in the revolution was not merely the history of an island nation, but the response to five centuries of colonial exploitation. At the point where history became a category that could be lived in a state of self-awareness, in the present, history turned itself into a symbol.

—JOSÉ QUIROGA, *CUBAN PALIMPSESTS* (2005)

STAYING IN STEP

There is a title sequence, then eleven images of the wedding of Luci Baines Johnson. The images are animated by panning, tilting, and zooming in and out on the bride and groom. President Johnson himself appears as the camera slowly zooms in on a red colorized image of him and his son-in-law. Three explicit images from *Playboy* magazine are intercut with an image of Johnson, who appears to be gazing at the women (as Álvarez playfully employs the Kuleshov effect). Creepy laughter. Religious iconography. More laughing. More wedding pictures, many of which are now bathed in red. The prologue closes with a five-shot sequence. First, the bride and groom cut their wedding cake. Second, an anamorphically

FIGURE 6.1. Paul Muni (symbolically) shooting up the wedding
of the daughter of Lyndon Baines Johnson in *LBJ*.

squeezed and red-colorized image of a famous scene from *Scarface* appears in which Paul Muni emerges from a cake firing rounds with his machine gun. The sequence concludes with a rapid succession of three shots (less than two seconds total) of magazine advertisements for Winchester guns and bullets.

This sequence, as I discussed in chapter 4, serves as the prologue to Álvarez's *LBJ*. There, I argued that the sequence establishes Álvarez's interest in the intricate relations between American politics and visual culture by means of an experimental montage style, innovative rostrum camera work with still images, and techniques of anamorphic squeezing and colorization. These experimental aesthetics, Álvarez believed, were necessary to deconstruct a continually adapting American visual iconography and to instruct viewers on strategies for media analysis.

In his review of the film, Manuel López Oliva celebrates Álvarez's expressivity, arguing that it is appropriate for a revolution that promised the combination of political commitment and artistic integrity. But he also notes that many people found the film too personalized and poetic, an unwelcome departure from Álvarez's previously more classical style.[1] Although such worries were common, Álvarez did not face the harsh criticism that met Dziga Vertov almost immediately upon the release of *Stride, Soviet!*, and *LBJ* did not contribute to the filmmaker's dismissal from the central, state-sponsored filmmaking agency. But *LBJ* did, like *Stride, Soviet!* and *A Sixth Part of the World*, employ a set of aesthetic and methodological strategies that came to be seen by many to communicate too personally, too complexly, too rapidly, too kaleidoscopically. This is evident both in the critical discourse and in the fact that, shortly thereafter, documentary filmmakers in Cuba began to mark themselves against such rapid juxtapositions and complex narrative and rhetorical structures. As in the Soviet Union by 1927, in Cuba by 1972, the earlier personal expressions came to be seen as inappropriate for historical moments in which institutionalization and collectivization policies took precedence. They came to be seen as insufficient service to the state, as historically out of step.[2]

In the Soviet Union, Esfir Shub's method and aesthetic were seen capable of countering the chaos of revolutionary change, her historical discourse aligning with a broader shift from subjective inspiration to (more) objective organization. Álvarez likewise began to shape social and historical imaginaries in ways distinct from his previous efforts. But whereas Shub endeavored to transform social and historical imaginaries by means of historical images, Álvarez's newsreels and documentaries of the period rely mostly on contemporary images. As in factography, Álvarez's newsreels and documentaries from 1972 to 1974 demonstrate how deeply "presentist" practices are imbricated in, in this case divergent, models of historical thought.

This chapter explores the shifts that take place in Álvarez's newsreel and documentary production from the period considered the height of achievement (1965–1971) to a period (1972–1974) seen by many as an artistic and political regression brought on by a loss of revolutionary utopianism. The massive failure of the ten-million-ton sugar harvest of 1971 that resulted in the increased institutionalization of Cuban society shaped the direction that nonfiction film took as filmmakers sought to remain "in step" with changing political-economic dynamics. The news-reel became a more commemorative and celebratory practice, discouraging interrogation of the present by carving a space for the revolution as an object of thought. This activity was informed by a specific temporal dimension. The films urged Cuban viewers to see the present from a state of remove, constantly imagining the present as a series of events and objects to be judged in the future.

The long chronicle documentaries—feature-length (and more) films following Castro on international excursions—that Álvarez made during this period marked a radical shift from his previous work. Their juxtaposition of extended observation with montage frameworks not only produced a new aesthetic but also sought to transform Cuban citizens' viewing habits. These films, however, have been seen as aesthetic regressions resulting from clampdowns on artistic expression, their realist form a capitulation to changing sociopolitical and cultural conditions. I argue that Álvarez's aesthetic and methodological transition can be better understood by turning to work in the history of science on objectivity. Conceiving of subjectivity and objectivity as relational and multifaceted functions as a tool for nuancing changes in Cuban nonfiction film history and opens to analysis the extraordinary range of Álvarezean juxtaposition.

As I discuss in the conclusion of the chapter, during this period newsreels and documentaries increasingly diverged in their purposes and practices. Whereas in the previous periods they remained complementary while at times shaping different dimensions of the social imaginary, during this period they operated on different orders. The structure of this chapter speaks to those distinctions, the first half focusing entirely on newsreels and the second half on documentaries.

ENCOUNTERING HISTORY IN THE ICAIC NEWSREEL

Anticipating one of the dominant modes of the early 1970s, a few newsreel editions from the end of the second period are entirely historical in focus. One, #438 (1969), concentrates on the Independence War leader and national poet José Martí and was issued prior to the opening of a museum dedicated to him (erected to mark the 100th anniversary of his birth). The film combines old photographs, found footage, paintings, and sketches by and about Martí (most of which are housed in the museum) as well as a recent interview with a young Mexican boy who discusses what he knows about Martí. A speech by Fidel narrates the film, filling in the details of the historical lesson. The film is structured by Fidel's speech—an increasingly common technique during the third period. A number of Martí's verses are sung in different languages, testifying to the internationalism of his life, work, and impact. The film concludes by reminding the audience that Fidel always saw the revolution as part of a lineage connected to Martí, as evidenced by his reference to Martí in the famous "History Will Absolve Me" speech of 1953.

The point on which the issue concludes was in fact a much more recent development in Cuban history, the reference to Martí becoming consistent only years later. Rafael Rojas marks 1968 as the year when Castro reinscribed the history of Cuba with a specific and enduring revolutionary legacy. In a speech on October 10, 1968, Castro asserted that Cuba has only had one revolution and it began in 1868 as a struggle against slavery and for independence from Spain. The struggle against North American imperialism and for socialism that succeeded in 1959 was a continuation of the earlier efforts.[3]

To be sure, Castro had always called on history as justification for and understanding of present actions. The "History Will Absolve Me" speech, José Quiroga argues, established a logic of historical thought that pervaded post-revolutionary Cuba. Castro concluded with the famous words, "Condemn me. It does not matter. History will absolve me." What Fidel offered, Quiroga writes, "was a future that was mostly an image of the present where *that* 'future' could be understood as 'history.'" There was a sense of debt and duty that marked the revolution from the outset: a debt to former revolutionaries who had struggled for the current citizens and a duty to struggle for those who would come after. From the moment (1954) of the circulation of the speech in pamphlet form, "the revolution always looked at the present from the point of view of the future. It turned the revolution into an encounter with history."[4] And yet the specificities of that encounter—the models of historical writing, the kinds of historical materials with which one worked, and the types of engagements they hoped to engender—were constantly contested.

The early 1970s saw a profound shift in the tenor of historical discourse, with utopian enthusiasm of the previous period "yielding to the ordered narratives of history."[5]

This historical sensibility infuses the period's newsreels, a media form that generally addresses contemporary issues and problems. In these years, however, the newsreel functioned as a "commemorative" and tradition-building practice, actively constructing a post-revolutionary history as it looked towards the future. And it did so by means of an array of national and international topics and themes. The films exhibit a marked trend away from the second period's focus on domestic problems whose solution required the sacrifice of the Cuban population. In its place came films that celebrate domestic production and international allies' war efforts, pay tribute to a tradition of Cuban revolutionary leaders and foreign dignitaries, and show solidarity with Latin American guerrilla movements. As such, the films indicate a significant change in state socialism and deflect attention from the struggles of contemporary Cuban social and economic life.

Commemoration and Celebration

A hostile international environment and the economic hardship that resulted in part from the failure to reach the ten-million-ton sugar production goal of 1971 prompted Cuba to strengthen its alliance with the Soviet Union and Eastern Europe in the early 1970s. The institutionalization and collectivization policies, which began in the late 1960s, took on a different character as Cuba adopted the Soviet economic model based on centralized planning wholesale. The government instituted a policy of "creating values" that understood the ultimate value to be completing the yearly plan, no matter how inefficient the process or how pragmatic the results. Juan Antonio Blanco explains: "It's like in the Soviet Union where they were measuring the productivity of a chair factory not by the number of chairs it made, or how comfortable the chairs were, or how cost-effective they were in producing them, but by the total weight of the chairs. So you go to the Soviet Union and you need a crane to carry a chair because they would make furniture as heavy as possible to 'overfulfill' their yearly plan."[6] This shift in economic models was accompanied by a new strategy of appeal. Rather than relying on Che-

inspired moral incentives that drew on citizens' sense of collective belonging, the government embraced material incentives that spoke more
to citizens' individual wants and needs. This was realized both in the
areas of production on which the issues focused as well as in the effort
to celebrate worker achievement.

Issue #592 (1973) speaks to the changed mode of address, drawing
on some of the discursive positions of the previous period while pointing to changes taking place in contemporary Cuban society. The newsreel charts the production of four foodstuffs: crackers/cookies, milk, ice
cream, and beer. Voice-over narration and workers testify to dramatic
production increases, attributing them to technological development
and hard work. A beer brewer points out that even though the factory
does not have the best equipment, it has guarantees that if something
breaks it will be fixed immediately. The result, as in the cracker factory, is that the workers have exceeded quotas and set new production
records. The visual focus of the films is factory production itself. Each
of the plants is presented as clean, organized, efficient, and active. As
new innovations are explained, the image-track offers evidence of their
functionality. Production equipment and the mechanisms coordinat-
ing them are shot from a range of angles and distances. Their beauty
is enshrined in their sharpness, their clean lines, their vibrancy and
efficiency. They are animated but not fetishized.

The significance of the issue is partially dependent on the products
themselves. In contrast to the previous period, dominated by attention to
agricultural production or industrial production of such necessary items
as transportation vehicles, weapons, or textiles, the interest in cookies,
beer, and ice cream is telling. The film promotes transforming the national structure of feeling from an urgent emphasis on basic needs (one
of national survival) to a more comfortable, and pleasurable, relationship
to daily life. Rather than a detailed exploration and reexamination of
process, #592 celebrates results. The sacrifice of work is replaced by the
celebration of achievement. The newsreel presents a government whose
treaties with socialist allies allow defective or broken equipment to be
fixed or replaced rapidly.[7] It addresses viewers who know that exceeding
quotas results in financial remuneration and offers them hope that they
can access the reward. The film thus paradoxically constructs a more

individualized subject through the process of institutionalization and collectivization—one whose advances are not entirely dependent on others, even though those gains ultimately rely on governmental action.

While newsreels celebrating contemporary production prompt viewers to reimagine a recent past, other issues during this period explicitly allude to a past further removed or construct a history for an imagined future. During this period, ICAIC produced a number of issues that celebrate the achievements of individual workers, worker brigades, teachers, schools, and factories by calling attention to their victories in national "competitions."[8] One example comes from the first part of issue #594 (1973). Following the titles is a sequence introducing the best women sugar-cane cutters. Running alongside classical music are images of women in the fields laboring, socializing, and completing tasks. The visuals highlight the dexterity of the women's hands and tightly framed smiling or concentrating faces. The voice-over narrates the story of their victory as the women testify that, like the factory workers of #592, they work hard and with regularity but do not overextend themselves.

In addition to groups of people, organizations are accorded celebrations. Issue #591 (1973) recounts the history of the University Students Federation on the fiftieth anniversary of the founding of the organization. The issue begins with idyllic images of children working, playing, studying, and laughing. Following the title sequence, the film cuts to Raul Roa, the minister of foreign affairs and a noted Cuban historian and intellectual, speaking on the steps at the University of Havana about the group's efforts over the years. Old photographs of Antonio Mella, the founder of the federation, and historical footage of earlier revolutionary action accompany Roa's recounting of the events. Roa describes the anti-Machado strike of 1933 and police aggression toward student protests in 1953 as images provide visible evidence of the events. The newsreel offers a history of revolutionary action taken by the University Students Federation, discusses its impact on Cuban history, and notes its continued influence with Fidel. But Roa's role in the film is significant—it is his speech that qualifies the newsreel as a contemporary event, making it a legitimate object of newsreel attention. Without it, the issue would feel more like a traditional historical documentary. In turn, the issue confers on Roa prestige and authority.

The tempered appeal of the newsreels of the early 1970s is perhaps most evident in an issue that, at first glance, would seem reminiscent of the earlier periods. Issue #599 (1973) is entirely devoted to the role of women in contemporary Cuban society. The film is monothematic, expresses a sense of urgency, and locates its primary domestic concerns within an internationalist perspective. It begins with images of babies being born and taken care of in an organized, well-maintained hospital. Cuban icon Silvio Rodriguez's gentle musical tribute to mothers runs alongside the images and establishes a laudatory tone. After the title sequence, the film cuts to an array of women representing all regions of the country entering a large auditorium in Havana. The topic of discussion is the role of women as workers. Some women give speeches, while others voice their opinions from the audience. The general line is that women who do not work need to "get out there" if Cuban society is to develop. The women testify passionately, and their voices often overlap.

Interspersed with coverage of the Conference of Working Women are images of a range of women workers: Vietnamese women, Cuban women who voluntarily supported them, and famous women in Cuban history. The music accompanying the images is an inspiring choral version of an old popular folk song flattering Cuban women. The film concludes with the declaration that, beginning in 1973, the country would celebrate International Women's Day.

This edition complicates the tradition-building trend in domestic newsreels by clearly addressing what many men and women saw as a critical issue in the development of Cuban society—the role of working women. It is presented as an urgent concern, a modern problem, and one whose solution requires all Cubans to rethink traditional gender roles. But this position is challenged by the way in which the film attends to multiple registers. The primary narration in the body of the film is the speeches and responses made by women at the convention. However, traditional Cuban and Vietnamese music continually interject and shape reception of the visuals. This latter strategy illustrates how the newsreel fits the move toward a more historical, tradition-building, celebratory newsreel practice shorn of any critical analysis of contemporary Cuban society—how I have been characterizing the issues from this period.

The tone of the conference itself is insistent, but the framework in which the conference is situated is laudatory and historical. The issue is book-ended by an opening that commends women who were both mothers and nurses (part of the labor force) and the government's commitment to their health and comfort and by a closing that recognizes International Women's Day. But the rhetorical structure of the issue does not allow the framing to solve the problem posed at the conference. The film maintains a dual perspective: one insisting that contemporary Cuban society transforms its traditional understandings of gender roles (enunciated by working women themselves) and another celebrating the achievements of women domestically and internationally. The film does not employ a problem-solution structure within which critique remains despite the solution proffered. Instead, the commemorative element stands alongside the social critique (although perhaps the celebratory tone of the opening and closing overrides the emotional urgency of the conference). It is likely that, had ICAIC covered the conference during an earlier period, the celebratory and historical element would have been greatly reduced or omitted entirely. But by the end of 1973, any attack on traditionalism, with its concomitant message of sacrifice, was tempered by a necessary commendation of Cuban achievement, one often linked to international struggles.

International Revolutionary Traditions and the Historians of the Future

The effort to commemorate and build traditions that emerges in the Cuban newsreels of the third period served not only to establish new "ordered narratives of history" but to create a space for these narratives by shaping citizens who looked at the present, not as a space of conflict, but as a space full of objects destined for analysis in the future—namely, objects that will be recognized as *historic* in the future. Their task was to "make history" by producing in the present, an achievement that required consistent, though not remarkable, laborious efforts. But in addition, they were urged to visualize and constantly imagine history being made. This process reinforced the power of the past and, as we see in newsreel issues from 1974, prompted people to locate the Cuban national trajectory in relation to other revolutionary traditions.

Throughout the 1960s and early 1970s, internationalism was projected in a range of nation-building discourses as integral to the construction of a Cuban national identity. Filmmakers paid particular attention to Cuba's historical and contemporary links with the Latin American continent, insisting that while imperialist policies divided the region, decolonization efforts united them. Historical fiction films made during what is critically considered the height of Cuban film production, 1965–1970, sought to "rescue their past from colonial and neo-colonial deformations."[9] And during the early to mid-1970s, a number of newsreels addressed Latin American unity from a historical perspective as well. They juxtaposed a range of historical visual material with contemporary footage or relied entirely on the historical material and voice-over narration.

In these films, Cuba is seen both as the last country in Latin America to achieve its freedom and as the liberated province of Latin America, inherently internationalist on account of the myriad of people who fought for its independence and as a consequence of its Marxist-Leninist roots. Issue #600 (1973), which examines student attempts to kill President Batista in the context of Latin American revolutionary action, typifies how integral the historical was to the articulation of pan–Latin American unity. The issue begins as jarring music gives way to the original radio broadcast report that students had stormed the Presidential Palace in an attempt to assassinate Batista. As the radio announcer narrates, the image-track displays children participating in a re-creation of the historic events—an increasingly common practice in Cuba in the early 1970s and one often represented in newsreels.[10] Following the title sequence, the film concurrently addresses Panamanian anger about U.S. policy on the canal, elections in Chile, Argentineans' desire to rid themselves of military dictatorship, and a Peruvian revolutionary leader victorious in his struggle against cancer. The final segment of the issue returns to Cuba and the historical performance, avowing that the blood of José Antonio Echeverría, the leader of the University Students Federation in 1957, led the way to freedom in Cuba and continues to inspire revolution in all of Latin America.

This sense of the inevitability of Latin American revolution was tempered, however, by recognition of the enemy's power. The realization in the early 1970s that the United States would go to considerable lengths to prevent another socialist revolution in the Americas strongly influenced Cuban policy toward Latin America and the Caribbean. As a result, Cuban international aid went primarily to progressive governments in Latin America and guerrilla movements fighting colonial powers in Africa.[11] This policy change, while not dramatically reflected in the newsreels, is accounted for in two ways. First, there is slightly more attention paid to guerrilla movements in Africa, most notably to Amílcar Cabral's liberation movement in Guinea Bissau, than there previously had been.[12] Second, issues such as the already discussed #600, #644 (1974) on the murders of innocent Bolivians by fascist police, or #645 (1974) on the difficulties facing socialist movements in the Dominican Republic make plain the power of the enemy to quash revolutionary struggle. The explicitness of the image-track, despite an excessively sanguine narrational address, speaks to the challenges facing continental revolution. While the newsreels on Latin American topics during this period are numerous, assert Cuban solidarity, are more likely to function as historical lessons than in any prior period (using maps, historical photographs, drawings, and paintings to make their arguments), and express the moral righteousness of Latin American revolution, they do not offer an unequivocal celebratory address. Instead, they provoke anger at the injustices they catalog while recognizing the challenges of their rectification.

The recognition of the complexity of contemporary Latin American politics in the newsreels considered above contrasts with representations of the Soviet Union and Eastern Bloc nations during the same period. Issues that deal with those topics are aesthetically and discursively more aligned with the celebratory domestic films of the period. They are historically pedagogical, look to the future in their efforts to build tradition, showcase the unity of the nation through shots of massive crowds and parades, assert Cuban independence, and, like the Latin American editions, draw parallels between Cuba's, the Soviet Union's, and East Germany's revolutionary roots.

Issues #642 (1974) and #643 (1974) focus on Soviet Premier Leonid Brezhnev's visit to Cuba in 1974. The former issue takes place on the anniversary of José Martí's birthday, indicated by voice-over as a parade marches past. A musical rendition of a Martí poem connects the pre-title, title, and first sequences as photographs and an abundance of film footage of Lenin appear on-screen. The narrator then explains how the people of Regla, a small island off the coast of Havana, had planted a tree to honor Lenin on the occasion of his death. After learning that people would go to the site to pay tribute to the Soviet leader, Cuban president Gerardo Machado (1925–1933) had the tree cut down. Now, the narrator asserts, on the anniversary of the Bolshevik Revolution, Cubans once again pay tribute and have replanted the tree. The first sequence ends with images of the site as energetic rock music booms in celebration of the reestablished tradition.

The second sequence of the issue celebrates the arrival of Brezhnev. The initial images are from an airplane, displaying the beauty of Cuba and the massive crowds gathered to meet the Soviet premier at the airport. The rest of the issue highlights the euphoria of the people greeting Brezhnev, follows him in the motorcade to Revolution Plaza, and reveals the enormous crowd and massive banners of famous revolutionary figures (Marx, Engels, Lenin, Martí, Che) on display opposite the podium.

Issue #643 is a double issue, running about twenty minutes, and picks up where the previous issue left off. Alongside yet another version of "The Internationale," Castro aims to establish the communist lineage of the Cuban Revolution, reminding that Cubans were forbidden to talk about communism in the early stages of the revolution. Now, he proclaims with pride, the people are free to express their gratitude to the USSR. Brezhnev maintains the emphasis on unity when he speaks in the next sequence about the everlasting bond between the nations. The image-track supports his claim with old footage of Che and Fidel signing various agreements with the USSR.

The last segment of the issue takes place at the Lenin School, the premier boarding high school in Cuba, located just outside Havana, and extends the discussion of unity by projecting an image of future cooperation. Castro and Brezhnev visit and tour the school. A celebration of fireworks and speeches wraps up their sojourn. The issue concludes with Castro speaking about the school and the ties between the nations. The film cuts to images of Lenin speaking as Castro's voice is heard beneath, uniting the two leaders and nations through the image-audio relation.

These issues work to establish a revolutionary link outside Cuba, expanding the historical purview. Previously, newsreels had emphasized a Cuban revolutionary tradition with Marx, Lenin, and select Latin American leaders. During this period, the linkages were made much more explicit and were much more directed, moving from Marx/Engels, Martí, Lenin, and Che to the present leaders, Brezhnev and Castro. Such a trajectory both secured the national idea and reinforced the bond between the nations. It argued that the nations were *already aligned* and that they shared a similar path. By fixing themselves to the Soviets, Cuba stabilized its past and its future. The path became a broader one, offering a different view of the landscape—one less inspired by new encounters and more secured by the scope of its historical vision.

As a whole, the newsreels of the third period became a commemorative practice, shaping social and historical imaginaries while discouraging interrogation of the present. If the newsreels of the first period sought to create a space in which viewers could see themselves as a collectivity and a force, and the issues of the second period sought to shape the laboring sensibilities and provide moral suasion for increased efforts, the newsreels of the third period sought to create a space for the revolution itself to be thought and for that to occur in a state of historical self-awareness. Cubans were to situate themselves—and the rest of Latin America—within a larger socialist revolutionary trajectory, recognizing themselves as the Latin American vanguard.

But the newsreels did not just exhibit historical information; they articulated and modeled the process of historicizing, of seeing through historically tinged lenses. This was achieved through a narrational address common to the newsreel form that reemerged in Cuba as a more conservative response to the experiments of the second period. It is thus the dynamics between the newsreels' unique historical thematics—their denial of contemporary social and economic problems, their disavowal of sacrifice, and their encouragement to imagine present objects and events as "future history"—and the contemporary enunciation that aims to produce such a subject. Within the logic of the newsreels, if anything was to be interrogated during this period, it was the Cuban subject. Sustaining Cuban subjectivity required an increasingly flexible historical *focus,* ordering historical narratives with an eye to the judgment of future historians.

DE AMÉRICA SOY HIJO AND NEW
DOCUMENTARY OBJECTIVITY

In the early 1970s, Álvarez made three extended documentaries that chronicled three of Castro's international trips: *De América soy hijo . . . y a ella me debo* (I am the son of America . . . and I am indebted to it, 1972, 195 minutes) details Fidel's tour of Chile in 1971; . . . *Y el cielo fue tomado por asalto* (. . . And heaven was taken by storm, 1973, 128 minutes) follows Fidel on his tour of East European and African nations in 1972; and *Los cuatro puentes* (The four bridges, 1974, 74 minutes) covers Fidel's participation in the Fourth Conference of Non-aligned Nations that took place in Algeria in September 1973. Although my focus will be on *De América soy hijo,* which articulates in a sophisticated way many of the issues and concerns of the other films, each of the films marks a sharp transition from the experimental collage films of the previous period.

John Mraz argues that these films signal a shift in Álvarez's work brought about by a transformation in historical periods. Mraz takes his cue from Georg Lukács's analysis of literature according to *narrative* or *descriptive* methods, arguing that the former corresponds to dynamic historical periods and the latter to periods in which the impulse to change is increasingly limited. Mraz categorizes Álvarez's chronicle films as descriptive, following the familiar story that they are the result of the increased institutionalization of Cuban society following the failure of the ten-million-ton sugar harvest and the adoption of the Soviet socialist economic model wholesale. He argues that they are "long, static, and frankly tedious reprises of Castro's speeches." In contrast, he describes the "dramatic form" of the films from 1965 to 1970 as corresponding to the sociopolitical effervescence of that period.[13]

At the broadest level, there is some merit to Mraz's distinctions. Álvarez's chronicle documentaries are a sharp and significant transition from his internationally renowned collage films of the late 1960s. They contain an array of descriptive sections and long takes and were indeed influenced by the increased institutionalization of Cuban society. But Mraz's correlation of the chronicle films with the "descriptive" practices of direct cinema omits the way in which the realist sections are framed within the films.[14] Most notably in *De América soy hijo* and *Y el cielo,*

Álvarez locates the extended "reprises of Castro's speeches" within an experimental montage framework that situates the present in relationship to Latin American colonial history. Moreover, the extended length and content of the observational segments, the overall length of the films, and their narrative structures challenge the sole applicability of the direct cinema model to these films.

This is significant for interrelated historical and conceptual reasons. On one hand, by aligning the chronicle documentaries with a filmmaking practice (direct cinema) that maintained explicit and implicit claims of non-mediation and objectivity, Mraz positions Álvarez (even if somewhat tacitly) as a filmmaker who appears to have abandoned the political aesthetic foundations he established in the 1960s.[15] (Assuming he did so as a result of changing cultural and political-economic conditions does not make it any better.) Such a trajectory fails to account for the ways in which cultural producers responded to shifting aesthetic expectations while maintaining radical political and perhaps even utopian dimensions to their work.

On the other hand, Mraz is correct that this shift is substantial and aligns, in certain ways, with a more descriptive, realist aesthetic emerging in multiple cultural fields such as literature, painting, and theater. To account for these dynamics, I argue that Álvarez's aesthetic and methodological shifts, like the transition to Shub in the USSR, encourages a reconception of documentary objectivity. In particular, I contend that such transitions to a modified or what can be called a "more realist" cinema can be illuminated, in part, by turning to Lorraine Daston and Peter Galison's work on the history of objectivity. The point is not to argue that Álvarez believed he was capturing or finding reality objectively (or objective reality) and just presenting that to audiences. Rather, what emerged is a moment in which, as Daston and Galison describe, "various forms of subjectivity came to be seen as dangerously subjective."[16] Álvarez's work of the third period, I will argue, points to the value in emphasizing the relationality of objectivity to subjectivity as well as to the usefulness in distinguishing the various strains of objectivity that have recently fused into a single concept. With such a focus, I hope not only to provide a more refined understanding of the trajectory of Álvarez's work but to reinsert into debates over documentary form and method a more historicized and multifaceted notion of objectivity.

This notion of objectivity in turn provides scholars of documentary and scholars of post-revolutionary socialist culture with tools for nuancing changes in documentary practices and their underlying ideologies while historicizing documentary subjectivity. It urges us to think carefully about the kinds of prohibitions that were supported, the types of subjective interventions that were tempered, and where, when, and how these were articulated both in films and criticism. And it does so by disentwining many of the suspect political, ethical, and epistemological claims associated with pure objectivity.

Daston and Galison's research on the epistemic virtues of modern science provides a useful point of entry for a new conception of documentary objectivity. Many scholars have aligned documentary with a scientific ethos, most notably Bill Nichols in his association of documentary with other "discourses of sobriety," such as science, economics, and medicine. However, while Daston and Galison's framework has the advantage of offering a multifaceted and historically rigorous approach to objectivity, any close consideration of Álvarez requires a modification of their concept of objectivity so as to account for its specific *cinematic* dimensions.

Objectivity Past and Present

While direct cinema's implicit and explicit claims of non-mediation and impartiality has made it the bad object for scholarship on documentary, dreams of and challenges to a notion of pure objectivity litter the history of film theory. A number of theorists and critics of cinema have addressed the ways in which the cinematic apparatus and certain aesthetic choices work to enforce a scientific ethos grounded in an objective, empiricist approach. For André Bazin, cinema's photographic basis ensures an ontological connection between an image and its object in the real world. Filmmakers exploit this uniqueness most productively when they employ an aesthetic of extended duration and deep focus. Such choices allow the spectator to experience a close, deep connection with objects in the real world.[17] For Bazin, cinema's existence in time—its potential to create an experience of duration and to satisfy the desire to preserve existence against time—is the terrain on which a truly realist cinema must be forged. The potential to create this experience prompts Bazin to describe cinema as "objectivity in time."[18] Whereas for Bazin this connection between the image and the real world has positive epistemological and even spiritual potential, for Jean-Louis Baudry (and many other film theorists doing psychoanalytically based film theory in the 1970s and 1980s) the cinematic apparatus and the dominant aesthetic practices work to enforce a problematic and ideological subject position. The combination of camera's monocular linear perspective[19] and the spectator's primary identification with the camera[20] creates an effect that is deeply empiricist. The camera and the realist aesthetics characteristic of the dominant cinema project a vision that is presuppositionless and transparent and that supports the centrality of the transcendental subject. A politically progressive cinema must counter this realist, narrative-centered model by challenging what have become the prevailing aesthetic and exhibition practices.[21] In so doing, cinema can undermine the dominant class, gender, racial, and ethnic positions that masquerade as natural, as emanating objectively from the historical world.[22]

This argument has deeply influenced studies of documentary, which have grown in depth and number as scholars have aligned with Bill Nichols's challenge to documentary's foundations in "the transparency and empowering capacity of language, the knowability of the visible world and the power to view it from a disinterested position of objectivity."[23] For Nichols, the idea of documentaries as objective, realist representations of the historical world points to a misunderstanding of the process of filmmaking, the history of documentary films themselves, and the insight provided by the poststructuralist critique of language systems. Michael Renov, author of *The Subject of Documentary*, likewise associates traditional understanding of documentary with objective representation and yet also notes how a shift in focus to the subjective has opened up vital lines of inquiry:

> The domain of nonfiction was typically fueled by a concern for objectivity, a belief that what was seen and heard must retain its integrity as a plausible slice of the social world. How else to persuade viewers to invest belief, to produce "visible evidence," and even induce social action? Nowadays

there are ample grounds for an active distrust of that hoped-for neutrality. . . . Given the waning of objectivity as a compelling social narrative, there appears to be ample grounds for a more sustained examination of the diverse expressions of subjectivity produced in nonfiction texts.[24]

Renov is not the only scholar whose recent work has centered on the subjective aspects of nonfiction film production. Robin Curtis, Jane Gaines, Chuck Kleinhans, Julia Lesage, Alisa Lebow, Catherine Russell, Linda Williams, Patricia Zimmerman, and numerous others have sought to expand approaches to documentary beyond its traditional association with a white, male, Western public imaginary. Such work has enriched documentary studies immensely as an interdisciplinary field.

So why would I want to reinfuse into the discussion a concept—objectivity—that is widely assumed to have been delegitimated? The answer is, in part, because what Daston and Galison demonstrate is the complexity and messiness of a concept has recently come to be seen as simple and clean. They argue that what currently constitutes a single concept of objectivity is in fact a fusion of different kinds—mechanical objectivity and structural objectivity being the primary ones—each with its own meaning and distinct history.[25] Working through their theoretical models in the context of not just the Cuban but the Soviet example as well, I have become increasingly convinced that rather than understanding objectivity as a naive approach to communicating knowledge about the historical world, the notion of objectivity as a multiplicity of practices and strategies, ones designed to counter the dangers of subjectivity, can reopen and invigorate the conversation about documentary form and method.

Daston and Galison point out that however the meanings of objectivity and subjectivity may have varied over the course of five hundred years, they have always been paired. "First and foremost," they write, "objectivity is the suppression of some aspect of the self, the countering of subjectivity. Objectivity and subjectivity define each other, like left and right or up and down. One cannot be understood, even conceived, without the other."[26] To understand what kind of documentary self[27] Cuban artists, critics, and state officials deemed necessary for the promotion of the revolutionary message requires an understanding of which aspects of the self were considered problematic in Cuba at the time.

A New Proximity: Methods and Forms

As in the Soviet Union in the late 1920s, Cuba in the early 1970s saw increased institutionalization and collectivization policies accompanied by a challenge to artistic individualism.[28] Ambrosio Fornet notes that the National Council of Culture reacted to what it saw as an excessively experimental artistic establishment in two ways. First, it promoted new young writers and artists by celebrating the value of amateurism. Second, it attempted to establish a "sort of criollo socialist realism"—not a traditional *Soviet* socialist realism, Luis Camnitzer contends, but a photo-realist hyperrealism. Although Camnitzer is primarily addressing Cuban painting, his arguments have relevance for a consideration of Cuban documentary. He writes, "The term *photo-realism* was used to underline a direct documentary contact with reality as offered by the camera and its use as support for the artwork, ensuring some mass-appeal."[29] The *documentary contact* afforded by the camera could support painting by linking the work to reality—a connection thought to speak to the needs and desires of viewers and politicians.

Arguments vary about the degree to which these trends affected cinema. Michael Chanan maintains that ICAIC was rather removed from the repercussions of the Padilla affair and its challenge to artistic freedom. He sees cinema and music as the only arts that avoided the aesthetic regressions to a stultified realism that plagued literary production and the plastic arts.[30] Mraz, as I outlined, takes a broad approach and argues that realist cinematic production in the 1970s was directly linked to a transformation in historical periods. Camnitzer likewise sees a strong link, though he postulates a less negative effect. He points to the category of "testimonial literature" instituted by Casa de las Américas as an example of a literary concept that has applicability to documentary film. Although not as far-reaching or multifaceted as Soviet factography, Cuban "testimonial" writing, like factography, emphasized the immediacy of diaries, reports, and other forms of representation of everyday experiences. Camnitzer notes that it had particular influence on Álvarez and describes its aesthetic as constituting "a lively and functional alternative to socialist realism, effectively responding to some of the needs of the revolutionary process at the time."[31]

The commitment to immediacy evident in Cuban testimonial literature only partially captures the way in which Álvarez makes use of realist aesthetics in his chronicle documentaries. In these films, immediacy and intimacy are countered by distance and stability. This is achieved both through aesthetic juxtaposition and by the embrace of a new method of production. Álvarez, as we saw in chapter 4, developed his reputation in part through his ability to work with found footage, specifically by animating still photographs taken by other people and integrating them with found live-action footage (*Now* is the great example of this). For Álvarez it was the move away from the found footage film and toward the chronicle film that was seen as an appropriate method of factual inscription in Cuba in the early 1970s. It was seen as a way of ensuring the communicability of the filmed material by attending to everyday reality, an issue of increasing importance, as Camnitzer describes, during the early 1970s. This new model of production was privileged for having a less personal perspective.

Daston identifies the desire for an "aperspectival" position as one of the fundamental and distinct roots of a scientific objectivity that has more recently fused into a single concept.[32] Aperspectival objectivity, Daston argues, emerged originally in moral and aesthetic philosophy during the eighteenth century. In the nineteenth century it spread to the natural sciences, as science came to consist in large part of communications that crossed boundaries of nationality, training, and skill. Daston writes, "The essence of aperspectival objectivity is communicability, narrowing the range of genuine knowledge to coincide with that of public knowledge."[33] Aperspectival objectivity may even sacrifice deeper, more rigorous knowledge in the service of communicability. One of the primary manners in which aperspectival objectivity achieved such aims was through a reliance on a scientific community. The existence of such a community, stretching over time and space, was seen as a necessity for scientific truth. A community of scientists would cancel individual errors.

At first glance, the notion of an "aperspectival" objectivity seems antithetical to any discussion of a politically committed cinema. The cinematic apparatus is a perspectival device, and the post-revolutionary Cuban nonfiction film project was activist in nature. But the move toward a less personal, less directorially perspectivized cinema was thought to enable a more comprehensible and authentic cinematic artifact for the wide population. And like a community of scientists, a community of "document-makers" or "fact-makers" could cancel individual errors or counter personal proclivities.

This is precisely the approach Álvarez employed in his chronicle films. Whereas in the 1960s Álvarez worked primarily with one or at most two others during shooting, *De América soy hijo* saw all nine of Álvarez's associates working on the film, most notably numerous camerapersons. Having all of them work on the film does not indicate a full-fledged embrace of what Fornet described as a move toward amateurism. Nor is the film a pure example of Camnitzer's "testimonial" writing. But it is a method that emphasizes a number of "visions" in the production phase, and it does privilege the immediacy of everyday reports and accounts. I have not been able to find a definitive statement explaining why Álvarez carried so many camerapersons. Certainly, the scope of the project was large. Having numerous people to cover events allowed for flexibility during production and postproduction. But it was the choice to embark on such a project and "cover" it in this manner that marks a new direction in Álvarez's method and aligns it with other Cuban cultural endeavors.

This shift in method does not indicate that Álvarez thought he had produced "objective" documentary films nor that he had fully ceded control of the projects to his co-contributors. The personal element remains, but it is located in a different space. More specifically, it emerges through the juxtaposition of the relationship between the image and the real world in an observational aesthetic and the effort to locate those moments within a montage framework. Álvarez organizes the space-time of the chronicle documentaries to establish a set of conflicts across sequences as well as between individual images and overriding narrative structures. In doing so, he offers competing and overlapping experiences of intimacy and stability. Rather than align immobilized visions or observed objects with a voyeuristic, contemplative, naive cinematic aesthetic and mobile, montage-based abstractions with active critical reflections, Álvarez marshals stylistic conflict to ensure legibility and yet retain artistic-political efficacy.

Central to such an achievement is work around the issue of time. His use of a more observational aesthetic that relies upon increased duration and spatial distance echoes what Daston and Galison describe as a "morality of prohibitions rather than exhortations."[34] It is this ethos that undergirds objectivity and is constitutive of an epistemic virtue that celebrates self-restraint in method and form. The embrace of a new prohibition on the documentary self applies to Álvarez himself, not to the audience. In fact, such restraint encourages a new effort on the part of the audience. If early Álvarezean aesthetics fragmented and dynamized space and time in the hopes of transforming viewers' perceptions and thought, Álvarez of the early 1970s stressed the conflict between such formal choices in the hopes of creating a new space for audience intuition. In so doing, he makes use of those subtle, contradictory, and at times overlapping psychic and bodily negotiations of presence and absence, immersion and contemplation, that mark the uniqueness of the film-viewing experience.

The conflicts in *De América soy hijo* occur most frequently at the level of section. *De América soy hijo* is a three-hour-and-fifteen-minute film dominated by two aesthetic strategies. The first is an array of extended observational sequences of Fidel preparing for and giving speeches, answering questions, fixing stage props, posing in photo opportunities, and generally milling around. Fidel and Salvador Allende shoot ducks from a boat. Fidel takes pictures at a Chilean dance performance. Fidel strokes llamas atop a mountain. Fidel spots sea lions on the Pacific coast. Fidel tours salt mines and industrial factories. Temporally, the observational sequences dominate this lengthy film. The second aesthetic strategy consists of collages of historical and ethnographic footage narrated with poetic voice-overs. These sequences open the film, emanate from Fidel's speeches, and locate the extended observations within an exegesis on Latin America's colonialist history and the neocolonialist forces marshaled against it at the moment. Animation sequences chastise imperialist governments for their treatment of poor people. Graphic text runs across the screen that does not correspond to any diegetic spoken word. Dramatically read voice-over narration performs José Martí's poetry. The key aesthetic issue to recognize is that the extended observational sequences maintain a certain autonomy in their own right. The uniqueness of *De América soy hijo* requires balancing the tension between those two analytic frameworks: the relative autonomy of the extended observational sections and their juxtaposition with the interrupting, framing montage sequences.

The thematic and spatiotemporal organization of the extended durational sections may trigger an alternating engagement/disengagement interaction with the material. To be precise, the opportunity to see Fidel, in all his immediacy and particularity, in situations unfamiliar to him and to Cubans, calls out for an attentive subject. To this end, Álvarez employed a sophisticated and challenging set of aesthetic and rhetorical strategies. His spatiotemporal logics provoke a sense of intimacy with the revolutionary leader while allowing for (even acknowledging) the need for critical and emotional distance. As such, *De América soy hijo* is both de-dramatized and hyper-dramatized cinema. But even as it collapses the mundane and the dramatic and challenges viewers with its organization and duration, the film's method and aesthetic declare the *availability* of Cuban leadership to the viewer's gaze. The inclusion of the seemingly unstructured and unrehearsed, what Stuart Hood refers to as the film's "untidy" detail, offers a promise of openness and honesty reinforced by Fidel's spoken words.[35] Whereas many earlier documentaries and newsreels show the battle cry, the inspiration, the spontaneity, and the results of the revolution, the institutionalization and bureaucratization of the early 1970s required seeing and hearing the dialogue, the everyday, the banal detail.

The unique aesthetic experience Álvarez seeks in *De América soy hijo* extends beyond its formal devices. *De América soy hijo* was one of the first feature-length Cuban documentaries Cuban audiences had the opportunity to see. Moreover, the combination of its chronicle structure and length served as a challenge to the viewing habits established by capitalism and which remained applicable to Cuba.[36] But the film's organizational strategies demonstrate a commitment to a clear narrative structure and rhetorical framework that evinces what Daston and Galison describe as objectivity's commitment to self-restraint. The resistant elements—the polysemy of rampant indexicality—emerged *after the legibility* of its narrative. Communicability clearly takes precedence over rhetorical complexity as Álvarez responded to the challenges posed by the structural and rhetorical complexity of the previous dominant documentary mode. Although the film combines historical and contemporary chronological frameworks, the relation between them is clearly delineated. The film opens with a lesson on the legacy of imperialism in Latin America. Found footage images narrated with voice-over provide the critical, historical foundation for locating the ensuing contemporary (extended duration) observational footage. It is the combination of the clear demarcation of these seemingly opposed styles and the precision of Álvarez's transhistorical and transnational argument that makes it easily comprehensible. Viewers must keep the established framework in mind, but the film itself does not rapidly tack back and forth between historical and contemporary moments. As a result, the chronotopic logics remain rather stable for a film with two seemingly opposed aesthetic strategies.

FROM OBJECTS TO THINGS

All of that is not to say, however, that De América soy hijo and Álvarez's chronicle films of the third period abandoned belief in the utopian potential of cinema to transform citizens. Álvarez's earlier experiments in film form and drastic manipulations of space and time offer perhaps more disjunctive modes of thought and experience than do the later films. But Álvarez's directorial restraints aimed not to foreclose the possibility of expansive meaning. Instead, these restraints sought to relocate this possibility and transform the process by which audiences engage documentary cinema.

Daston and Galison paint their image of objectivity by describing the practices and debates that drive these new epistemological frameworks and by maintaining that they come attached with far-reaching moral implications. But in 1970s Cuba, the shifts had not crystallized to the point where they were necessarily indicative of any totalizing condemnation of the epistemology associated with Álvarez's previous dominant forms. While earlier Álvarezean subjectivity needed to be countered, its politics remained aligned with the revolutionary agenda. It was his tactics that no longer worked. In particular, his method and aesthetics failed to provide the points of contact seen to be necessary for the newly imagined Cuban citizenry. Like modern scientists committed to objectivity, the Álvarez of the early 1970s embraced a more realist aesthetic that "would present a scattering of individual phenomena that would cover the range of the normal, leaving it to the reader to accomplish intuitively what the . . . maker no longer deemed to do explicitly."[37] These tactics created the opportunity for new connections across time and space. They required an active viewer looking to transcend historical and geographical boundaries. They upheld nonfiction film's truth claims by not deforming their inscriptions while doing the work of (trans)national identity building.

In creating the conditions for these new connections, Álvarez's films hold the potential to transform subject-object relations. *De América soy hijo* urges the possibility of new connections among Cubans and between Cubans and Chileans. And it does so outside Cuban national space. Its more extended duration, stable perspectives, and intelligible structure work to locate images within an approved and easily legible political argument while creating space (and desire) for a leap into recent history and across regional divides. It allows citizens with varying access to images and news a range of *contacts* with figures. It challenges familiar dichotomies by urging interrogation and allowing the time and space for it to take place. And it does so while insisting, always, on situatedness.

In the early 1970s, this new subjectivity could be understood to ally with and speak most powerfully to a new social, national, and historical imaginary. It was its located, more contextualized indexicals that offered this possibility. It was the legibility of its temporalities, which provided the stability, in time-space, for transhistorical and transnational leaps. As in the third period in the USSR, at this point in the Cuban postrevolutionary nonfiction film trajectory, thick-things-in-context were thought to move more fluidly across times and spaces and from profilmic space to viewer.

The paradox of this new documentary self is that in reining in directorial expressivity, in embracing methods and inscription strategies associated with aperspectival and mechanical objectivity, but doing so in a framework that reworks dominant models of proximity, it creates the potential of removing the objectness from the object. It is neither the abandonment of utopian dreams nor a repressive aesthetic shift imposed from above. It provides new post-revolutionary things—things that speak both then and now and create points of contact that urge connections between Cuban citizens and national projects. *De América soy hijo* is thus a fascinating nation-building mélange—a condensation of the paradoxes of nation-building and cinema with their numerous possibilities and foreclosures.

NOTES

Introduction

1. Trotsky, *Literature and Revolution,* 207.
2. E. Guevara, "Socialism and Man in Cuba," 218.
3. Gutkin, *Cultural Origins of the Socialist Realist Aesthetic,* 17–18.
4. Chuzhak, "Pisatel'skaia pamiatka," in *October* 118 (Fall 2006): 80.
5. Ibid.
6. Guevara, "Socialism and Man in Cuba," 219.
7. Frias, "Entrevista con Manuel Perez," 42, cited in Mraz, "Film and History in Revolutionary Cuba," 36.
8. Gaonkar, "Toward New Imaginaries," 5.
9. For analyses of Cuban documentary in English that focus on the post-revolutionary period, see Mraz, "Film and History in Revolutionary Cuba"; Burton, "Revolutionary Cuban Cinema," 17–20; and Chanan, *Cuban Cinema,* 184–246. For articles that focus on Álvarez, see Hess, "Santiago Álvarez"; and Mraz, "Santiago Álvarez." For an account of the ICAIC newsreel by someone who was the longtime head of film production at ICAIC, see Fraga, "Cuba's Latin American Weekly Newsreel." For articles that deal specifically with Gomez's work, see Lesage, "*One Way or Another*"; and Lord, "Temporality and Identity."
10. C. Taylor, *Modern Social Imaginaries,* 23.
11. Gaonkar, "Toward New Imaginaries," 4.
12. See, for example, Beller, *Cinematic Mode of Production;* and Hansen, "The Mass Production of the Senses."
13. Anderson, *Imagined Communities,* chapter 1.
14. Ibid., 12.
15. Bhabha, "Introduction," 1.
16. I discuss the importance of the Bay of Pigs invasion and the nonfiction films made about it at length in chapter 2.
17. Wachtel, *Making a Nation, Breaking a Nation,* 233–34.
18. Wachtel charts the differing makeups of a number of nation-states by varying levels of stability. For example, Sweden and Poland, as uninational, uniethnic, and unicultural, are the most stable, while China and India, as multinational, multiethnic, and multicultural, are the least stable. Cuba would fall into the "more

stable" category, whereas the Soviet Union would fall into the "unstable" category. The chart is not meant to definitively predict whether a country would or would not fall apart.

19. For Soviet examples, see Kiaer and Naiman, *Everyday Life in Early Soviet Russia;* Kotkin, *Magnetic Mountain;* and the work of Hellbeck, esp. "Fashioning the Stalinist Soul." For a Cuban example that pertains directly to cinema, see Amaya, *Screening Cuba.*

20. Kiaer and Naiman, "Introduction," 7.

21. Kiaer and Naiman describe the desire to be a Soviet subject as one of "central characteristics of Soviet subjectivity." Ibid., 18.

22. Marx writes, "What we have to deal with here is a communist society, not as it has *developed* on its own foundations, but, on the contrary, just as it *emerges* from capitalist society; which is thus in every respect, economically, morally, and intellectually, still stamped with the birthmarks of the old society from whose womb it emerges." *Critique of the Gotha Programme,* 320.

23. Arendt, *On Revolution,* 31.

24. Salazkina, *In Excess,* 17.

25. Fitzpatrick, *Cultural Front,* 17.

26. Ibid., 91–114.

27. Tsivian, *Silent Witnesses.*

28. Burton, "Revolutionary Cuban Cinema," 17. See also the introduction to Perez's *Material Ghost,* where he talks about his moviegoing childhood in Havana.

29. For more information on cinema and Soviet nationalities, see Yangirov, "Soviet Cinema in the Twenties"; and Sarkisova, "Envisioned Communities."

30. Kepley, "Soviet Cinema and State Control," 4–8.

31. Ibid., 10.

32. See Kepley, "Origins of Soviet Cinema" and "Soviet Cinema and State Control."

33. For a recent analysis that takes a new and productive look at how the relationship between the media and the public sphere was conceived by, among others, Walter Lippmann and John Dewey—whose conceptions were foundational for the development of documentary—see Kahana, *Intelligence Work.*

34. These are the frameworks most often cited in these contexts. Certainly there are other ways of conceiving the purposes and essences of nonfiction film practice. Perhaps the most influential formulation is Michael Renov's four tendencies of documentary: to record, reveal, or preserve; to persuade or promote; to analyze or interrogate; and to express. Renov, "Toward a Poetics of Documentary."

35. Hicks, *Dziga Vertov,* 8.

36. Chanan, *Santiago Álvarez,* 6.

37. Nichols reconsiders the origins of documentary, emphasizing its formation as a unique genre in the 1920s. Rather than claiming that documentary's origins reside solely in the photographic realism of early actuality films, Nichols highlights in addition the development of rhetorical strategies, narrative structure, and the modernist practices associated with Vertov and other experimental artists concerned with negotiating the effects of the aesthetic form itself with a concern for social and political impact. Nichols, "Documentary Film and the Modernist Avant-

Garde." Hicks contends that Vertov's influence over the history of documentary is as formative as John Grierson's and Robert Flaherty's.

38. MacKay, "Film Energy," 49. His reference to this "conceptual knot" cites Rosen, "Document and Documentary," in *Change Mummified*, 234.

39. For a wonderful collection of essays that examines this tradition, see Waugh, *"Show Us Life."*

40. Gaonkar, "Toward New Imaginaries," 5.

41. C. Taylor, *Modern Social Imaginaries*, 164.

42. The terms "played" and "non-played," however, do not simply translate into fiction and nonfiction. For example, Shub argues that her films use real material, but she organizes it in such a way that they can be considered "played." In that way, the division is more about imposing narrative or sequential structure than the "quality" of material. For more information, see Taylor and Christie, *Film Factory*, esp. 225–32; and Ben Brewster, "From *Novy-lef* with an Introduction."

43. *Ciclón* and *De América soy hijo . . . y a ella me debo* are two films that I was not given additional copies of but that have just recently received distribution. My analysis relies on my initial viewings at ICAIC.

1. *Kino-Nedelia*, Early Documentary, and the Performance of a New Collective

1. The only information about this "somewhat mysterious" film comes from Vertov's writings. See three still images from the film in Tsivian, *Lines of Resistance*, 76.

2. Film and cultural historians have increasingly paid attention to the relationship between the new collective sensory experience of modernity, articulated in an everyday aesthetic produced by modernization and its products, and early cinema's particular mediation of that collective sensory experience. For Miriam Hansen, it is Hollywood cinema, with its mass of moviegoers, that best exemplifies this dynamic, producing a modern global vernacular. Hansen, Yuri Tsivian, Susan Buck-Morss, and Masha Salazkina all address the compatibility between the registration of the "mass production of the senses"—to use Hansen's famous phrase—in the American context and in the Soviet avant-garde. Whereas these early newsreels and documentaries cannot unquestionably be categorized under that rubric, I want to argue that they require accounting for what Zhang Zhen has described as a shift from a text-based to an affective-based paradigm of cinema, especially given their exhibition context. See Hansen, "Mass Production of the Senses"; Tsivian, "Between the Old and the New"; Buck-Morss, *Dreamworld and Catastrophe*; Salazkina, *In Excess*; and Zhen, *Amorous History of the Silver Screen*, 3.

3. Lenin himself emphasized the effort to "rouse discontent and indignation." See his *What Is to Be Done?*, 409–10. Some of G. V. Plekhanov's writings can be found in Harding's anthology *Marxism in Russia*. For recent discussions of the distinctions made in the Russian and Soviet context, see R. Taylor, *Film Propaganda*, 28–29; and Lenoe, *Closer to the Masses*, 28, though Lenoe's excellent account does not discuss cinema.

4. Hicks, *Dziga Vertov*, 6–7.

5. Vertov himself argues that, formally, the *Kino-Nedelia* series was not a significant departure from the pre-revolutionary newsreel. Vertov, *Kino-Eye,* 42. Feldman and Hicks see glimpses of the Vertov to come only in late issues of *Kino-Nedelia.* Feldman, *Evolution of Style,* 47–48; and Hicks, *Dziga Vertov,* 6 and n. 10, 18–19.

6. Rosen, "Now and Then."

7. For the history of nonfiction film in Russia prior to the revolution, see Leyda, *Kino*; Roberts, *Forward Soviet!*; and Feldman, *Evolution of Style.* The most extensive analysis of pre-revolutionary nonfiction film in Russian is untranslated and comes from Vishnevskii, *Dokumentaln'ye filmy dorevoliutsionnoi Rossii.*

8. Roberts, *Forward Soviet!,* 12.

9. See, for example, the *Russian Military Newsreel* series. Hicks, *Dziga Vertov,* 5.

10. Roberts, *Forward Soviet!,* 13–14.

11. For more information on Russian Cubo-Futurism, see Pike, "Introduction"; Stapanian, *Mayakovsky's Cubo-Futurist Vision;* and Gray, *Russian Experiment in Art.*

12. Feldman, *Evolution of Style,* 12. Both Feldman and Tsivian explore the relationship between Vertov's early childhood and late teen experiments, the contemporary artistic currents, and Vertov's future cinematic experiments. See Feldman, *Evolution of Style,* 11–22; and Tsivian, *Lines of Resistance,* 22–24.

13. Feldman, *Evolution of Style,* 12–13, 14–15.

14. Feldman details the changing of the name:

> Sometime in 1917, Denis Arkadievich Kaufman adopted the pseudonym Dziga Vertov. The varied implications of that pseudonym are a good indication of the complexities of the man who chose it. "Dziga" is not only a child's toy top, but it is also related to a Ukrainian word describing gypsies. "Vertov" is the adjectival form of the Russian word "vertet" meaning to spin or twirl. Thus "Dziga Vertov" is often translated as "Spinning Top" or "Spinning Gypsy." "Vertet," however, is also used to describe the action of rewinding film. According to Jay Leyda, Vertov himself thought of "Dziga" as the sound made by film rewound on an editing table, while "Vertov" described the rewinding itself. . . . Optimally, one may begin a consideration of the artist's work by combining all these implications and defining "Dziga Vertov" as a phrase uniting the image of spinning gypsies with physical film stock on an editing table.

Feldman, *Evolution of Style,* 1.

15. Vance Kepley argues that historians who emphasize centralization in these early years and attribute it to Lenin's leadership are being teleological in their thinking. The idea that the decree was inevitable and the perfect marriage of Bolshevism and cinema, Kepley argues, is historically inaccurate in failing to account for the "unintended consequences and institutional contradictions" that conditioned the decision and, as such, contributes to the polarization of Soviet cinema from the West. The decree was less ideological in nature than a "stop-gap device to help an industry through an inevitable period of capital consumption." See Kepley, "Soviet Cinema and State Control," quote from p. 4, and "Origins of Soviet Cinema," quote from p. 66.

16. Lunacharsky in fact imagined two parallel industries—the private sector and the state-sponsored films—existing alongside each other. Distribution-wise, he

hoped that private theaters would hire state-made films because of their quality, but he thought there was a possibility they would need to open a state-run theater in each major city to ensure access. Kepley, "Soviet Cinema and State Control," 8.

17. All of the issues exist in whole or in part in the Russian State Archive of Kino and Photo Documents (RGAKFD). In many, the intertitles have been completely or partially lost. See Tsivian's annotated filmography in *Lines of Resistance,* 403, for details about the films that exist in whole or in fragments and that are missing intertitles. The incompleteness of the run and lack of access to these films have certainly contributed to the lack of critical attention on the series.

18. Aleksandr Deriabin supplied this data. Although there is limited information about the distribution and exhibition of the series, there are accounts of a number of film screenings taking place in public squares, especially in urban areas. These screenings often included a number of issues at a time, so the traditional model of newsreel seriality does not seamlessly apply. Such an exhibition history urges us to consider the topics, thematics, aesthetics, and rhetorics of the series as a totality rather than isolate individual issues. This is even more appropriate for a newsreel series that has such a fragile history. Many of the issues were cut up after their initial release and the material was used for other purposes. When they were put back together, it is not at all assured that the stories assumed the same order and the editing the same structure.

19. The *kinocs* were a group of filmmakers, led by Vertov, Kaufman, and Ivan Beliakov (the "Council of Three"), who aimed to eliminate fiction filmmaking and sought the eventual de-professionalization of nonfiction film production.

20. The most vocal proponent of world revolution in the USSR at the time was of course Leon Trotsky. His fullest articulation can be found in Trotsky, *Permanent Revolution.*

21. The Congress made this assertion in their resolution "On Political Propaganda and Cultural Enlightenment Work in the Countryside." Roberts, *Forward Soviet!,* 19.

22. Ibid., 10–11.

23. And they have a notable history in the development of cinema. From the birth of cinema, films, and news films in particular, have covered such celebrations. Audiences were thus familiar with these kinds of moving visual representations, making their distinctions from previous models, I would argue, more legible.

24. Lenin, "Two Tactics of Social Democracy," 113, cited in von Geldern, *Bolshevik Festivals,* 42.

25. Von Geldern, *Bolshevik Festivals,* 43.

26. Jameson, "Cognitive Mapping."

27. Lunacharsky, for one, was absolutely committed to the preservation of art. In fact, he had resigned his post after hearing (incorrectly, it turns out) that the St. Basil's and Uspensky Cathedrals had been destroyed. He published his resignation November 2, 1917, in *Novaya Zhizn',* writing, "I cannot bear it. My cup is full. I am powerless to stop this awfulness. It is impossible to work under the pressure of thoughts that are driving me mad." For more on Narkompros and Lunacharsky himself in the immediate post-revolutionary years, see Fitzpatrick, *Commissariat of Enlightenment.*

28. Arendt, *On Revolution*, 31.

29. Lunacharsky, "Tasks of the State Cinema."

30. One more fascinating aspect to Soviet monument-building is that, as Yuri Tsivian points out in his notes to the Pordenone catalog (p. 30), most of these early edifices were made of nondurable materials. It is thus ironic that evidence of monumental art, usually thought to be materially stabile, was preserved through the fragile medium of film. But the use of such fragile materials opens up two fascinating strategic possibilities, each of which is imbricated with questions of historicity: either the Bolsheviks deemed the immediacy of the monuments' erection more important than its overall stability, or their physical instability was considered a positive—a history easily capable of being rewritten if the need arose (though this is perhaps teleological). I discuss the value of malleable material for history (re)construction in depth in part 2.

31. Tsivian, *Notes to the 23rd Pordenone Silent Film Festival Catalogue*, 31. It's also important to note that references to foreign governments are made continually in the series, most often in an attempt to indicate the stable leadership of the Bolsheviks. The second story in episode #4 presents the Bolsheviks receiving a Bulgarian envoy as evidence of the increased normalization of international relations. Moreover, this normalization is accompanied by an assertion of international alignments. In episode #5, for example, we see alliances with a Serbian leadership that has continually supported revolutionary efforts.

32. "In the Cinema Committee," *Kommunar*, November 3, 1918, in Tsivian, *Lines of Resistance*, 38.

33. Although I could not find data about the attendance at this screening, a comparable screening in Moscow squares in 1922 (run by four mobile cinema units) claims to have had 10,000 viewers. "The VFKO Mobile Cinemas," in Tsivian, *Lines of Resistance*, 75.

2. A Cinema Looking for People

1. Chris Marker, *L'avant-scène du cinema* 6 (1961), quoted in Chanan, *Cuban Cinema*, 193.

2. Amaya, *Screening Cuba*, 15. For further discussions of the influence of "Palabras" on Cuban film policy and debate, see ibid., 3–30; and Chanan, *Cuban Cinema*, 139–41.

3. Burton, "Film and Revolution in Cuba," 124. Originally published as "Revolutionary Cuban Cinema," in *Jump Cut* 19 (1978): 17–20.

4. "Cuba : Ley 169," 13.

5. Alfredo Guevara, *Revolución es lucidez* (Havana: Ediciones ICAIC, 1998), 53, quoted in Chanan, *Cuban Cinema*, 53. Emphasis mine.

6. On this point, see Stefan Morawski's discussion of Sánchez Vázquez in *Inquiries into the Fundamentals of Aesthetics*, 234–35.

7. Sánchez Vázquez, "Vanguardia Artistica y Vanguardia Politica." His writings have been published in Sánchez Vázquez, *Art and Society*. For further discussion of his reception in Cuba, see Amaya, *Screening Cuba*, 44–45; Chanan, *Cuban Cinema*, 173 and 269–71; and Mosquera, "Estética y Marxismo en Cuba."

8. Chanan, *Cuban Cinema*, 147.

9. Gutiérrez Alea and Julianne Burton, "Individual Fulfillment and Collective Achievement: An Interview with T. G. Alea." Cited in Chanan, *Cuban Cinema*, 161–62.

10. Pier Paolo Pasolini, *Le Ceneri di Gramsci* (Milan: Garzanti Press, 1957). For a discussion of Pasolini's critique of the Italian neorealist project, see Restivo, *Cinema of Economic Miracles*, 8.

11. Quoted in Chanan, *Cuban Cinema*, 35. My emphasis. Birri in fact made some of the most experimental films in Latin American cinema history in the late 1960s and early 1970s and remained actively and critically engaged with the Cubans. He made two films about Che Guevara—*Mi hijo el Che* (1985) and *Che, ¿muerte de una utopía?* (1997).

12. Burton, "Democratizing Documentary," 374.

13. Ibid., 375–76.

14. Fernandez, "Cuba and *lo Cubano*," 98.

15. The first films, Lindsay Anderson's *O Dreamland*, Tony Richardson and Karel Reisz's *Momma Don't Allow*, and Lorenza Mazzetti and Denis Horne's *Together*, were screened February 5–8, 1956, at the National Theatre in London. Subsequent programs include Reisz's *We Are the Lambeth Boys* (1958) and Anderson's *Every Day Except Christmas* (1967).

16. Lambert, "Free Cinema," 173.

17. Gutiérrez Alea, "El free cinema." For a synopsis of Alea's arguments, see Chanan, *Cuban Cinema*, 186–88.

18. Conversation with Lazara Herera, Santiago Álvarez's wife, March 2004.

19. Álvarez, "5 Frames Are 5 Frames, Not 6, but 5," 17.

20. For biographical information on Álvarez and his role in Nuestro Tiempo, I relied on the above-cited interview with Álvarez ("5 Frames Are 5 Frames, Not 6, but 5") in *Cineaste* as well as Michael Chanan's *Cuban Cinema*, 105–109. García Espinosa offers support for this idea of Nuestro Tiempo and ICAIC as committed to communism in the early days when he says, "ICAIC set out from the beginning to create a communist political awareness. This was before Fidel defined the Revolution as socialist." Julio García Espinosa, quoted in Chanan, *Cuban Cinema*, 124.

21. Jorgé Fraga claims that during the late 1960s, ICAIC printed only sixty copies of each newsreel since they lacked the raw stock to print more. Since the country had 500 permanent theaters and 400 mobile film units, there was a lag time of three to four weeks in some locations. Fraga, "Cuba's Latin American Weekly Newsreel," 241.

22. Bhabha, "Introduction," 1.

23. As early as 1953 in his famous "History Will Absolve Me" speech, Castro proclaimed the need for comprehensive education reform. In the first year following the victory of the rebels, the government built more than 3,000 new public schools; 7,000 new teachers entered the system to instruct over 300,000 students attending school for the first time.

24. This contrasts with the Chinese effort to "reunite" urban youths with rural life by "sending them down" to the countryside during the Cultural Revolution—a project seen by many to have been absolutely disastrous.

25. Paulston, "Education." While this is the rate Paulston gives for the nation, at its height the literacy rate prior to the campaign reached 43 percent in the countryside.

26. In the early morning hours of April 17, 1961, approximately 1,400 men began to arrive at Girón Beach on the southern coast of Cuba in an attempt to overthrow the Castro government. Trained in Guatemala by the CIA and supplied with weapons by the United States, Brigade 2506 hoped to secure a beachhead and travel by land to meet the internal resistance movement centered in the Escambray Mountains eighty miles away. Instead, lacking the air support they thought they would receive from the United States Air Force, the invasion was thoroughly defeated by Cuban forces in seventy-two hours. The attack further destabilized the already tenuous relations between the two governments. In the process, it solidified the alliance between Cuba and the Soviet Union.

27. This was not just a common strategy at the time but what Tzvi Medin identifies as "existence as confrontation," one of the three discursive platforms of the revolution that served to legitimize it. In this discourse, the ideals of the military infuse everyday life. Medin, *Cuba*, 31.

28. González, "Relationship with the Soviet Union."

29. Rafael Quintero quoted in Blight and Kornbluh, *Politics of Illusion*, 17. The text in which Quintero is quoted emanates from a conference held in 1996 that brought together some of the major players in the CIA-sponsored attempted overthrow of Castro in April 1961. CIA, FBI, and White House officials convened with Cuban resistance fighters and Latin American studies scholars in a fascinating reassessment of the events of 1960–1961. The collection, described by the editors as a "critical oral history," features the exchanges that took place at the conference as well as the recently declassified documents (from both the U.S. and Cuban side), which partially drove the meeting in the first place.

30. This strategy is an early example of Álvarez's appropriation of popular music for straight and biting purposes. I address numerous examples in chapter 4.

31. On the mobile cinemas, see Pereira and Pardo, "La Pantalla Movíl"; and Falicov, "Mobile Cinemas in Cuba."

32. Falicov, "Mobile Cinemas in Cuba," 106–107.

33. Widdis, *Visions of a New Land*, 76–96.

34. *Cine Cubano* 1, no. 3 (Havana, 1960). For more on Ivens's time in Cuba, see Waugh, "Joris Ivens' Work in Cuba." *Cine Cubano* not only regularly published work about film technique and carried film reviews but also contained highly theoretical interviews with filmmakers such as Ivens, Richardson, Agnes Varda, and Marker. It also published theoretical essays that considered the work of, among others, Eisenstein, Lukács, Brecht, Garcia Espinosa, and Gutiérrez Alea. For more on the context of film criticism in Cuba (and on the response to Cuban films in the United States) during the Cold War, see Amaya, *Screening Cuba*.

35. Waugh argues that the film is informed by Ivens's and 1950s French documentary directors' interest in the travelogue and the lyrical essay mode. On this account, it was especially well received in France. Waugh, "Joris Ivens' Work in Cuba," 25–26.

36. José Massip's recount of his experiences with Ivens is found in *Cine Cubano* 1, no. 3 (Havana, 1960): 24–28.

37. Waugh, "Joris Ivens' Work in Cuba," 26, 29.

38. The film garnered the Golden Dove prize at the Leipzig Film Festival, an award Álvarez would win four additional times in the 1960s.

39. Anonymous, "El cine revolucionario, factor de educación permanente," 67; Falicov, "Mobile Cinemas in Cuba," 106. Emphasis added.

3. The Dialectics of Thought and Vision in the Films of Dziga Vertov

1. Tsivian, *Lines of Resistance*, 407.

2. Tsivian analyzes the political economy of meat in *Kino-Eye* as well, though we come to somewhat different conclusions. Tsivian, *Lines of Resistance*, 11–12.

3. Vertov, "Kinocs: A Revolution," in *Kino-Eye: The Writings of Dziga Vertov*, 15–16.

4. Ibid., 15.

5. Beller discusses how Vertov's *Man with a Movie Camera* denaturalizes how money works and shows how it can circulate differently in *Cinematic Mode of Production*, ch. 1. Although *Kino-Eye* is not noted for its reflexivity in the ways *Man with a Movie Camera* has been, I believe that its efforts offer a glimpse of what Vertov more fully establishes—making evident "the possibilities of social transparency regarding mode of production, collectivity, and critique"—in his famous 1929 film. Beller, *Cinematic Mode of Production*, 129.

6. For more on kino-eye and "life caught unaware" *(zhizn' vrasplokh)* as a theory and method of production, see Vertov's writing in *Kino-Eye* and in Drobashenko, *Stat'i, Dnevniki, Zamysly*; and secondary sources such as Petric, "Dziga Vertov as Theorist"; Feldman, *Evolution of Style*; Roberts, *Forward Soviet!*, ch. 2; and Hicks, *Dziga Vertov*, 22–38. Hicks's discussion of Vertov's various techniques for filming is excellent.

7. In 1926 Vertov wrote, "There are no Goskino-Calendars. There are no twenty-three Kino-Pravdas. There is no film Kino-Eye. There are no films about the Moscow Soviet, the State Trading Organization, and so on. You just think there are. There is the Kino-Eye movement, there are articles and public speeches of Kino-Eye, there is the constant and scientific work of Kino-Eye, but there are no individual films." Vertov, "Kino-Eye."

8. Lenin, "Directive on Cinema Affairs."

9. Lunacharsky, "Conversation with Lenin." To remind, at this point people are not making distinctions between newsreel and documentary but between nonfiction film (unplayed) and fiction film (played). "Newsreel" thus stands in for nonfiction practice, in particular films that highlight their agitational and propagandistic potential.

10. As I discussed in the introduction to part 1, the decision to nationalize was driven more by pragmatic than ideological forces and was limited in its effectiveness. See Kepley, "Origins of Soviet Cinema" and "Soviet Cinema and State Control."

11. There is disagreement as to who actually produced the *Kino-Pravda* series. Tsivian argues that Goskino produced the whole run and that those who credit the VFKO (the All-Russia Photographic and Cinematic Department of the People's

Commissariat of Enlightenment) do so incorrectly. Taylor and Christie, however, establish the birth of Goskino in December 1922—six months after the first issue of *Kino-Pravda*. See Tsivian, *Lines of Resistance*, 409; and Taylor and Christie, *Film Factory*, 53.

12. R. Taylor, *Politics of the Soviet Cinema*, 54–55.

13. Ibid., 63.

14. Vertov, "Kino-Pravda."

15. Tsivian, *Notes*, 38; Hicks, *Dziga Vertov*, 7.

16. Remember that because of the struggle with stock shortages and circulation routes, viewers often saw more than one issue at a time. Such exhibition protocols further encouraged integration not only within but across issues.

17. Vertov uses a metaphor of the new, revolutionary social *body* in describing his representation of the travel to the exhibition, arguing that the issues show the "'blood circulation' [*krovoobrashchenie*] brought about by the idea of the agricultural exhibition." Vertov, "O Kinopravde," (1923), quoted in Widdis, *Visions of a New Land*, 107.

18. For more on the context of the commission of *A Sixth Part of the World*, see Sarkisova, "Across One Sixth of the World"; MacKay and Musser, *Notes*; and Widdis, *Visions of a New Land*, 108–11. The practice of state corporations patronizing nonfiction cinema to sell an image of it to the broadest possible audience was actually quite common in the 1920s. See Sarkisova, "Across One Sixth of the World," 26. I would argue that this practice needs to be considered in any historical reassessment of the relationship between sponsorship and nonfiction film conceived broadly.

19. MacKay and Musser develop this idea of the "visual bond" and "decoding" as the "two different though related notions of totalization" in their "notes." I address and further develop this idea later in the chapter. MacKay and Musser, *Notes*, 57.

20. This sense of rhythm is itself a Whitmanesque gesture. For a comparable example, see the intertitles in D. W. Griffith's *Intolerance*. Vertov was deeply interested in poetry and in fact wrote poems in the style of Whitman and Mayakovsky throughout his life.

21. Widdis, *Visions of a New Land*, 110.

22. Hirsch, *Empire of Nations*.

23. Martin, "An Affirmative Action Empire," 76.

24. Michelson, "Introduction"; Beller, *Cinematic Mode of Production*, 38.

25. Vertov, "From Kino-Eye to Radio-Eye," in *Kino-Eye*, 87–88.

26. Widdis, *Visions of a New Land*, 2.

27. Ibid., 121. On the "new blood circulation," she is citing Isaak Babel' from *Neft'*, in *Sochineniia*, vol. 2 (Moscow: Khudozhestvennaia literatura, 1992).

28. In one example from *Kino-Pravda* #17, the intertitle LENIN accompanies a train. The word is written in traditional Constructivist font and is the largest title in the episode. Varying the font size was one of the strategies Rodchenko used to create a sense of dynamism and emphasis. In the famous Lenin *Kino-Pravda* (#21), Vertov overlays the title ON THE RAILS OF LENINISM onto a low-angle shot of a train and its track. Once again, the leader's name stands out from the other words.

29. Gray, *Russian Experiment in Art*, 243–48.

30. In fact, it is arguable that the exaltation of technology was precisely the place in which Bolsheviks and 1920s avant-garde artists most closely aligned.

31. Vladimir Lenin, *Polnoe sobranie, sochinenii*, 5th ed., vol. 26 (Moscow, 1970), 116. Cited in Stites, *Revolutionary Dreams*, 147.

32. Frederick Taylor lays out his ideas in *Principles of Scientific Management*. I have also relied on discussions of Taylor's ideas in Merkle, *Management and Ideology*; and Rabinbach, *Human Motor*, 238–41.

33. For more on the adoption of Taylorism in the Soviet Union, see Maier, "Between Taylorism and Technocracy"; and Stites, *Revolutionary Dreams*, 145–64.

34. Rabinbach, *Human Motor*, 272.

35. Merkle, *Management and Ideology*, 103.

36. For the information on Gastev, I am relying on Bailes, "Alexei Gastev and the Soviet Controversy over Taylorism."

37. Gastev, "O tendentsiyakh proletarskoi kul'tury," quoted in Bailes, "Alexei Gastev and the Soviet Controversy over Taylorism," 378.

38. Stites, *Revolutionary Dreams*, 146.

39. For a breakdown of mobile cinema screenings in Moscow in the summer of 1922, see "Peredvizhki VFKO."

40. Gan was editor-in-chief of the Constructivist journal *Kino-Fot* who imagined Vertov's *Kino-Pravda* series to be filmed Constructivism. During 1922–1923, the journal published essays by Gan himself that celebrated Vertov's cinematic achievements and gave Vertov a voice by publishing his first manifesto, an interview, and a few short essays. For more on Gan and Vertov during this period, see Tsivian, *Lines of Resistance*, 2–3.

41. Gan, "'Levyi front' i kinematografiya."

42. Gan, "10-ia 'Kino-Pravda.'"

43. On Kerzhentsev and other "Timeists," see Stites, *Revolutionary Dreams*, 155–59.

44. MacKay and Musser, *Notes*, 57.

45. Tsivian, "Turning Objects, Toppled Pictures," 110.

46. This sense of the organic is prevalent throughout Vertov's work and, as both Malcolm Turvey and Annette Michelson point out, function in tandem with his sense of mechanization. See Michelson's "Introduction" to *Kino-Eye*, xli; and Turvey's essay "Between the Organism and the Machine" for a more extensive consideration of this issue.

47. Urazov, "Excerpts from *Shestaia chast mira*."

48. Shklovsky, "Ikh nastoiashchee."

49. Brik, "Protiv zhanrovykh kartinok."

50. Some, like Vitaly Zhemchuzhny, find this to be a step in the right direction. He writes, "*A Sixth Part of the World* cannot be called newsreel. . . . In newsreel the events are always individualized. Mention of the place and time, stress of characteristic details are compulsory. In *A Sixth Part of the World* the showing of an individual event is subordinated to the thematic intention of the film." This allows the emergence of "a completely original phenomenon." Zhemchuzhny, "Shestaia chast mira." The quote, along with the fact that others echo his sentiments, indicates the

influence of Shklovsky's position and the increasing interest in shifting discussions from newsreel to the idea of documentary, an issue I explore more fully in chapter 6.

51. A. Zorich, "O Shestoi chasti mira."

52. Aseev, "Shestaia chast . . . vozmozhnostei."

53. Gr, "Shestaia chast mira."

54. Sosnovsky, "Shestaia chast mira," 221.

55. Sovkino replaced Goskino in 1924 as part of another effort to centralize and become more efficient.

56. "Why Dziga Vertov Has Been Dismissed from Sovkino." For the entire debate, see Tsivian, *Lines of Resistance,* 252–56.

57. Sosnovsky, "Shestaia chast mira," 220.

4. (Non)Alignments and the New Revolutionary Man

1. Guevara originally wrote the essay on a three-month overseas trip (mostly to Africa) in the form of a letter to Carlos Quijano, editor of the weekly Uruguayan journal *Marcha.* It was published first there under the title "From Algiers, for *Marcha:* The Cuban Revolution Today" on March 12, 1965. It is available in *Che Guevara Reader,* 212–30.

2. *79 primaveras* was made at a time when many sectarians were aggressively condemning the influence of "Western" rock music. Álvarez challenged this position in many of his films not only by including Western rock music and its antiwar and counterculture associations in his films but by using music by Cuban artists who were critiqued for being influenced by it (such as the Cuban folk singer Silvio Rodriguez).

3. Conversation with Mario Piedra in Havana, July 2004.

4. Of course, the Cubans were not the first to note the ideological content of these newsreels. They received considerable criticism, especially William Randolph Hearst's *News of the Day,* throughout their history from the Left, which accused them of promoting militarism and celebrating anti-communist speeches. The most in-depth discussion of the American newsreel is Fielding, *American Newsreel.*

5. Álvarez always considered himself first and foremost a journalist. In an interview with *Hablemos de Cine,* a Peruvian film journal, in 1970, Álvarez says, "I'm a journalist above all. My first vocation, before I thought about film, was journalism. And I've always craved to be doing journalism. I stumbled upon film and found out how to use it journalistically." But elsewhere he qualifies, "A newsreel is essentially a product which provides information. That's certain but it isn't all. And even though this may be its principle characteristic, there's no reason either to neglect it or to turn it into a social chronicle of socialism, following the conventional line of a sequence of news items without connection." See Chanan, *Santiago Álvarez,* 6, 18, 19.

6. Hess makes the point about graffiti in "Santiago Álvarez," 392.

7. But *Now,* more than any other Álvarez film during this period, expands the address somewhat to speak to people beyond Cuba's borders. Hess argues that the skill with which Álvarez coordinates his cuts in relation to a particular lyric in *Now* contributes significantly to the organization of the film. The English-

language lyrics, he argues, are so precisely coordinated with the visuals that they clearly add another layer of meaning. English speakers would have been able to comprehend the lyrics of the song, note the precision of their temporal placement, and have the ability to place the photographs in context, since they were able to read the placards. Moreover, Hess writes, "early [American] travelers to Cuba's new revolution smuggled copies of *Now* into the country and it saw yeoman service on the underground circuit in the mid-and late-1960s." Hess, "Santiago Álvarez," 395–97 and 387–88. Given the circulation of the film (the possibility of which may have occurred to Álvarez in the process of production), I think it is likely that Álvarez constructed the film on two tracks—one for a Spanish-speaking audience and one for an English-speaking audience. That would account for the music-lyric relation and recognize Álvarez's commitment to speaking for the Cuban government to the Cuban people.

8. Carlos Moore became the most vocal critic of the Cuban government's record on racial issues in Cuba. See Moore, *Castro, the Blacks, and Africa*.

9. In Latin America, Tuesday the 13th has the equivalent connotations of Friday the 13th in the United States.

10. A number of scholars have remarked on the predominance of historical discourse in post-revolutionary Cuba. Most literary, filmic, and theatrical examples demonstrate the inevitability of the revolution by envisioning it as a natural result of a continuous commitment to sacrifice and struggle for freedom. ICAIC and other cultural institutions encouraged historical topics. ICAIC in fact approved historical topics at a much higher rate than those that addressed contemporary society. The government even established the Department of Historical Assessment of the Cuban Institute of Radio and Television to assist writers and directors in producing historical work. Álvarez, perhaps due to his commitment to journalism, was much less likely to take on entirely historical topics. Rather, he locates understandings of contemporary social and political events within a historical purview while deepening alignments with other peoples involved in revolutionary struggles. For more on Cuban cinema's attention to historical discourse during this period, see Mraz, "Film and History in Revolutionary Cuba"; and Barnard, "Death Is Not True."

11. Mesa-Lago and Zephirin, "Central Planning," 158–59.

12. For detailed statistical information and analysis of the shifting economic policies in Cuba from 1959 to 1970, see Mesa-Lago, "Economic Policies and Growth."

13. Leontieff, for one, attributes the inefficiency and low productivity of the Cuban economy to Fidel's "mini-planning." Leontieff contends that the lack of overall economic coordination made such problems highly foreseeable. Leontieff, "Notes on a Visit to Cuba."

14. Fidel Castro quoted in Bernardo, *Theory of Moral Incentives in Cuba*, 2.

15. In his 1961 article "Cuba: Historical Exception or Vanguard in the Anticolonial Struggle?," Che answered the question "What is underdevelopment?" in the following way:

A dwarf with an enormous head and swollen chest is "underdeveloped," insofar as his fragile legs and short arms don't match the rest of his anatomy.

He is the product of an abnormal and distorted development. That is what we are in reality—we, who are politely referred to as "underdeveloped." In truth, we are colonial, semicolonial or dependent countries, whose economies have been deformed by imperialism, which has peculiarly developed only those branches of industry or agriculture needed to complement its own economy.

16. To be sure, this constant fear of military invasion was not unjustified. Following the U.S. Marines invasion of the Dominican Republic in 1965, many in Cuba were convinced that the United States would launch a full-scale invasion of the island. Information has recently come available acknowledging that Johnson had developed a plan to assassinate Castro and follow it up with a major invasion. See, for example, Blight and Kornbluh, *Politics of Illusion.*

17. Medin, *Cuba,* 29 and 31.

18. Horowitz, "Introduction." Similar moral incentives were connected to volunteer labor in the Soviet Union following the Bolshevik Revolution. For a discussion of the "communist *subbotniki*" (volunteer Saturday labor), see Chase, "Voluntarism, Mobilization, and Coercion."

19. Halperin, *The Taming of Fidel Castro,* 21, 93–111. See also Mraz, "Film and History in Revolutionary Cuba," 64–108.

20. González, *Cuba under Castro,* 134.

21. In addition to *Año 7,* Álvarez speaks to Che's model of international revolution in other documentaries and special issue newsreels of the period such as *Solidaridad Cuba y Vietnam, Cerro Pelado* (1966), and *La escalada de chantaje.*

22. Like *Año 7, Hanoi, martes 13* avows its support for the Guevaran position immediately in the title sequence. Following the prologue, titles announce that ICAIC Y OSPAAAL PRESENTA the film. Although the Tricontinental Conference was well attended, there is no evidence that the organization it founded, OSPAAAL, had much practical effect. Its support for the film was entirely symbolic, offering a frame of reference for the issues about to be considered.

23. For information on Guevara, see James, *Ché Guevara;* Sauvage, *Che Guevara;* and Halperin, *Taming of Fidel Castro,* 112–31.

24. Chanan, *Cuban Cinema,* 232.

25. Castro, *Che,* 78–79.

26. While the legend of Che has certainly accrued over the years and taken on a life of its own, his sexual and charismatic appeal was widely testified to well before he died.

27. Fidel, *Che,* 78.

28. Amaya, *Screening Cuba,* xii.

29. For a discussion of the long-running television program, see the interview "Film Criticism in Cuba" that Jorge Silva conducted with Colina in *Jump Cut.*

30. Ibid., 32. It was very common for Cubans filmmakers to do critical and theoretical work as well. The production/criticism divisions often found in the West were much less rigid in Cuba.

31. Many critics have argued that this syncretic aspect of Cuban cinema is what distinguishes it from other national outputs and unites it with other Cuban cultural traditions. Chanan *(Cuban Cinema)* and Burton ("Film and Revolution in Cuba") are two of the most prominent examples.

32. Although an argument can be made that Álvarez accuses Johnson of murder, I agree with Chanan and Hess that such an analysis misses the overall point of the film, which does not emphasize that kind of reductionism.

33. Álvarez describes this editorial practice as "anticipatory," arguing that by introducing a theme and then returning to it, audiences become energized and engaged. He employed this technique in both newsreels and documentaries throughout his work in the 1960s and 1970s.

34. This caricaturizing and ensuing film clip is doubled later in the film when an image of Johnson is altered so that he is wearing armor and appears as a medieval knight. That image is then followed by a squeezed movie clip from an exotic, period adventure film.

35. The "Kuleshov effect," resulting from Lev Kuleshov's experiments with editing in the early 1920s at his workshop in Moscow, is based on the notion that leaving out the establishing shot triggers viewers to create coherent geographies, construct complete bodies, and even project emotion or desire from fragments or shots seemingly unrelated. It has been taken up by numerous film historians, filmmakers, and film scholars in a variety of ways, the most common being an emphasis on filmmakers' ability to construct meaning rather than to find meaning in the pro-filmic world. For a fascinating set of essays on the "Kuleshov effect," see the special issue of *Iris* 4, no. 1 (1986).

36. C. Taylor, *Modern Social Imaginaries*, 25.

37. It is important to remember that viewers were watching newsreels and documentaries as part of the same theatrical film program. This increases the potential for them to be both seen as part of a related project and recognized as distinct discursive objects.

38. Álvarez's work is not the only example of this dynamic. Nicolás Guillén Landrián's *Coffea Arábiga* (Coffee Arabica, 1968) likewise speaks to the relationship between productivism, economic mobilization, and nonfiction film, doing so self-consciously and, at times, highly critically. Guillén Landrián's style of isolating and animating still photographs; his use of didactic intertitles and dramatic shifts in mood, tone, rhythm, and texture; his audio distortions and playfulness with rock music; and his rapidly and rhythmically edited sequences of coffee cultivation are remarkably resonant with Álvarez's work of the period. For our purposes, it is inconsequential whether *Coffea Arábiga* functions as critique of how nonfiction films about mobilization efforts should be made (thus a critique of Álvarez's work of the period) or whether it serves as a fascinating and unique semi-homage (supported by some of Guillén Landrián's personal touches). The film establishes the degree to which Álvarez's vision, realized in both newsreels and documentary films, had pervaded the culture of ICAIC and even the nation as a whole.

5. Esfir Shub, Factography, and the New Documentary Historiography

1. Vertov, "We: Variant of a Manifesto," in *Kino-Eye*, 8.
2. "Discussion of Vertov's Film *Stride, Soviet!*," 176.
3. Fore, "Introduction," 5–6.
4. Tret'iakov, "From the Photo-Series," in *October* 118 (2006): 73.

5. Mikhail Iampol'skii, "Reality at Second Hand," 161.

6. Hicks, *Dziga Vertov,* 39–40; Boltianskii, "Kino-khronika za 10 let," 14.

7. For more on media ideologies and their connection to linguistic anthropological work on language ideologies, see Gershon, "Media Ideologies."

8. Dickerman, "Fact and the Photograph," 138. For information on party cultural policy during this period, see Fitzpatrick, "'Soft' Line on Culture and Its Enemies"; B. Taylor, *Art and Literature under the Bolsheviks,* 31–46; and Dickerman, "Fact and the Photograph," 136–38. Realism, of course, is one of the key terms of Soviet cultural debate going back to the middle of the nineteenth century. A principal category for thinking through realism in the Russian/Soviet context, one that has special resonance in thinking about cinema and nonfiction film in particular, is the concept of *byt. Byt,* an important term but one difficult to translate, refers to everyday life, daily routine, lifestyle, and even (going back to the medieval period) household belongings. Whether it's a restructuring of "old byt," a critically realist response to contemporary byt, or the imagining of a new ideal byt in the future, the differences and overlaps between the factographic approach to byt and the proletarian realist approach to byt crystallized in the 1930s as Socialist Realism became the dominant aesthetic approach. For two particularly insightful analyses of the representation of byt, see Boym, *Common Places;* and Gutkin, *Cultural Origins of the Socialist Realist Aesthetic.*

9. Tret'iakov, "New Leo Tolstoy."

10. Tret'iakov, "Our Cinema," in *October* 118 (2006): 33.

11. Tret'iakov, "New Leo Tolstoy." To be sure, the worker-correspondent *(rabkor)* movement did not originate at this point but, as Kenez demonstrates in *Birth of the Propaganda State,* emerged almost immediately after the Bolsheviks assumed power. For more on the history of the movement and its development through the 1920s, see Gorham, *Speaking in Soviet Tongues;* and Lenoe, *Closer to the Masses.*

12. Tret'iakov, "To Be Continued."

13. Ibid.; Tret'iakov, "Biography of the Object," 61.

14. Groys, "Birth of Socialist Realism," 129.

15. Tret'iakov, "New Leo Tolstoy," 49. See also Chuzhak, "Pisatel'skaia pamiatka."

16. Tret'iakov, "New Leo Tolstoy"; Fore, "Introduction." As Fore, writes, "Tret'iakov's texts take as their point of departure the observation that factography both facilitated, and was itself conditioned by, a revolution in language." Fore, "Introduction," 8. The most extended collection of Tret'iakov's essays on cinema is in Tret'iakov, *Kinematograficheskoe Nasledie.*

17. Tret'iakov, "To Be Continued," 54.

18. By the term "second-hand" material, Iampol'skii is emphasizing the fact that the filmmakers/editors encounter material that *has already been seen* by others. For more on this idea of the film factory-archive, see Malitsky, "Esfir Shub and the Film Factory-Archive."

19. *The Fall of the Romanov Dynasty* is the only one of the three with widespread distribution. *The Great Way* is available only in select archives—at the Russian State Archive of Literature and Art (RGALI) and the Österreichisches Filmmuseum, Vienna (where I obtained a research copy), and perhaps some others, while *The Russia of Nicholas II and Lev Tolstoy* is, in the words of Graham Roberts, an "unseen" film.

Roberts, *Forward Soviet!*, 67. Although Shub is rightfully known as a pioneer of the found footage or compilation documentary, Vertov was in fact one of the inaugurators of the practice with his *Anniversary of the Revolution* (1918) and *The History of the Civil War* (1921). But in the intervening years, Vertov had moved away from such practices. He continued to make use of found material selectively and regularly reused some of his own footage, but he deviated from compilation as his governing concept.

20. For more on Shub, see in particular Petric, "Esfir Shub"; and Roberts, *Forward Soviet!* For Shub's own writing, see her autobiography, *Zhizn' moia—kinematograf,* or translated excerpts from the book and other writings in Taylor and Christie, *Film Factory.*

21. Osip Brik, "The *Lef* Arena, Comrades: Fight Out Your Ideas!" *Novy Lef* 4 (1928), in Brewster, *Screen Reader 1,* 315.

22. Vertov, of course, always entered the editing process with a plan in mind. But by then, for Brik, the damage had already been done.

23. I develop this line of thinking about objectivity and directorial restrain in Malitsky, "A Certain Explicitness."

24. Kenez, *Cinema and Soviet Society,* 90–91.

25. R. Taylor, *Politics of the Soviet Cinema,* 99, 101.

26. Tret'iakov, "Lef and Film," 305, 306. Emphasis added.

27. Shklovsky, "Kuda shagaet Dziga Vertov?," 152.

28. Tret'iakov, "Lef and Film," 307.

29. Bauman and Briggs, "Poetics and Performance," 72–73. See also Silverstein and Urban, "Natural History of Discourse."

30. Bauman and Briggs, "Poetics and Performance," 73.

31. Ibid.

32. Barthes, *Camera Lucida,* 96.

33. Peirce, *Collected Papers,* 159.

34. Ibid.

35. On the "deictic field," see Hanks, "Indexical Ground of Deictic Reference" and "Explorations in the Deictic Field."

36. Metz, *Film Language,* 67. Emphasis added.

37. It strikes me that theorizations of deixis have become increasingly cinematic in their thought. Although Hanks's formulations do not directly speak to the uniqueness of cinematic temporality, his recent work on the "deictic field" does seem to open up space for translation so as to be applicable to cinema.

38. For a recent reconsideration of indexicality as a theoretically useful tool in understanding cinematic ontology, see the special issue of *differences* 18 (2007) edited by Mary Ann Doane. And for a more extended consideration of the cinematic index as deictic and its relation to index as trace, see Doane, "Indexical and the Concept of Medium Specificity," esp. 135–40.

39. Bauman and Briggs, "Poetics and Performance," 74.

40. For more on the distinction between the "experimental science pursued by factographers and the abstract calculus of Western rationalism," see Fore, "Introduction."

41. Brik, "Blizhe k Factu," quoted in Dickerman, "Fact and the Photograph," 143. Emphasis added.

42. I'd like to thank (and promote) Yuri Tsivian's "cinemetrics" machine for providing the technology to obtain such information. For access, go to: http://www.cinemetrics.lv/.

43. Deleuze, *Cinema 2*, 185. See also Corrigan, "Forgotten Image between Two Shots," where he discusses Chris Marker's photo-essay *The Koreans* in relation to the "conjunctive 'and'" (41–61).

44. Corrigan, "Forgotten Image between Two Shots," 50.

45. Shub, *Zhizn' moia—kinematograf*, 268, quoted in Iampol'skii, "Reality at Second Hand," 163.

46. Tret'iakov, "Our Cinema," 37.

47. Implicit in this point is a comparison to factory workers who need to improvise in order to complete their tasks (not an uncommon experience in the USSR at the time).

48. Tret'iakov, "Our Cinema," 37.

49. Hanks, "Indexical Ground of Deictic Reference," 62, 51.

50. In 1928, Brik modified his stance somewhat, accepting Shklovsky's insistence that filmed material needs to be organized. But while Shklovsky argued for full-scale plots, Brik continued to call for looser, thematically driven scripts.

51. For other analyses of factography as a method of accumulating and communicating historical knowledge, see Kozlov, "Historical Turn in Late Soviet Culture"; and V. Tupitsyn, *Museological Unconscious*. Whereas Kozlov emphasizes factography's accumulation of detail and minutiae that was meant "to complement rather than revolutionize existing worldviews" (578), Tupitsyn calls attention to the neofactographers who "give preference to the *other*" of photographic history—the accidentally preserved photographs that testify to an unofficial record, that of fragments of everyday life that reveal the ordinary moments and experiences of others.

52. This is Anatoli Lunacharsky, the Commissar of Enlightenment who oversaw the film industry, stressing Bukharin's comments in a speech to film industry workers. Interestingly, 1928 was the first year that box office returns from Soviet films actually exceeded those from foreign imports. Lunacharsky, "Speech to Film Workers," 196.

53. Ibid., 197.

54. Stepanova, "Photomontage," 236.

55. Ibid.

56. See also M. Tupitsyn, *Soviet Photograph*. One of the ways in which the photographer goes about achieving the desired snapshot effect is to "pack" or "compress" the material in a photograph, overloading the image so as to create a "maximum condensation." See in particular the photographs and Tupitsyn's discussion of Boris Ignatovich.

57. Rodchenko, "Against the Synthetic Portrait," 239–40.

58. Ibid., 240.

59. Stepanova quoted in Buchloh, "From Faktura to Factography," 91.

60. It is Tret'iakov's essay *in relation* to the photo-essay that demonstrates the factographic approach. I am not taking the photo-essay itself as an exemplar of the factographic model, as it was not understood by any of the leading critics to be so.

61. Tret'iakov, "From the Photo-Series," 73; Brik, "Photography vs. Painting."

62. Tret'iakov, "From the Photo-Series," 74.

63. Ibid., 75.

64. Ibid.

65. Ibid., 77. To be clear, Tret'iakov still believes there is a place for the photo-series, and the extended photo-observation is to augment, not replace, the photo-series. The photo-series is capable of defining the object of study, even if it requires the extended photo-observation to articulate its development.

66. The fullest treatment of this documentary subgenre can be found in Kilborn, *Taking the Long View*.

67. Chuzhak, "Pisatel'skaia pamiatka." See also Fore's introduction to Chuzhak's essay, 78–79.

68. Gunning, "What's the Point of an Index?"

69. Doane, "Indexical and the Concept of Medium Specificity," 140.

70. Buchloh, "From Faktura to Factography," 103.

71. For more on studies of the Soviet cinema audience conducted by Sovkino, the state-run film organization of the time, and ODSK, see R. Taylor, *Politics of the Soviet Cinema,* 87–101.

72. Shklovsky, "Kinoki I Nadpisi."

73. Ibid., 154.

74. Ibid., 153.

75. Tret'iakov, "From the Photo-Series," 76.

76. I am not arguing against Buchloh here, who focused his attention on pho-tomontage practices. Rather, I am claiming that the terrain changes when photo-essays and found footage documentaries become part of the equation.

6. The Object of Revolutionary History

1. López Oliva, "Imagenes de *L.B.J.*"

2. Sergei Eisenstein's critique of Vertov speaks to this concern between the purposes of cultural activity and shifting political-economic dynamics. Eisenstein argued that Vertov was still making films as if it were wartime communism (1918–1920) or the immediately preceding years when they were living in the period of the New Economic Policy. He writes, "Today, we are not living in 1920, and not living in 1923. . . . The New Economic Policy is giving birth to new forms of tactics in the unending class struggle between eternally inimical class forces. In the new conditions the artistically primitive tactical pluperfect [Vertovian articulation] misfires." Eisenstein, "Letter to the Editor of *Film Technik.*"

3. Rojas, *Isla sin fin.* For more on Cuban efforts to establish a new revolution-ary lineage and trajectory at this point in history and the implications of such ef-forts, see L. Pérez, "Toward a New Future, from a New Past"; and Quiroga, *Cuban Palimpsests,* 25–50.

4. Quiroga, *Cuban Palimpsests,* 29.

5. Ibid., 47.

6. Blanco and Benjamin, "From Utopianism to Institutionalization," 437.

7. One of the major recurring problems of the early 1960s was a lack of replace-able parts for production equipment. Factories and farms would often be shut down for extended periods due to the breakdown of a piece of U.S.-manufactured equip-

ment. Because of the embargo, Cubans either had to improvise a technological so-lution or reform the means of production. Neither choice was as efficient as simply replacing the broken part. For a detailed discussion of the transformation of the Cuban economy following the revolution, see Boorstein, *Economic Transformation of Cuba*.

8. The emergence of editions celebrating competition winners is reminiscent of Soviet Stakhanovism. Like the films about workers "overfulfilling" quotas, these films appear to address the present while precluding its examination. Their primary function is to construct tradition—a practice always predicated on looking to the future. ICAIC director Fausto Canel argues that Cubans are in fact "nostalgic for the future." Canel quote from Mraz, "Film and History in Revolutionary Cuba," 16.

9. Ibid., 46.

10. The Soviets were of course known for historical recreations on a grand scale, including the storming of the Winter Palace on the third anniversary of the revolu-tion. The performance included 125 ballet dancers, 100 circus people, 1,750 students, 260 secondary actors, 150 assistants, and tanks and armored cars. It was performed in front of 100,000 spectators. For more on Soviet festivals, see Von Geldern, *Bol-shevik Festivals;* Stites, *Revolutionary Dreams,* 97–100; and Kleberg, *Theatre as Action*.

11. LeoGrande, "Cuban-Soviet Relations and Cuban Policy in Africa," 15.

12. The extent of Cuban intervention in Guinea Bissau, however, was rarely publicized. A Cuban friend who viewed a newsreel on Guinea Bissau with me re-lated that her father had actually been sent to fight with the guerrillas in the West African nation. The family had been told he was on a sailing expedition. It was not until years later that he confessed, to the shock of his family, what his service had actually been.

13. Mraz, "Santiago Álvarez," 131–49, quote from 146.

14. Mraz nuances this comparison by noting that the political intentions of the two practices were radically different; he does not simply argue that Álvarez be-came a direct cinema practitioner.

15. For more on the direct cinema's claims to objectivity, the critique it pro-voked, and the counterclaims asserted, see Winston, *Claiming the Real,* 148–63.

16. Daston and Galison, "Image of Objectivity," 82.

17. This understanding of Bazin has been complicated in recent years, but it remains the predominant reading. Some influential challenges are Morgan, "Re-thinking Bazin"; Rosen, *Change Mummified;* and Gunning, "Moving Away from the Index."

18. Bazin, *What Is Cinema?,* 1:14.

19. Baudry, "Ideological Effects."

20. Metz, *The Imaginary Signifier,* 56.

21. A noteworthy example of this line of thought comes from Wollen, "Godard and Counter Cinema."

22. For a critical analysis of film theory since 1968 that engages the critique of realism, see Rodowick, *Crisis of Political Modernism*.

23. Nichols, *Representing Reality,* 63.

24. Renov, *Subject of Documentary,* xvii.

25. Daston and Galison, *Objectivity*.

26. Ibid., 36–37.

27. While there are certainly other models of selfhood—the self as governor of mental faculties, as negotiator of personal experience, and as site for exploration of conscious, subconscious, and unconscious processes, for example—I am, like Renov, focused on the self imagined as a subjectivity.

28. The Heberto Padilla affair, in particular, caused many to question the openness of Cuban revolutionary cultural policy that supporters considered its hallmark. In 1971, Padilla, a poet, was arrested and detained for twenty-eight days for what was considered inappropriate intellectual activity—both in his original writing and in his defenses of ostracized colleagues. Following Padilla's arrest and his Stalinesque public self-criticism, many international onlookers felt that Fidel had betrayed the original vision and fallen under Soviet influence not only economically but culturally. Ambrosio Fornet argues that the most lamentable outcome of the Padilla affair was that party dogmatists found support for the notion that only monolithic thinking could guarantee the continued success of the revolution.

29. Camnitzer, *New Art of Cuba*, 9. It is important to note that most recent cultural historians understand Soviet socialist realism as hyperrealist. See Gutkin, *Cultural Origins of the Socialist Realist Aesthetic*. The term itself, however, covers an array of meanings. The hyperrealisms of Soviet Socialist Realism, Cuban 1970s painting, and contemporary digital culture are certainly not identical.

30. Chanan, *Cuban Cinema*, 314.

31. Camnitzer, *New Art of Cuba*, 9.

32. Daston, "Objectivity and the Escape from Perspective." The argument that Daston makes in this article does not get taken up in her and Galison's *Objectivity*. That text is concerned more with the creation of new epistemic virtues in modern science, namely objectivity (especially its dominant strand—mechanical objectivity), its primary epistemic precursor (truth to nature), its primary successor (trained judgment), and the manners in which such virtues coexist and interact.

33. Daston, "Objectivity and the Escape from Perspective," 600.

34. Daston and Galison, "Image of Objectivity," 122.

35. Hood, "Murder on the Way."

36. That is not to say that viewers did not get an "emotional charge" from *De América soy hijo*. In fact, research demonstrates that they went to see the film in droves, continually filling up seven cinemas in Havana for two months. Álvarez discusses this in "5 Frames Are 5 Frames, Not 6, but 5."

37. Daston and Galison, *Objectivity*, 186.

BIBLIOGRAPHY

Álvarez, Santiago. "Arte y Compromiso." *El Mundo,* Havana (1968). Reprinted in *Hojas de Cine: Testimonios y Documentos Del Nuevo Cine Latinoamericano,* vol. 3. Mexico City: Secretaría de Educación Pública, Universidad Autónoma Metropolitana, Fundación Mexicana de Cineastas, 1988. 35–37.

———. "Cinema as One of the Mass Communications Media." *Cine Cubano,* nos. 49–51 (1968). Reprinted in *Santiago Álvarez,* edited by Michael Chanan. BFI Dossier, no. 2. London: British Film Institute, 1980. 27–30.

———. "5 Frames Are 5 Frames, Not 6, but 5: An Interview with Santiago Álvarez." *Cineaste* 6, no. 4 (Spring 1975): 17–23.

———. "Interview: From Hanoi to Yungay." *Hablemos de Cine,* nos. 55–56 (1970). Reprinted in *Santiago Álvarez,* edited by Michael Chanan. BFI Dossier, no. 2. London: British Film Institute, 1980. 13–22.

———. "Motivaciones de un Aniversario o Respuesta Inconclusa a un Cuestionario que no Tiene Fin." *Revista Cine Cubano,* nos. 54–55 (1969). Reprinted in *Santiago Álvarez, Cronista Del Tercer Mundo,* edited by Edmundo Aray. Caracas, Venezuela: Cinemateca Nacional, 1983. 102–106.

Amad, Paula. *Counter-Archive: Film, the Everyday, and Albert Kahn's Archives de la Planète.* New York: Columbia University Press, 2010.

Amaya, Hector. *Screening Cuba.* Urbana: University of Illinois Press, 2010.

Anderson, Benedict R. *Imagined Communities: Reflections on the Origin and Spread of Nationalism.* 1983. Rev. and extended ed. New York: Verso, 1991.

Anonymous. "El cine revolucionario, factor de educación permanente." *Cine Cubano,* nos. 66–67 (1971): 61–67.

Anoschenko, Aleksandr. "Kinokoki" [The kinococci]. *Kino-Nedelia,* February 19, 1924. Reprinted in *Lines of Resistance: Dziga Vertov and the Twenties,* edited by Yuri Tsivian. Russian texts translated by Julian Graffy. Pordenone, Italy: Le Giornate del Cinema Muto Press, 2004. 90–92.

Aray, Edmundo, ed. *Santiago Álvarez, Cronista Del Tercer Mundo.* Caracas, Venezuela: Cinemateca Nacional, 1983.

Arendt, Hannah. *On Revolution.* New York: Viking, 1963.

———. *The Origins of Totalitarianism.* New York: Harcourt Brace, 1951.

Aseev, Nikolai. "Shestaia chast . . . vozmozhnostei" [A sixth part of the . . . potential]. *Kino,* October 26, 1926. Reprinted in *Lines of Resistance: Dziga Vertov and the Twenties,* edited by Yuri Tsivian. Russian texts translated by Julian Graffy. Pordenone, Italy: Le Giornate del Cinema Muto Press, 2004. 200.

Bailes, Kendall. "Alexei Gastev and the Soviet Controversy over Taylorism, 1918–24." *Soviet Studies* 39, no. 3 (1977): 373–94.

Barnard, Timothy. "Death Is Not True: Form and History in Cuban Film." In *The New Latin American Cinema,* edited by Michael T. Martin. Vol. 2. Detroit: Wayne State University Press, 1997. 143–54.

Barnouw, Erik. *Documentary: A History of the Non-Fiction Film.* Rev. ed. Oxford: Oxford University Press, 1983.

Barthes, Roland. *Camera Lucida: Reflections on Photography.* Translated by Richard Howard. New York: Hill and Wang, 1981.

Baudry, Jean-Louis. "Ideological Effects of the Basic Cinematographic Apparatus." In *Film Theory and Criticism,* edited by Leo Braudy and Marshall Cohen. 7th ed. Oxford: Oxford University Press, 2009. 355–65.

Bauman, Richard, and Charles Briggs. "Poetics and Performance as Critical Perspectives on Language and Social Life." *Annual Review of Anthropology* 19 (1990): 59–88.

Baxandall, Lee, ed. *Radical Perspectives in the Arts.* Harmondsworth, U.K.: Penguin, 1972.

Bazin, André. *Bazin at Work: Major Essays and Reviews from the Forties and Fifties.* Translated by Bert Cardullo. Edited by Alan Piette and Bert Cardullo. New York: Routledge, 1997.

———. "The Myth of Stalin in the Soviet Cinema." Translated by Bert Cardullo. Edited by Alan Piette and Bert Cardullo. *New Orleans Review* 15, no. 3 (1988): 5–17.

———. *What Is Cinema?* Translated and edited by Hugh Gray. 2 vols. Berkeley: University of California Press, 1967.

Beller, Jonathan. *The Cinematic Mode of Production.* Lebanon, N.H.: University of New England Press, 2006.

Benjamin, Walter. *Illuminations.* Translated by Harry Zohn. Edited by Hannah Arendt. New York: Schocken Books, 1986.

———. *Moscow Diary.* Translated by Richard Sieburth. Edited by Gary Smith. Cambridge, Mass.: Harvard University Press, 1969.

Bernardo, Robert M. *The Theory of Moral Incentives in Cuba.* Tuscaloosa: University of Alabama Press, 1971.

Bhabha, Homi. "Introduction: Narrating the Nation." In *Nation and Narration,* edited by Homi Bhabha. New York: Routledge, 1990. 1–7.

Birri, Fernando. "For a Nationalist, Realist, Critical, and Popular Cinema." In *New Latin American Cinema,* edited by Michael T. Martin. Volume 1. Detroit: Wayne State University Press, 1997. 95–98.

Blanco, Juan Antonio, and Medea Benjamin. "From Utopianism to Institutionalization." In *The Cuba Reader: History, Culture, Politics,* edited by Aviva Chomsky, Barry Carr, and Pamela Maria Smorkaloff. Durham: Duke University Press, 2003. 433–42.

Blasier, Cole, and Carmelo Mesa-Lago. *Cuba in the World.* Pittsburgh: University of Pittsburgh Press, 1979.

Blight, James G., and Peter Kornbluh. *Politics of Illusion: The Bay of Pigs Invasion Reexamined*. Boulder, Colo.: Lynne Rienner, 1998.

Blium, Vladimir. "Shagai, Soviet!" [Stride, Soviet!]. *Izvestia*, April 6, 1926. Reprinted in *Lines of Resistance: Dziga Vertov and the Twenties*, edited by Yuri Tsivian. Russian texts translated by Julian Graffy. Pordenone, Italy: Le Giornate del Cinema Muto Press, 2004. 157–60.

Bluem, A. William. *Documentary in American Television: Form, Function and Method*. New York: Hastings House, 1965.

Bogdanov, Alexander. *Red Star: The First Bolshevik Utopia*. Bloomington: Indiana University Press, 1984.

Boltianskii, Grigorii. "Kino-khronika za 10 let" [Film chronicle for ten years]. *Sovietskoe Kino* [Soviet cinema] 7 (1927), 14–15.

Boorstein, Edward. *The Economic Transformation of Cuba*. New York: Monthly Review Press, 1968.

Bowlt, John E. *Russian Art of the Avant-Garde: Theory and Criticism, 1902–1934*. New York: Viking Press, 1976.

Boym, Svetlana. *Common Places: Mythologies of Everyday Life in Russia*. Cambridge, Mass.: Harvard University Press, 1994.

Braverman, Harry. *Labor and Monopoly Capital: The Degradation of Work in the Twentieth Century*. New York: Monthly Review Press, 1975.

Brewster, Ben. "From *Novy-lef* with an Introduction." *Screen* 12, no. 4 (Winter 1971–72): 59–91.

———, ed. and trans. *Screen Reader I: Cinema/Ideology/Politics*. 1927. London: Society for Education in Film and Television, 1977.

Brik, Osip. "Blizhe k Factu" [Close to the fact]. *Novyi Lef* 2 (1927): 34.

———. "Fikstatsia Facta" [The fixation of fact]. *Novyi Lef* 11–12 (1927): 48–50.

———. "The *Lef* Ring: Comrades! A Clash of Views." *Novyi Lef* 4 (1928): 27–36. Reprinted in *The Film Factory: Russian and Soviet Cinema in Documents 1896–1939*, translated and edited by Richard Taylor and Ian Christie. Cambridge, Mass.: Harvard University Press, 1988. 225–26.

———. "Photography vs. Painting." *Sovetskoie Foto* 2 (1926). Reprinted in *Rodchenko*, edited by David Elliot. Oxford: Oxford University Press, 1979. 90–91.

———. "Protiv zhanrovykh kartinok" [Against genre pictures]. *Kino*, July 5, 1927. Reprinted in *Lines of Resistance: Dziga Vertov and the Twenties*, edited by Yuri Tsivian. Russian texts translated by Julian Graffy. Pordenone, Italy: Le Giornate del Cinema Muto Press, 2004. 275.

Brooks, Jeffrey. *Thank You, Comrade Stalin! Soviet Public Culture from Revolution to Cold War*. Princeton, N.J.: Princeton University Press, 2000.

Brown, Edward James. *Russian Literature since the Revolution*. Rev. and enl. ed. Cambridge, Mass.: Harvard University Press, 1982.

Buchloh, Benjamin. "From Faktura to Factography." *October* 30 (1984): 82–119.

Buchsbaum, Jonathan. *Cinema and the Sandinistas: Filmmaking in Revolutionary Nicaragua*. Austin: University of Texas Press, 2003.

Buck-Morss, Susan. *Dreamworld and Catastrophe: The Passing of Mass Utopia in East and West*. Cambridge, Mass.: MIT University Press, 2000.

Burton, Julianne. *Cinema and Social Change in Latin America: Conversations with Filmmakers*. Austin: University of Texas Press, 1986.

———. "Democratizing Documentary: Modes of Address in Latin American Cinema, 1958–1972." In *"Show Us Life": Toward a History and Aesthetics of the Committed Documentary*, edited by Thomas Waugh. Metuchen, N.J.: Scarecrow Press, 1984. 344–83.

———. "Film and Revolution in Cuba." In *New Latin American Cinema*, edited by Michael T. Martin. Vol. 2. Detroit: Wayne State University Press, 1997. 123–42.

———. "Individual Fulfillment and Collective Achievement: An Interview with Tomás Gutiérrez Alea." *Cineaste* 8, no. 1 (1977): 8–15.

———. "Revolutionary Cuban Cinema." *Jump Cut* 19 (1978): 17–20.

———, ed. *The Social Documentary in Latin America*. Pittsburgh: University of Pittsburgh Press, 1990.

Camnitzer, Luis. *New Art of Cuba*. Austin: University of Texas Press, 1994.

Casaus, Victor. "Conversacion con Santiago Álvarez." *Revista Cine Cubano*, nos. 78, 79, 80, Havana (1973). Reprinted in *Santiago Álvarez, Cronista Del Tercer Mundo*, edited by Edmundo Aray. Caracas, Venezuela: Cinemateca Nacional, 1983. 146–56.

Castoriadis, Cornelius. *The Imaginary Institution of Society*. Translated by Kathleen Blamey. Cambridge, Mass.: MIT Press, 1998.

Castro, Fidel. *Che: A Memoir by Fidel Castro*. Melbourne, Australia: Ocean Press, 1994.

———. *Fidel Castro Speaks*. Edited by James Petras and Martin Kenner. New York: Grove Press, 1969. Online at http://www.walterlippmann.com/fc-02-04-1962 .html (accessed June 17, 2008).

———. "Words to the Intellectuals." In *Radical Perspectives in the Arts*, edited by Lee Baxandall. Harmondsworth, U.K.: Penguin, 1972, 267–98.

Chakravarty, Sumita S. *National Identity in Indian Popular Cinema, 1947–1987*. Austin: University of Texas Press, 1993.

Chanan, Michael. *Cuban Cinema*. Minneapolis: University of Minnesota Press, 2003.

———. *Santiago Álvarez*. BFI Dossier, no. 2. London: British Film Institute, 1980.

———. *Twenty-Five Years of the New Latin American Cinema*. London: Channel Four Television, BFI Books, 1983.

Chase, William. "Voluntarism, Mobilization, and Coercion: *Subbotniki* 1919–1921." *Soviet Studies* 41 (January 1989): 111–28.

Christie, Ian. "Introduction." In *The Film Factory: Russian and Soviet Cinema in Documents 1896–1939*, translated and edited by Richard Taylor and Ian Christie. Cambridge, Mass.: Harvard University Press, 1988. 1–17.

Christie, Ian, and John Gillett. *Futurism/Formalism/FEKS: "Eccentrism" and Soviet Cinema, 1918–1936*. London: British Film Institute, 1978.

Chu, Yingchi. *Chinese Documentaries: From Dogma to Polyphony*. New York: Routledge, 2007.

Chuzhak, Nikolai, ed. *Literatura fakta* [Literature of fact]. Moskva: Federatsiia, 1929.

———. "Pisatel'skaia pamiatka" [A writer's handbook]. In *Literatura fakta*, edited by Nikolai Chuzhak. Moscow: Federatsiia, 1929. 9–28. Reprinted in *October* 118 (Fall 2006): 78–94, translated by Devin Fore and Douglas Greenfield.

Clark, Katerina. "Engineers of Human Souls in an Age of Industrialization." In *Social Dimensions of Soviet Industrialization,* edited by William Rosenberg and Lewis Siegelbaum. Bloomington: Indiana University Press, 1993, 248–64.

Colina, Enrique. "Entrevista a Santiago Álvarez." *Cine Cubano,* nos. 58–59 (1969). Reprinted in *Santiago Álvarez, Cronista Del Tercer Mundo,* edited by Edmundo Aray. Caracas, Venezuela: Cinemateca Nacional, 1983. 83–89.

Corrigan, Timothy. "The Forgotten Image between Two Shots: Photos, Photograms, and the Essayistic." In *Still Moving: Essays between Cinema and Photography,* edited by Karen Beckman and Jean Ma. Durham, N.C.: Duke University Press, 2008. 41–61.

"Cuba: Ley 169: Creación del Instituto de Arte e Industria Cinematográficos, ICAIC." *Hojas de Cine: Testimonios y Documentos Del Nuevo Cine Latinoamericano,* vol. 3. Mexico City: Secretaría de Educación Pública, Universidad Autónoma Metropolitana, Fundación Mexicana de Cineastas, 1988. 13–19.

Daston, Lorraine. "Objectivity and the Escape from Perspective." *Social Studies of Science* 22, no. 4 (1992): 597–618.

Daston, Lorraine, and Peter Galison. "The Image of Objectivity." *Representations* 40 (Fall 1992): 81–128.

———. *Objectivity.* Cambridge, Mass.: Zone Books, 2007.

Davis, Horace Bancroft. *Toward a Marxist Theory of Nationalism.* New York: Monthly Review Press, 1978.

Deleuze, Gilles. *Cinema 2: The Time-Image.* Translated by Hugh Tomlinson and Robert Galeta. Minneapolis: University of Minnesota Press, 1989.

Derrida, Jacques. *Archive Fever: A Freudian Impression.* Translated by Eric Prenowitz. Chicago: University of Chicago Press, 1996.

Diaz, Jesus. "Asaltar el Cielo: Funcion de la Cultura Revolucionaria." *Revista Cine Cubano,* nos. 84–85 (1974). Reprinted in *Santiago Álvarez, Cronista Del Tercer Mundo,* edited by Edmundo Aray. Caracas, Venezuela: Cinemateca Nacional, 1983. 169–72.

Dickerman, Leah. "The Fact and the Photograph." *October* 118 (2006): 132–52.

"Discussion of Vertov's Film *Stride, Soviet!* by the Presidium Committee of the Moscow Soviet." RGALI 2091-1-6, March 18, 1926. Reprinted in *Lines of Resistance: Dziga Vertov and the Twenties,* edited by Yuri Tsivian. Russian texts translated by Julian Graffy. Pordenone, Italy: Le Giornate del Cinema Muto Press, 2004. 176–77.

Djilas, Milovan. *Tito: The Story from Inside.* New York: Harcourt, Brace, Jovanovich, 1980.

D'Lugo, Marvin. "'Transparent Women': Gender and Nation in Cuban Cinema." In *New Latin American Cinema,* edited by Michael T. Martin. Volume 1. Detroit: Wayne State University Press, 1997. 155–66.

Doane, Mary Ann. *The Emergence of Cinematic Time: Modernity, Contingency, the Archive.* Cambridge, Mass.: Harvard University Press, 2002.

———. "The Indexical and the Concept of Medium Specificity." *differences* 18, no. 1 (2007): 128–52.

———. "The Object of Theory." In *Rites of Realism,* edited by Ivone Margulies. Durham: Duke University Press, 2003. 80–89.

Drobashenko, Sergei, ed. *Stat'i, Dnevniki, Zamysly* [Writings, diaries, projects]. Moscow: Iskusstvo, 1966.

Eagle, Herbert. *Russian Formalist Film Theory*. Ann Arbor: University of Michigan, 1981.

Efimova, Alla, and Lev Manovich, eds. *Tekstura: Russian Essays on Visual Culture*. Chicago: University of Chicago Press, 1993.

Eikhenbaum, Boris. *The Poetics of Cinema*. Translated by Richard Taylor. Oxford: RPT Publications, 1982.

Eisenstein, Sergei. *Film Form: Essays in Film Theory*. Translated and edited by Jay Leyda. New York: Harcourt Brace Jovanovich, 1977.

———. *The Film Sense*. Translated and edited by Jay Leyda. New York: Harcourt Brace Jovanovich, 1942.

———. *Immoral Memories: An Autobiography*. Translated by Herbert Marshall. Boston: Houghton Mifflin, 1983.

———. "Letter to the Editor of *Film Technik*," 26 February 1927. RGALI 1923-1-910. Reprinted in *Lines of Resistance: Dziga Vertov and the Twenties*, edited by Yuri Tsivian. Russian texts translated by Julian Graffy. Pordenone, Italy: Le Giornate del Cinema Muto Press, 2004. 144.

Ellis, Jack C. *The Documentary Idea: A Critical History of English-Language Documentary Film and Video*. Englewood Cliffs, N.J.: Prentice Hall, 1989.

Enrique, Leon. "Notas por el Decimo Aniversario Noticiero ICAIC." *Revista UPEC*, July 1970. Reprinted in *Santiago Álvarez, Cronista Del Tercer Mundo*, edited by Edmundo Aray. Caracas, Venezuela: Cinemateca Nacional, 1983. 112–15.

Ermolinsky, Sergei. "Shagai, Soviet!" [Stride, Soviet!] *Komsomolskaia Pravda*, June 29, 1926, 4. Reprinted in *Lines of Resistance: Dziga Vertov and the Twenties*, edited by Yuri Tsivian. Russian texts translated by Julian Graffy. Pordenone, Italy: Le Giornate del Cinema Muto Press, 2004. 165.

Falicov, Tamara. "Mobile Cinemas in Cuba: The Forms and Ideology of Traveling Exhibitions." *Public* 40 (2010): 104–8.

Feldman, Seth. *Dziga Vertov, a Guide to References and Resources*. Boston: G. K. Hall, 1979.

———. *Evolution of Style in the Early Work of Dziga Vertov*. New York: Arno Press, 1977.

Fernández, Damián. "Cuba and lo Cubano." In *Cuba, the Elusive Nation: Interpretations of National Identity*, edited by Damián Fernández and Madeline Cámara Betancourt. Gainesville: University of Florida Press, 2000. 79–99.

Fevralsky, Aleksandr. "Shagai, Soviet!" [Stride, Soviet!]. *Pravda*, March 12, 1926. Reprinted in *Lines of Resistance: Dziga Vertov and the Twenties*, edited by Yuri Tsivian. Russian texts translated by Julian Graffy. Pordenone, Italy: Le Giornate del Cinema Muto Press, 2004. 161.

Fielding, Raymond. *The American Newsreel, 1911–1967*. Norman: University of Oklahoma Press, 1972.

Fitzpatrick, Sheila. *The Commissariat of Enlightenment: Soviet Organization of Education and the Arts under Lunacharsky, October 1917–1921*. Cambridge: Cambridge University Press, 1970.

——. *The Cultural Front: Power and Culture in Revolutionary Russia*. Ithaca, N.Y.: Cornell University Press, 1992.

——. *The Russian Revolution*. Oxford: Oxford University Press, 1992.

——. "The 'Soft' Line on Culture and Its Enemies: Soviet Cultural Policy 1922–1927." *Slavic Review* 2 (1974): 267–87.

Fore, Devin. "Introduction." *October* 118 (2006): 3–10.

——. "The Operative Word in Soviet Factography." *October* 118 (2006): 95–131.

Fraga, Jorgé. "Cuba's Latin American Weekly Newsreel: Cinematic Language and Political Effectiveness." In *The Social Documentary in Latin America,* edited by Julianne Burton. Pittsburgh: University of Pittsburgh Press, 1990. 239–50.

Franqui, Carlos. *Diary of the Cuban Revolution*. New York: Viking Press, 1980.

Freire, Paulo. *Cultural Action for Freedom*. Monograph Series, no. 1. Cambridge, Mass.: Harvard Educational Review, 1970.

——. *Education for Critical Consciousness*. 1st American ed. New York: Seabury Press, 1973.

——. *Pedagogy of the Oppressed*. New York: Seabury Press, 1970.

Frias, Isaac Leon. "Entrevista con Manuel Perez" [Interview with Manuel Perez]. *Hablemos de ciné*, Lima, Peru, no. 70 (April 1979): 29–45.

Gabriel, Teshome H. *Third Cinema in the Third World: The Aesthetics of Liberation*. Ann Arbor, Mich.: UMI Research Press, 1982.

Gaines, Jane. "Political Mimesis." In *Collecting Visible Evidence,* edited by Jane Gaines and Michael Renov. Minneapolis: University of Minnesota Press, 1999. 84–102.

Gaines, Jane, and Michael Renov, eds. *Collecting Visible Evidence*. Minneapolis: University of Minnesota Press, 1999.

Galiano, Carlos. "*One Way or Another*: The Cuban Revolution in Action." *Granma Weekly Review,* November 20, 1977. Reprinted in *Jump Cut* 19 (1978): 33.

Gan, Alexei. "'Levyi front' i kinematografiya" [The 'Left Front' and cinema]. *Kino-Fot*, no. 5, December 10, 1922, 1–3. Reprinted in *The Film Factory: Russian and Soviet Cinema in Documents 1896–1939,* translated and edited by Richard Taylor and Ian Christie. Cambridge, Mass.: Harvard University Press, 1988. 75–77.

——. "10-ia 'Kino-Pravda'" [The tenth "Kino-Pravda"]. *Kino-Fot*, no. 4, 1922. Reprinted in *Lines of Resistance: Dziga Vertov and the Twenties,* edited by Yuri Tsivian. Russian texts translated by Julian Graffy. Pordenone, Italy: Le Giornate del Cinema Muto Press, 2004. 55.

Gaonkar, Dilip. "Toward New Imaginaries: An Introduction." *Public Culture* 14, no. 1 (2002): 1–19.

García Espinosa, Julio. "For an Imperfect Cinema." In *New Latin American Cinema,* edited by Michael T. Martin. Volume 1. Detroit: Wayne State University Press, 1997. 71–82.

——. "Meditations on Imperfect Cinema . . . Fifteen Years Later." In *New Latin American Cinema,* edited by Michael T. Martin. Volume 1. Detroit: Wayne State University Press, 1997. 83–85.

Gellner, Ernest. *Nations and Nationalism*. Ithaca, N.Y.: Cornell University Press, 1983.

Gershon, Ilana. "Media Ideologies: An Introduction." *Journal of Linguistic Anthropology* 20, no. 2 (2010): 283–93.

González, Edward. *Cuba under Castro: The Limits of Charisma*. Boston: Houghton Mifflin, 1974.

———. "Relationship with the Soviet Union." In *Revolutionary Change in Cuba*, edited by Carmelo Mesa-Lago. Pittsburgh: University of Pittsburgh Press, 1971. 81–105.

González, Edward, and David F. Ronfeldt. *Castro, Cuba, and the World*. Santa Monica, Calif.: Rand, 1986.

Gorham, Michael. *Speaking in Soviet Tongues: Language Culture and the Politics of Voice in Revolutionary Russia*. DeKalb: Northern Illinois University Press, 2003.

Gough, Maria. *The Artist as Producer: Russian Constructivism in Revolution*. Berkeley: University of California Press, 2005.

Goulding, Daniel. *Liberated Cinema: The Yugoslav Experience, 1945–2001*. Bloomington: Indiana University Press, 2002.

Gr. "Shestaia chast mira" [A sixth part of the world]. *Uralskii rabochii*, January 25, 1927. Reprinted in *Lines of Resistance: Dziga Vertov and the Twenties*, edited by Yuri Tsivian. Russian texts translated by Julian Graffy. Pordenone, Italy: Le Giornate del Cinema Muto Press, 2004. 207.

Gray, Camilla. *The Russian Experiment in Art, 1863–1922*. New York: H. N. Abrams, 1971.

Groys, Boris. "The Birth of Socialist Realism from the Spirit of the Russian Avant-Garde." In *The Culture of the Stalin Period*, edited by Hans Gunther. London: Macmillan Press, 1990, 193–218.

———. *The Total Art of Stalinism: Avant-Garde, Aesthetic Dictatorship, and Beyond*. Princeton, N.J.: Princeton University Press, 1992.

Guevara, Alfredo. "El Cine Cubano." Havana (1963). Reprinted in *Hojas de Cine: Testimonios y Documentos Del Nuevo Cine Latinoamericano*, vol. 1. Mexico City: Secretaría de Educación Pública, Universidad Autónoma Metropolitana, Fundación Mexicana de Cineastas, 1988. 21–34.

———. "Reflexiones en Torno a una Experienca Cinematografica I." *Bohemia*, Havana (January 1969). Reprinted in *Hojas de Cine: Testimonios y Documentos Del Nuevo Cine Latinoamericano*, vol. 3. Mexico City: Secretaría de Educación Pública, Universidad Autónoma Metropolitana, Fundación Mexicana de Cineastas, 1988. 39–45.

Guevara, Ernesto (Che). *The Che Guevara Reader*. Edited by David Deutschmann. 2nd ed. Melbourne, Australia: Ocean Press, 2003.

———. "Cuba: Historical Exception or Vanguard in the Anticolonial Struggle?" In *The Che Guevara Reader*, edited by David Deutschmann. 2nd ed. Melbourne, Australia: Ocean Press, 2003. 130–42.

———. "Socialism and Man in Cuba." In *The Che Guevara Reader*, edited by David Deutschmann. 2nd ed. Melbourne, Australia: Ocean Press, 2005. 212–30.

Gunning, Tom. "Moving Away from the Index: Cinema and the Impression of Reality." *differences* 18, no. 1 (2007): 29–53.

———. "What's the Point of an Index? Or, Faking Photographs." In *Still Moving: Essays between Cinema and Photography,* edited by Karen Beckman and Jean Ma. Durham, N.C.: Duke University Press, 2008. 23–40.

Gusman, Boris. "V serdtse krestianina Lenin zhiv" [Lenin is alive in the heart of the peasant]. *Pravda,* April 3, 1925. Reprinted in *Lines of Resistance: Dziga Vertov and the Twenties,* edited by Yuri Tsivian. Russian texts translated by Julian Graffy. Pordenone, Italy: Le Giornate del Cinema Muto Press, 2004. 51.

Gutiérrez Alea, Tomás. "El free cinema y la objetividad." *Cine Cubano* 4 (1961): 35–39.

———. "Individual Fulfillment and Collective Achievement: An Interview with T. G. Alea." Interview by Julianne Burton. *Cineaste* 8, no. 1 (1977), 8–15, 59.

———. "The Viewer's Dialectic." In *New Latin American Cinema,* edited by Michael T. Martin. Volume 1. Detroit: Wayne State University Press, 1997. 108–31.

Gutkin, Irina. *The Cultural Origins of the Socialist Realist Aesthetic, 1890–1934.* Evanston, Ill.: Northwestern University Press, 1999.

Halperin, Maurice. *The Taming of Fidel Castro.* Berkeley: University of California Press, 1981.

Hanks, William. "Explorations in the Deictic Field." *Current Anthropology* 46, no. 2 (2005): 191–220.

———. "The Indexical Ground of Deictic Reference." In *Rethinking Context: Language as an Interactive Phenomenon,* edited by Alessandro Duranti and Charles Goodwin. Cambridge: Cambridge University Press, 1992. 43–76.

Hansen, Miriam. "Introduction." In *Theory of Film,* by Siegfried Kracauer. Princeton, N.J.: Princeton University Press, 1997. vii–xiv.

———. "The Mass Production of the Senses: Classical Cinema as Vernacular Modernism." *Modernism-Modernity* 6, no. 2 (1999): 59–77.

Hanson, Stephen E. *Time and Revolution: Marxism and the Design of Soviet Institutions.* Chapel Hill: University of North Carolina Press, 1997.

Harding, Neil, ed. *Marxism in Russia: Key Documents 1879–1906.* Translated by Richard Taylor. Cambridge: Cambridge University Press, 2008.

Harrison, Charles, and Paul Wood, eds. *Art in Theory, 1900–2000: An Anthology of Changing Ideas.* Malden, Mass.: Blackwell, 2003.

Hellbeck, Jochen. "Fashioning the Stalinist Soul: The Diary of Stepan Podlubnyi, 1931–1939." In *Stalinism: New Directions,* edited by Sheila Fitzpatrick. New York: Routledge, 2000. 77–116.

Heller, Agnes. "Paradigm of Production: Paradigm of Work." *Dialectical Anthropology* 6 (1981): 71–79.

Hess, John. "No Mas Habermas, or . . . Rethinking Cuban Cinema in the 1990s." *Screen* 40, no. 2 (1999): 203–11.

———. "Santiago Álvarez: Ciné-agitator for the Cuban Revolution and the Third World." In *"Show Us Life": Toward a History and Aesthetics of the Committed Documentary,* edited by Thomas Waugh. Metuchen, N.J.: Scarecrow Press, 1984. 384–402.

Hicks, Jeremy. *Dziga Vertov: Defining Documentary Film.* London: I. B. Tauris, 2007.

Hirsch, Francine. *Empire of Nations.* Ithaca, N.Y.: Cornell University Press, 2005.

Hjort, Mette, and Scott MacKenzie, eds. *Cinema and Nation*. London: Routledge, 2000.

Hobsbawm, E. J. *Nations and Nationalism since 1780: Programme, Myth, Reality*. Cambridge: Cambridge University Press, 1990.

Hojas de Cine: Testimonios y Documentos Del Nuevo Cine Latinoamericano. Mexico City: Secretaría de Educación Pública, Universidad Autónoma Metropolitana, Fundación Mexicana de Cineastas, 1988.

Hood, Stuart. "Murder on the Way." *New Statesman*, 18 April 1980, 596-97.

Horowitz, Irving Louis. "Introduction." In *The Theory of Moral Incentives in Cuba*, by Robert Bernardo. Tuscaloosa: University of Alabama Press, 1971. xvi–xviii.

———. "The Political Sociology of Cuban Communism." In *Revolutionary Change in Cuba*, edited by Carmelo Mesa-Lago. Pittsburgh: University of Pittsburgh Press, 1971. 127–41.

Iampol'skii, Mikhail. *The Memory of Tiresias: Intertextuality and Film*. Berkeley: University of California Press, 1998.

———. "Reality at Second Hand." *Historical Journal of Film, Radio, and Television* 11, no. 2 (1991): 161–72.

Issari, Mohammad Ali, and Doris Atkinson Paul. *What Is Cinéma Vérité?* Metuchen, N.J.: Scarecrow Press, 1979.

Ivens, Joris. *The Camera and I*. New York: International Publishers, 1974.

James, Daniel. *Ché Guevara: A Biography*. New York: Stein and Day, 1969.

Jameson, Fredric. "Cognitive Mapping." In *Marxism and the Interpretation of Culture*, edited by Cary Nelson and Lawrence Grossberg. Urbana: University of Illinois Press, 1988. 347–57.

———. *The Geopolitical Aesthetic: Cinema and Space in the World System*. Bloomington: Indiana University Press, 1995.

Kahana, Jonathan. *Intelligence Work: The Politics of American Documentary*. New York: Columbia University Press, 2008.

Kei, Di. "Kino-khronika 'Pravdy'" [The "Pravda" newsreel]. *Pravda*, June 28, 1922. Reprinted in *Lines of Resistance: Dziga Vertov and the Twenties*, edited by Yuri Tsivian. Russian texts translated by Julian Graffy. Pordenone, Italy: Le Giornate del Cinema Muto Press, 2004. 40.

Kenez, Peter. *The Birth of the Propaganda State: Soviet Methods of Mass Mobilization, 1917–1929*. Cambridge: Cambridge University Press, 1985.

———. *Cinema and Soviet Society, 1917–1953*. Cambridge: Cambridge University Press, 1992.

Kepley, Vance, Jr. "The Origins of Soviet Cinema: A Study in Industry Development." In *Inside the Film Factory: New Approaches to Russian and Soviet Cinema*, edited by Richard Taylor and Ian Christie. London: Routledge, 1991. 60–79.

———. "Soviet Cinema and State Control: Lenin's Nationalization Decree Reconsidered." *Journal of Film and Video* 42, no. 2 (Summer 1990): 3–14.

Khan-Magomedov, S. O. *Konstruktivizm: Kontseptsiia Formoobrazovaniia* [Constructivism: Concept formation]. Moscow: Stroiizdat, 2003.

Kiaer, Christina, and Eric Naiman, eds. *Everyday Life in Early Soviet Russia*. Bloomington: Indiana University Press, 2006.

———. "Introduction." In *Everyday Life in Early Soviet Russia*, edited by Christina Kiaer and Eric Naiman. Bloomington: Indiana University Press, 2006. 1–22.

Kilborn, Richard. *Taking the Long View: A Study of Longitudinal Documentary.* Manchester, U.K.: University of Manchester Press, 2010.

Kleberg, Lars. *Theatre as Action: Soviet Russian Avant-Garde Aesthetics.* Translated by Charles Rougle. London: Macmillan, 1993.

Koltsov, Mikhail. "U ekrana" [In front of the screen]. *Pravda*, November 28, 1922. Reprinted in *Lines of Resistance: Dziga Vertov and the Twenties*, edited by Yuri Tsivian. Russian texts translated by Julian Graffy. Pordenone, Italy: Le Giornate del Cinema Muto Press, 2004. 41–46.

Kotkin, Stephen. *Magnetic Mountain: Stalinism as a Civilization.* Berkeley: University of California Press, 1995.

Kozlov, Dennis. "The Historical Turn in Late Soviet Culture: Retrospectivism, Factography, Doubt, 1953–91." *Kritika: Explorations in Russian and Eurasian History* 2, no. 3 (2001): 577–600.

Lambert, Gavin. "Free Cinema." *Sight and Sound* 25 (Spring 1956): 173–77.

Latour, Bruno. *Pandora's Hope.* Cambridge, Mass.: Harvard University Press, 1999.

Lefebvre, Henri. *Everyday Life in the Modern World.* New York: Harper and Row, 1971.

Lenin, Vladimir. "Directive on Cinema Affairs." In *Samoe vazhnoe is vzekh iskusstv: Lenin o kino* [The most important of all arts: Lenin on film], edited by A. M. Gak. Moscow, 1973, 42. Reprinted in *The Film Factory: Russian and Soviet Cinema in Documents 1896–1939*, translated and edited by Richard Taylor and Ian Christie. Cambridge, Mass.: Harvard University Press, 1988. 56.

———. "Two Tactics of Social Democracy in the Democratic Revolution." In *Collected Works*, vol. 9. Moscow: Progress Publishers, 1962. 15–140.

———. *What Is to Be Done?* In *Collected Works*, vol. 5. Moscow: Foreign Languages Publishing House, 1961. 347–530.

Lenoe, Matthew. *Closer to the Masses: Stalinist Culture, Social Revolution, and Soviet Newspapers.* Cambridge, Mass.: Harvard University Press, 2004.

LeoGrande, William. "Cuban-Soviet Relations and Cuban Policy in Africa." In *Cuba in Africa*, edited by Carmelo Mesa-Lago and June S. Belkin. Pittsburgh: Center for Latin American Studies Press, 1982, 13–49.

Leontieff, Wassily. "Notes on a Visit to Cuba." *New York Review of Books* 13 (1969): 19.

Lesage, Julia. "*One Way or Another*. Dialectical. Revolutionary. Feminist." *Jump Cut* 20 (May 1979): 20–23.

Leyda, Jay. *Kino: A History of the Russian and Soviet Film.* 3rd ed. Princeton, N.J.: Princeton University Press, 1983.

Lodder, Christina. *Russian Constructivism.* New Haven, Conn.: Yale University Press, 1983.

Lopez, Ana M. "*The Battle of Chile*: Documentary, Political Process, and Representation." In *The Social Documentary in Latin America*, edited by Julianne Burton. Pittsburgh: University of Pittsburgh Press, 1990. 267–88.

López Oliva, Manuel. "Imagenes de *L.B.J.*" *El Mundo*, Havana (December 1968). Reprinted in *Santiago Álvarez, Cronista Del Tercer Mundo*, edited by Edmundo Aray. Caracas, Venezuela: Cinemateca Nacional, 1983. 53–54.

Lord, Susan. "Temporality and Identity in Sara Gómez' Documentaries." In *Women Filmmakers: Refocusing,* edited by Jacqueline Levitin, Judith Plessis, and Valerie Raoul. Vancouver: University of British Columbia Press, 2003. 249–63.

Lukács, Georg. *Realism in Our Time: Literature and the Class Struggle.* New York: Harper and Row, 1964.

———. *Studies in European Realism.* New York: Grosset and Dunlap, 1964.

———. *Writer and Critic, and Other Essays.* New York: Grosset and Dunlap, 1971.

Lunacharsky, Anatoli. "Conversation with Lenin." In *Lenin i kino,* ed. G. M. Botyanskii. Moscow and Leningrad, 1925, 16–19. Reprinted in *The Film Factory: Russian and Soviet Cinema in Documents 1896–1939,* translated and edited by Richard Taylor and Ian Christie. Cambridge, Mass.: Harvard University Press, 1988. 56–57.

———. "Revolyutsionnaya ideologiya I kino—tezisy" [Revolutionary ideology and cinema—theses]. *Kino-Nedelia* 46 (1924). Reprinted in *The Film Factory: Russian and Soviet Cinema in Documents 1896–1939,* translated and edited by Richard Taylor and Ian Christie. Cambridge, Mass.: Harvard University Press, 1988. 109.

———. "Speech to Film Workers." *Zhizn Iskusstvo* 4, no. 24 (1928). Reprinted in *The Film Factory: Russian and Soviet Cinema in Documents 1896–1939,* translated and edited by Richard Taylor and Ian Christie. Cambridge, Mass.: Harvard University Press, 1988. 195–97.

———. "The Tasks of the State Cinema in the RSFSR." *Kinematograf* Moscow (1919), 5–7. Reprinted in *The Film Factory: Russian and Soviet Cinema in Documents 1896–1939,* translated and edited by Richard Taylor and Ian Christie. Cambridge, Mass.: Harvard University Press, 1988. 47–49.

MacKay, John. "Film Energy: Process and Metanarrative in Dziga Vertov's *The Eleventh Year* (1928)." *October* 121 (Summer 2007): 41–78.

MacKay, John, and Charles Musser. *Notes to the 23rd Pordenone Silent Film Festival Catalogue.* Pordenone, Italy: Le Giornate del Cinema Muto Press, 2004. 57–58.

Maier, Charles S. "Between Taylorism and Technocracy." *Journal of Contemporary History* 6, no. 2 (1970): 27–61.

Makovskaia, N. "2000 metrov v strane bolshevike" [2,000 meters in the land of the Bolsheviks]. *Trud,* March 17, 1926, 4. Reprinted in *Lines of Resistance: Dziga Vertov and the Twenties,* edited by Yuri Tsivian. Russian texts translated by Julian Graffy. Pordenone, Italy: Le Giornate del Cinema Muto Press, 2004. 162.

Malitsky, Joshua. "A Certain Explicitness: Objectivity, History, and the Documentary Self." *Cinema Journal* 50, no. 3 (Spring 2011): 26–44.

———. "Esfir Shub and the Film Factory-Archive: Soviet Documentary from 1925–1928." *Screening the Past* 17 (December 2004). http://www.latrobe.edu.au /screeningthepast/.

———. "Ideologies in Fact: Still and Moving-Image Documentary in the Soviet Union, 1927–1932." *Journal of Linguistic Anthropology* 20, no. 2 (Fall 2010): 352–71.

Malitsky, Joshua, and Ilana Gershon. "Actor-Network Theory and Documentary Studies." *Studies in Documentary Film* 4, no. 1 (Spring 2010): 65–78.

Manovich, Lev. *The Language of New Media.* Cambridge, Mass.: MIT Press, 2001.

Margulies, Ivone. "Bodies Too Much." In *Rites of Realism: Essays on Corporeal Cinema,* edited by Ivone Margulies. Durham, N.C.: Duke University Press, 2003. 1–23.

———. *Nothing Happens: Chantal Akerman's Hyperrealist Everyday.* Durham, N.C.: Duke University Press, 1996.

———, ed. *Rites of Realism: Essays on Corporeal Cinema.* Durham, N.C.: Duke University Press, 2003.

Martin, Michael T., ed. *New Latin American Cinema.* 2 vols. Detroit: Wayne State University Press, 1997.

Martin, Terry. *The Affirmative Action Empire: Nations and Nationalism in the Soviet Union, 1923–1939.* Ithaca, N.Y.: Cornell University Press, 2001.

———. "An Affirmative Action Empire: The Soviet Union as the Highest Form of Imperialism." In *A State of Nations: Empire and Nation-Making in the Age of Lenin and Stalin,* edited by Ronald Grigor Suny and Terry Martin. New York: Oxford University Press, 2001. 67–90.

Marx, Karl. *Capital: A Critique of Political Economy.* Volume 1. Introduced by Ernest Mandel. Translated by Ben Fowkes. New York: Penguin Books, 1976.

———. *Critique of the Gotha Programme, Part 1.* In *Karl Marx: Selected Writings,* edited by Lawrence Simon. Indianapolis: Hackett Publishing. 315–32.

Marx, Karl, and Friedrich Engels. *Marx and Engels on Literature and Art: A Selection of Writings.* Edited by Stefan Morawski. St. Louis, Mo.: Telos Press, 1973.

Medin, Tzvi. *Cuba: The Shape of Revolutionary Consciousness.* Boulder, Colo.: L. Rienner Publishers, 1990.

Merkle, Judith A. *Management and Ideology: The Legacy of the International Scientific Management Movement.* Berkeley: University of California Press, 1980.

Mesa-Lago, Carmelo. "Economic Policies and Growth." In *Revolutionary Change in Cuba,* edited by Carmelo Mesa-Lago. Pittsburgh: University of Pittsburgh Press, 1971. 277–338.

———. *The Economy of Socialist Cuba: A Two-Decade Appraisal.* Albuquerque: University of New Mexico Press, 1981.

———, ed. *Revolutionary Change in Cuba.* Pittsburgh: University of Pittsburgh Press, 1971.

Mesa-Lago, Carmelo, and Carl Beck, eds. *Comparative Socialist Systems: Essays on Politics and Economics.* Pittsburgh: University of Pittsburgh Center for International Studies, 1975.

Mesa-Lago, Carmelo, and June S. Belkin, eds. *Cuba in Africa.* Pittsburgh: Center for Latin American Studies Press, 1982.

Mesa-Lago, Carmelo, and Luc Zephirin. "Central Planning." In *Revolutionary Change in Cuba,* edited by Carmelo Mesa-Lago. Pittsburgh: University of Pittsburgh Press, 1971. 145–84.

Metz, Christian. *Film Language: A Semiotics of the Cinema.* Translated by Michael Taylor. New York: Oxford University Press, 1974.

———. *The Imaginary Signifier: Psychoanalysis and the Cinema.* Translated by C. Britton, A. Williams, B. Brewster, and A. Guzzetti. Bloomington: Indiana University Press, 1982.

Michelson, Annette. "Introduction." In *Kino-Eye: The Writings of Dziga Vertov,* by Dziga Vertov. Translated by Kevin O'Brien. Edited by Annette Michelson. Berkeley: University of California Press, 1984. xv–lxi.

———. "*The Man with the Movie Camera:* From Magician to Epistemologist." *Artforum* 10, no. 7 (March 1972): 60–72.

Moore, Carlos. *Castro, the Blacks, and Africa.* Los Angeles: University of California Press, 1988.

Morawski, Stefan. *Inquiries into the Fundamentals of Aesthetics.* Cambridge, Mass.: MIT Press, 1974.

Morgan, Daniel. "Rethinking Bazin: Ontology and Realist Aesthetics." *Critical Inquiry* 32, no. 3 (2006): 441–81.

Mosquera, Gerardo. "Estética y Marxismo en Cuba" [Aesthetics and Marxism in Cuba]. *Cuadernos Americanos* [American notebooks] 5, no. 29 (September–October 1991): 169–86.

Mraz, John. "Film and History in Revolutionary Cuba: 1965–1970." Diss., University of California at Santa Cruz, 1986.

———. *Nacho López, Mexican Photographer.* Minneapolis: University of Minnesota Press, 2003.

———. "Santiago Álvarez: From Dramatic Form to Direct Cinema." In *The Social Documentary in Latin America,* edited by Julianne Burton. Pittsburgh: University of Pittsburgh Press, 1990. 131–49.

Nichols, Bill. *Blurred Boundaries: Questions of Meaning in Contemporary Culture.* Bloomington: Indiana University Press, 1994.

———. "Documentary Film and the Modernist Avant-Garde." *Critical Inquiry* 27, no. 4 (2001): 580–610.

———. *Representing Reality: Issues and Concepts in Documentary.* Bloomington: Indiana University Press, 1991.

Nietzsche, Friedrich. *Unfashionable Observations.* Edited and translated by Richard T. Gray. Stanford, Calif.: Stanford University Press, 1995.

O'Regan, Tom. *Australian National Cinema.* New York: Routledge, 1996.

Paulston, Richard G. "Education." In *Revolutionary Change in Cuba,* edited by Carmelo Mesa-Lago. Pittsburgh: University of Pittsburgh Press, 1971. 385–87.

Peirce, Charles Sanders. *Collected Papers of Charles Sanders Peirce.* Vol. 2. Edited by Charles Hartshorne and Paul Weiss. Cambridge, Mass.: Harvard University Press, 1932.

"Peredvizhki VFKO" [The VFKO mobile cinemas]. *Kino-Fot,* no. 2, 1922, 7. Reprinted in *Lines of Resistance: Dziga Vertov and the Twenties,* edited by Yuri Tsivian. Russian texts translated by Julian Graffy. Pordenone, Italy: Le Giornate del Cinema Muto Press, 2004. 75–77.

Pereira, Manuel, and José Manuel Pardo. "La Pantalla Movíl" [The mobile screen]. *Cine Cubano* 95 (1979): n.p.

Perez, Gilberto. *The Material Ghost: Films and Their Medium.* Baltimore, Md.: Johns Hopkins University Press, 2000.

Pérez, Louis, Jr. "Toward a New Future, from a New Past: The Enterprise of History in Socialist Cuba." *Cuban Studies* 15, no. 1 (1985): 1–13.

Pérez-Stable, Marifeli. *The Cuban Revolution: Origins, Course, and Legacy*. New York: Oxford University Press, 1993.

Petric, Vlada. *Constructivism in Film: The Man with the Movie Camera: A Cinematic Analysis*. Cambridge: Cambridge University Press, 1987.

———. "Dziga Vertov as Theorist." *Cinema Journal* 18, no. 1 (1978): 29–44.

———. "Esfir Shub: Film as Historical Discourse." In *"Show Us Life": Toward a History and Aesthetics of the Committed Documentary*, edited by Thomas Waugh. Metuchen, N.J.: Scarecrow Press, 1984. 21–46.

Pick, Zuzana M. *The New Latin American Cinema: A Continental Project*. Austin: University of Texas Press, 1993.

Pike, Christopher. "Introduction." In *The Futurists, the Formalists, and the Marxist Critique*, edited by Christopher Pike. London: Ink Links, 1979, 1–40.

Pineda Barnett, Enrique. " . . . Y el Cielo Fue Tomado Por Asalto." *La Habana* (1973). Reprinted in *Santiago Álvarez, Cronista Del Tercer Mundo*, edited by Edmundo Aray. Caracas, Venezuela: Cinemateca Nacional, 1983. 162–68.

Pines, Jim, and Paul Willemen, eds. *Questions of Third Cinema*. London: British Film Institute, 1989.

Plekhanov, G. V. "Propaganda among the Workers." In *Marxism in Russia: Key Documents 1879–1906*, edited by Neil Harding. Translated by Richard Taylor. Cambridge: Cambridge University Press, 2008. 59–67.

Quiroga, José. *Cuban Palimpsests*. Minneapolis: University of Minnesota Press, 2005.

Quiros, Oscar. "Critical Mass of Cuban Cinema: Art as the Vanguard of Society." *Screen* 37, no. 3 (1996): 279–93.

Rabinbach, Anson. *The Human Motor: Energy, Fatigue, and the Origins of Modernity*. Berkeley: University of California Press, 1990.

Ratliff, William E. *Castroism and Communism in Latin America, 1959–1976: The Varieties of Marxist-Leninist Experience*. Washington, D.C.: American Enterprise Institute for Public Policy Research, 1976.

Renov, Michael. *The Subject of Documentary*. Minneapolis: University of Minnesota Press, 2004.

———, ed. *Theorizing Documentary*. New York: Routledge, 1993.

———. "Toward a Poetics of Documentary." In *Theorizing Documentary*, edited by Michael Renov. New York: Routledge, 1993. 12–36.

Restivo, Angelo. *The Cinema of Economic Miracles: Visuality and Modernization in the Italian Art Film*. Durham, N.C.: Duke University Press, 2002.

Roberts, Graham. *Forward Soviet! History and Non-fiction Film in the USSR*. London: I. B. Tauris, 1999.

Rodchenko, Aleksandr. "Against the Synthetic Portrait, for the Snapshot." In *Photography in the Modern Era: European Documents and Critical Writings, 1913–1940*, edited by Christopher Phillips. 1928. New York: The Metropolitan Museum of Art/Aperture, 1989. 238–43.

Rodowick, David Norman. *The Crisis of Political Modernism: Criticism and Ideology on Contemporary Film Theory*. Berkeley: University of California Press, 1988.

Rodriguez Aleman, Mario. "Y el Cielo Fue Tomado Por Asalto." *Granma*, Havana (April 1973). Reprinted in *Santiago Álvarez, Cronista Del Tercer Mundo*, edited by Edmundo Aray. Caracas, Venezuela: Cinemateca Nacional, 1983. 156–59.

Rojas, Rafael. *Isla sin fin: Contribución a la critica del nacionalismo cubano* [Island without end: Contributions to the critique of Cuban nationalism]. Miami: Ediciones Universal, 1998. 188–215.

Rosen, Philip. *Change Mummified: Cinema, Historicity, Theory.* Minneapolis: University of Minnesota Press, 2001.

———. "History, Textuality, Nation: Kracauer, Burch, and Some Problems in the Study of National Cinema." *Iris* 2, no. 2 (1984): 69–84.

———. "Now and Then: Conceptual Problems in Historicizing Documentary Imaging." *Canadian Journal of Film Studies* 16, no. 1 (2007): 29.

Rosenberg, William G., and Lewis H. Siegelbaum, eds. *Social Dimensions of Soviet Industrialization.* Bloomington: Indiana University Press, 1993.

Rosenthal, Alan, ed. *New Challenges for Documentary.* Berkeley: University of California Press, 1988.

Salazkina, Masha. *In Excess.* Chicago: University of Chicago Press, 2009.

Sánchez Vázquez, Adolfo. *Art and Society: Essays in Marxist Aesthetics.* New York: Monthly Review Press, 1973.

———. "Vanguardia Artistica y Vanguardia Politica." In *Literatura y arte Nuevo en Cuba,* edited by Mario Benedetti, Alejo Carpentier, Julio Cortázar, and Miguel Barnet. Barcelona: Editorial Laia, 1977, 91–96.

Sarkisova, Oksana. "Across One Sixth of the World: Dziga Vertov, Travel Cinema, and Soviet Patriotism." *October* 121 (Summer 2007): 25–27.

———. "Envisioned Communities: Representations of Nationalities in Non-Fiction Cinema in Soviet Russia, 1923–1935." Diss., Central European University, 2004.

Sauvage, Léo. *Che Guevara: The Failure of a Revolutionary.* Englewood Cliffs, N.J.: Prentice-Hall, 1973.

Scarpaci, Joseph, Roberto Segre, and Mario Coyula. *Havana: Two Faces of the Antillean Metropolis.* Chapel Hill: University of North Carolina Press, 2002.

Schmutzler, Robert. *Art Nouveau.* New York: Abrams, 1978.

Serge, Victor. *Memoirs of a Revolutionary.* Translated by Peter Sedgwick. Iowa City: University of Iowa Press, 2002.

Shklovsky, Viktor. "Ikh nastoiashchee" [Their present time]. In *Lines of Resistance: Dziga Vertov and the Twenties,* edited by Yuri Tsivian. Russian texts translated by Julian Graffy. Pordenone, Italy: Le Giornate del Cinema Muto Press, 2004. 271.

———. "Kinoki I Nadpisi" [The cine-eyes and intertitles]. *Kino* (1926). Reprinted in *The Film Factory: Russian and Soviet Cinema in Documents 1896–1939,* translated and edited by Richard Taylor and Ian Christie. Cambridge, Mass.: Harvard University Press, 1988. 153–54.

———. "Kuda shagaet Dziga Vertov?" [Where is Dziga Vertov striding?]. *Sovetskii ekran,* August 14, 1926, 4. Reprinted in *The Film Factory: Russian and Soviet Cinema in Documents 1896–1939,* translated and edited by Richard Taylor and Ian Christie. Cambridge, Mass.: Harvard University Press, 1988. 151–52.

———. "*Lef* and Film." In *Screen Reader 1: Cinema/Ideology/Politics,* translated and edited by Ben Brewster. 1927. London: Society for Education in Film and Television, 1977. 309. 309.

———. *Mayakovsky and His Circle.* Edited by Lily Feiler. New York: Dodd, Mead, and Company, 1972.

———. *Theory of Prose*. Translated by Benjamin Sher. Normal, Ill.: Dalkey Archive Press, 1991.

———. *Third Factory*. Translated by Richard Sheldon. Chicago: Dalkey Archive Press, 2002.

———. *Zoo: Or, Letters Not about Love*. Ithaca, N.Y.: Cornell University Press, 1971.

Shub, Esfir. "This Work Cries Out." *Kino*, no. 11 (1928). Reprinted in *The Film Factory: Russian and Soviet Cinema in Documents 1896–1939*, translated and edited by Richard Taylor and Ian Christie. Cambridge, Mass.: Harvard University Press, 1988. 217.

———. "We Do Not Deny the Element of Mastery." *Novyi Lef* 11–12 (1927): 58–59. Reprinted in *The Film Factory: Russian and Soviet Cinema in Documents 1896–1939*, translated and edited by Richard Taylor and Ian Christie. Cambridge, Mass.: Harvard University Press, 1988. 185–87.

———. *Zhizn' moia—kinematograf* [Cinematography—my life]. Moskva: Iskusstvo, 1972.

Silva, Jorge. "Film Criticism in Cuba: Interview with Enrique Colina." Translated by Julianne Burton. *Jump Cut* 22 (May 1980): 32–33.

Silverstein, Michael, and Greg Urban. "The Natural History of Discourse." In *Natural Histories of Discourse*, edited by Michael Silverstein and Greg Urban. Chicago: University of Chicago Press, 1996. 1–17.

Solanas, Fernando, and Octavio Getino. "Towards a Third Cinema: Notes and Experiences for the Development of a Cinema of Liberation in the Third World." In *New Latin American Cinema*, edited by Michael T. Martin. Volume 1. Detroit: Wayne State University Press, 1997. 33–58.

Sosnovsky, L. "Shestaia chast mira" [A sixth part of the world]. *Rabochaia gazeta* [Workers gazette], January 5, 1927. Reprinted in *Lines of Resistance: Dziga Vertov and the Twenties*, edited by Yuri Tsivian. Russian texts translated by Julian Graffy. Pordenone, Italy: Le Giornate del Cinema Muto Press, 2004. 220–21.

Stanojevic, Petar. "Film Journal in a Federative Manner." In *Filmske Novosti, 1944–2004*, edited by Božidar Zečević. Belgrade, SJU, 2004, 89–94.

Stapanian, Juliette R. *Mayakovsky's Cubo-Futurist Vision*. Houston, Tex.: Rice University Press, 1986.

Stepanova, Varvara. "Photomontage." In *Photography in the Modern Era: European Documents and Critical Writings, 1913–1940*, edited by Christopher Phillips. 1928. New York: The Metropolitan Museum of Art/Aperture, 1989. 234–38.

Stites, Richard. *Revolutionary Dreams: Utopian Vision and Experimental Life in the Russian Revolution*. Oxford: Oxford University Press, 1989.

Stollery, Martin. "Eisenstein, Shub and the Gender of the Author as Producer." *Film History* 14, no. 1 (2002): 87–99.

Suny, Ronald Grigor. "The Empire Strikes Out: Imperial Russia, 'National' Identity, and Theories of Empire." In *A State of Nations: Empire and Nation-Making in the Age of Lenin and Stalin*, edited by Ronald Grigor Suny and Terry Martin. New York: Oxford University Press, 2001. 23–66.

———. *The Soviet Experiment: Russia, the USSR, and the Successor States*. Oxford: Oxford University Press, 2011.

Taylor, Brandon. *Art and Literature under the Bolsheviks.* Vol. 2, *Authority and Revolution, 1924–1932.* New York: Columbia University Press, 1953.

Taylor, Charles. *Modern Social Imaginaries.* Durham, N.C.: Duke University Press, 2004.

Taylor, Frederick Winslow. *The Principles of Scientific Management.* 1911. New York: Norton, 1967.

Taylor, Richard. *Film Propaganda: Soviet Russia and Nazi Germany.* 2nd rev. ed. London: I. B. Tauris, 1998.

———. *The Politics of the Soviet Cinema, 1917–1929.* Cambridge: Cambridge University Press, 1979.

Taylor, Richard, and Ian Christie, eds. *The Film Factory: Russian and Soviet Cinema in Documents 1896–1939.* Cambridge, Mass.: Harvard University Press, 1988.

———. *Inside the Film Factory: New Approaches to Russian and Soviet Cinema.* London: Routledge, 1991.

Thompson, John B. "Ideology and the Social Imaginary." *Theory and Society* 11, no. 5 (1982): 659–81.

Tret'iakov, Sergei. "The Biography of the Object." 1929. Reprinted in *October* 118 (2006): 57–62.

———. "From the Photo-Series to Extended Photo-Observation." *Proletarskoe Foto* 4 (1931). Reprinted in *October* 118 (2006): 71–77.

———. *Kinematograficheskoe Nasledie: Stat'i, Ocherki, Stenogrammy Vystuplenii, Doklady. Stsenarii* [Cinematic heritage: Articles, essays, speeches, reports, scripts]. Sankt Peterburg: Nestor-istoriia, 2010.

———. "Lef and Film." 1927. Reprinted in *Screen Reader 1: Cinema/Ideology/Politics,* translated and edited by Ben Brewster. London: Society for Education in Television, 1977. 305–8.

———. "The New Leo Tolstoy." *Novyi Lef* 1 (1927). Reprinted in *October* 118 (2006): 45–50.

———. "Our Cinema." *Novyi Lef* 5 (1928). Reprinted in *October* 118 (2006): 29–44.

———. "To Be Continued." 1928. Reprinted in *October* 118 (2006): 51–56.

Trotsky, Leon. *Literature and Revolution.* 1925. Edited by William Keach. Translated by Rose Strunsky. Chicago: Haymarket Books, 2005.

———. *The Permanent Revolution.* Translated by Max Schachtman. New York: Pioneer Publishers, 1931.

Tsivian, Yuri. "Between the Old and the New: Soviet Film Culture in 1918–1924." *Griffithiana* 55/56 (1996): 15–63.

———. *Early Cinema in Russia and Its Cultural Reception.* Translated by Alan Bodger. Edited by Richard Taylor. Chicago: University of Chicago Press, 1994.

———, ed. *Lines of Resistance: Dziga Vertov and the Twenties.* Russian texts translated by Julian Graffy. Pordenone, Italy: Le Giornate del Cinema Muto Press, 2004.

———. *Notes to the 23rd Pordenone Silent Film Festival Catalogue.* Pordenone, Italy: Le Giornate del Cinema Muto Press, 2004.

———. *Silent Witnesses: Russian Films 1908–1919.* London: British Film Institute, 1990.

———. "Turning Objects, Toppled Pictures: Give and Take between Vertov's Film and Constructivist Art." *October* 121 (Summer 2007): 92–110.

———. "The Wise and Wicked Game: Re-editing and Soviet Film Culture of the 1920s." *Film History* 8 (1996): 327–43.

Tupitsyn, Margarita. *The Soviet Photograph.* New Haven, Conn.: Yale University Press, 1996.

Tupitsyn, Victor. *The Museological Unconscious: Communal (Post)Modernism in Russia.* Cambridge, Mass.: MIT Press, 2009.

Turvey, Malcolm. "Between the Organism and the Machine." *October* 121 (Summer 2007): 5–18.

Urazov, Izmail. "Excerpts from *Shestaia chast mira*" [*A sixth part of the world*]. Moscow, 1926. Reprinted in *Lines of Resistance: Dziga Vertov and the Twenties,* edited by Yuri Tsivian. Russian texts translated by Julian Graffy. Pordenone, Italy: Le Giornate del Cinema Muto Press, 2004. 184.

———. "Shagai Soviet." RGALI 2091-1-87. Reprinted in *Lines of Resistance: Dziga Vertov and the Twenties,* edited by Yuri Tsivian. Russian texts translated by Julian Graffy. Pordenone, Italy: Le Giornate del Cinema Muto Press, 2004. 163.

Vertov, Dziga. "Kino-Eye." RGALI 2091-2-196, January 1926. Reprinted in *Lines of Resistance: Dziga Vertov and the Twenties,* edited by Yuri Tsivian. Russian texts translated by Julian Graffy. Pordenone, Italy: Le Giornate del Cinema Muto Press, 2004. 259.

———. *Kino-Eye: The Writings of Dziga Vertov.* Translated by Kevin O'Brien. Edited and with an introduction by Annette Michelson. Berkeley: University of California Press, 1984.

———. "Kino-Pravda." *Kino-Fot,* no. 6, January 8, 1923, 13. Reprinted in *The Film Factory: Russian and Soviet Cinema in Documents 1896–1939,* translated and edited by Richard Taylor and Ian Christie. Cambridge, Mass.: Harvard University Press, 1988. 84.

———. "Novoe techenie v kinematografi" [A new current in cinema]. *Pravda,* July 15, 1923. Reprinted in *Lines of Resistance: Dziga Vertov and the Twenties,* edited by Yuri Tsivian. Russian texts translated by Julian Graffy. Pordenone, Italy: Le Giornate del Cinema Muto Press, 2004. 82–84.

———. "Vertov's Response to the Cuts Suggested by the Presidium Committee." RGALI 2091-1-8, March 1926. Reprinted in *Lines of Resistance: Dziga Vertov and the Twenties,* edited by Yuri Tsivian. Russian texts translated by Julian Graffy. Pordenone, Italy: Le Giornate del Cinema Muto Press, 2004. 177.

"The VFKO Mobile Cinemas." *Kino-Fot,* no. 2, 1922, 7. Reprinted in *Lines of Resistance: Dziga Vertov and the Twenties,* edited by Yuri Tsivian. Russian texts translated by Julian Graffy. Pordenone, Italy: Le Giornate del Cinema Muto Press, 2004. 75.

Vishnevskii, Veniamin. *Dokumentaln'ye filmy dorevoliutsionnoi Rossii 1907–1916* [Documentary films in pre-revolutionary Russia]. Moscow: Muzeĭ kino, 1996.

Von Geldern, James. *Bolshevik Festivals.* Berkeley: University of California Press, 1993.

Wachtel, Andrew. *Making a Nation, Breaking a Nation: Literature and Cultural Politics in Yugoslavia.* Stanford, Calif.: Stanford University Press, 1998.

———. *An Obsession with History: Russian Writers Confront the Past.* Stanford, Calif.: Stanford University Press, 1994.

Warner, Michael. *Publics and Counterpublics.* New York: Zone Books, 2005.

Waugh, Thomas. "Joris Ivens' Work in Cuba." *Jump Cut* 22 (May 1980): 25–29.

———, ed. *"Show Us Life": Toward a History and Aesthetics of the Committed Documentary.* Metuchen, N.J.: Scarecrow Press, 1984.

"Why Dziga Vertov Has Been Dismissed from Sovkino." *Vechernaia Moskva,* January 14, 1927. Reprinted in *Lines of Resistance: Dziga Vertov and the Twenties,* edited by Yuri Tsivian. Russian texts translated by Julian Graffy. Pordenone, Italy: Le Giornate del Cinema Muto Press, 2004. 254.

Widdis, Emma. *Visions of a New Land: Soviet Film from the Revolution to the Second World War.* New Haven, Conn.: Yale University Press, 2003.

Willemen, Paul. *Looks and Frictions: Essays in Cultural Studies and Film Theory.* London: British Film Institute, 1994.

Winston, Brian. *Claiming the Real: The Griersonian Documentary and Its Legitimations.* London: British Film Institute, 1995.

———. "Direct Cinema: The Third Decade." In *New Challenges for Documentary,* edited by Alan Rosenthal. Berkeley: University of California Press, 1988. 517–29.

———. *Lies, Damn Lies and Documentaries.* London: British Film Institute, 2000.

Wollen, Peter. "Godard and Counter Cinema: Vent d'*Est*." *Afterimage* 4 (Autumn 1972): 6–17.

Xavier, Ismail. *Allegories of Underdevelopment: Aesthetics and Politics in Modern Brazilian Cinema.* Minneapolis: University of Minnesota Press, 1997.

Yangirov, Rashit. "Soviet Cinema in the Twenties: National Alternatives." Translated by Richard Taylor. *Historical Journal of Film, Radio and Television* 11, no. 2 (1991): 129–39.

Z., A. "Na vechere 'Kino-Pravdy'" [At an evening of "Kino-Pravda"]. *Pravda,* September 2, 1922. Reprinted in *Lines of Resistance: Dziga Vertov and the Twenties,* edited by Yuri Tsivian. Russian texts translated by Julian Graffy. Pordenone, Italy: Le Giornate del Cinema Muto Press, 2004. 41.

Zakharov, Alexander. "Mass Celebrations in a Totalitarian System." In *Tekstura: Russian Essays on Visual Culture,* edited by Alla Efimova and Lev Manovich. Chicago: University of Chicago Press, 1993. 201–18.

Zhemchuzhny, Vitaly. "Shestaia chast mira." *Novyi Zritel,* no. 42 (145), October 19, 1926, 16. Reprinted in *Lines of Resistance: Dziga Vertov and the Twenties,* edited by Yuri Tsivian. Russian texts translated by Julian Graffy. Pordenone, Italy: Le Giornate del Cinema Muto Press, 2004. 196–199.

Zhen, Zhang. *An Amorous History of the Silver Screen: Shanghai Cinema, 1896–1937.* Chicago: University of Chicago Press, 2005.

Zorich, A. "O Shestoi chasti mira" [On A sixth part of the world]. *Gudok,* January 8, 1927. Reprinted in *Lines of Resistance: Dziga Vertov and the Twenties,* edited by Yuri Tsivian. Russian texts translated by Julian Graffy. Pordenone, Italy: Le Giornate del Cinema Muto Press, 2004. 223.

FILMOGRAPHY

In addition to providing information on the films discussed in the book, this filmography offers detailed information about the breadth of newsreel and documentary films produced by Dziga Vertov and Santiago Álvarez during the period under consideration. It relies on some published sources, including Yuri Tsivian's *Lines of Resistance*.

The Soviet Union

NEWSREELS/FILM JOURNALS

Kino-Nedelia (Film-Week)
> Issue nos. 1–43 (May 1918–June 1919). Produced by Moscow Film Committee of the People's Commissariat of Enlightenment. Directed by Mikhail Koltsov, Nikolai Tikhonov, Yevgenii Shneider, and Dziga Vertov.

Kino-Pravda (Film-Truth)
> Issue nos. 1–23 (June 1922–March 1925). Produced by Goskino, Moscow. Directed by Dziga Vertov.

State Kino-Calendar
> Issue nos. 1–57 (April 1923–May 1925). Produced by Goskino. Directed by Dziga Vertov.

NAMED ISSUES OF *KINO-PRAVDA*

Kino-Pravda #13: *Yesterday, Today, Tomorrow: A Film Poem Dedicated to the October Celebrations/October Kino-Pravda*, 1922
> 3 reels. 900 meters. Directed and edited by Dziga Vertov. Intertitles by Aleksandr Rodchenko.

Kino-Pravda #16: *Spring Kino-Pravda: A Picturesque, Lyrical Newsreel*, 1923
> 3 reels. 1100 meters. Directed by Dziga Vertov.

Kino-Pravda #17: *For the First Soviet Agricultural, Handicraft, and Industrial Exhibition*, 1923
> 1 reel. 332 meters. Directed by Dziga Vertov. Edited by Elizaveta Svilova.

Kino-Pravda #18: *A Movie Camera Race over 299 Meters and 14 Minutes and 50 Seconds in the Direction of Soviet Reality*, 1924
> 1 reel. 299 meters. Directed by Dziga Vertov. Edited by Aleksandr Goldobin.

Kino-Pravda #19: Black Sea—Arctic Ocean—Moscow / A Movie Camera Race from Moscow to the Arctic Ocean, 1924
    1 reel. 358 meters. Directed by Dziga Vertov. Edited by Aleksandr Goldobin.
Kino-Pravda #20: Pioneer Pravda, 1924
    1 reel. 352 meters. Directed by Dziga Vertov. Camera by Mikhail Kaufman.
Kino-Pravda #21: Lenin Kino-Pravda / A Film Poem about Lenin, 1925
    3 reels. 800 meters. Produced by Kultkino. Directed by Dziga Vertov. Camera by Grigorii Giber, Aleksandr Levitsky, Aleksandr Lemberg, Petr Novitsky, Eduard Tisse, and others.
Kino-Pravda #22: Peasant Kino-Pravda / Lenin Is Alive in the Heart of the Peasant, 1925
    2 reels. 606 meters. Directed by Dziga Vertov. Camera by Mikhail Kaufman, Aleksandr Lemberg, and Ivan Beliakov.
Kino-Pravda #23: Radio Pravda, 1925
    4 reels. 1400 meters. Directed by Dziga Vertov. Camera by Mikhail Kaufman, Aleksandr Lemberg, and Ivan Beliakov. Animation design by Aleksandr Bushkin.

DOCUMENTARY FILMS

The Anniversary of the Revolution, 1918
    12 reels. 2710 meters. Produced by Moscow Film Committee of the People's Commissariat of Enlightenment. Directed by Dziga Vertov and Alexei Savelev.
The Brain of Soviet Russia, 1919
    1 reel. 317 meters. Produced by Moscow Film Committee of the People's Commissariat of Enlightenment. Directed by Dziga Vertov.
The Battle of Tsaritsyn, 1919
    1 reel. 350 meters. Produced by Moscow Film Committee of the People's Commissariat of Enlightenment and the Revolutionary Military Soviet. Directed by Dziga Vertov. Camera by Aleksandr Lemberg.
The Trial of Mironov, 1919
    1 reel. 300 meters. Produced by Moscow Film Committee of the People's Commissariat of Enlightenment. Directed by Dziga Vertov. Camera by Petr Ermolev.
The Exhumation of the Remains of Sergius of Radonezh, 1919
    2 reel. 166 meters. Produced by Moscow Film Committee of the People's Commissariat of Enlightenment. Directed by Dziga Vertov and Lev Kulshov.
The Red Star Literary-Instructional Agit-Steamer of the All-Russia Central Executive Committee, 1919
    2 reels. 335 meters. Produced by Moscow Film Committee of the People's Commissariat of Enlightenment. Directed by Dziga Vertov. Camera by Aleksandr Lemberg and Petr Ermolev.
The Agit-Train of the All-Russia Central Executive Committee, 1921
    1 reel. Produced by Moscow Film Committee of the People's Commissariat of Enlightenment. Directed by Dziga Vertov.
The History of the Civil War, 1921
    13 reels. 3643 meters. Produced by VFKO (the All-Russia Photographic and Cinematic Department) and Narkompros (the People's Commissariat of Enlightenment). Directed by Dziga Vertov.

The Trial of the Right Socialist Revolutionaries, 1922
> 3 reels. 671 meters. Produced by VFKO (the All-Russia Photographic and Cinematic Department) and Narkompros (the People's Commissariat of Enlightenment). Directed by Dziga Vertov. Assisted by Elizaveta Svilova. Camera by Mikhail Kaufman and Aleksandr Levitsky.

You Give Us the Air!, 1923
> Issue 1: 1 reel. 652 meters. Issue 2: 1 reel. 280 meters. Issue 3: 1 reel. 280 meters. Produced by Goskino. Directed by Dziga Vertov. Camera by Mikhail Kaufman and Ivan Beliakov. Intertitles and diagrams by Ivan Beliakov.

Today, 1923
> 1 reel. 195 meters. Produced by Goskino. Directed by Dziga Vertov. Camera by Mikhail Kaufman. Animation by Ivan Beliakov and Boris Volkov.

Automobile (GUM), 1923
> 2 reels. 600 meters. Produced by Goskino. Directed by Dziga Vertov and Mikhail Doronin.

The 1st of May in Moscow / The 1st of May Celebration in Moscow, 1923
> 1 reel. 403 meters. Produced by Proletkino. Directed by Dziga Vertov. Camera by Petr Novitsky.

Soviet Toys, 1924
> 1 reel. 350 meters. Produced by Goskino. Directed by Dziga Vertov. Camera by Aleksandr Dorn. Animation by Ivan Beliakov and Aleksandr Ivanov.

Humoresques, 1924
> 1 reel. 60 meters. Produced by Goskino. Directed by Dziga Vertov. Camera by Ivan Beliakov. Production design by Aleksandr Bushkin. Animation by Boris Egerev and Boris Volkov.

Kino-Eye on Its First Reconnaissance: First Episode of the Cycle "Life Off-Guard," 1924
> 6 reels. 1627 meters. Produced by Goskino. Directed by Dziga Vertov. Camera by Mikhail Kaufman. Edited by Elizaveta Svilova.

The First October without Ilich, 1925
> 3 reels. 895 meters. Produced by Goskino. Directed by Dziga Vertov. Camera by Mikhail Kaufman. Edited by Elizaveta Svilova.

Stride, Soviet! / The Moscow Soviet in the Present, Past, and Future / The Moscow Soviet, 1926
> 7 reels. 1650 meters. Produced by Goskino. Directed by Dziga Vertov. Assisted by Elizaveta Svilova. Camera by Ivan Beliakov. Location scouting by Ilya Kopalin.

A Sixth Part of the World: A Kino-Eye Race around the USSR: Export and Import by the State Trading Organization of the USSR, 1926
> 7 reels. 1718 meters. Produced by Goskino and Sovkino. Directed by Dziga Vertov. Assisted by Elizaveta Svilova. Head camera by Mikhail Kaufman. Additional camera by Ivan Beliakov, Samuel Benderskii, Petr Zotov, Nikolai Konstantinov, Aleksandr Lemberg, Nikolai Strukov, and Iakov Tolchan. Location scouting by Aleksandr Kagarlitskii, Ilya Kopalin, and Boris Kudinov.

The Fall of the Romanov Dynasty, 1927
> 1700 meters. 90 minutes. Produced by Sovkino. Written and directed by Esfir Shub. Released March 11.

The Great Way, 1927
   2350 meters. 116 minutes. Produced by Sovkino. Written and directed by Esfir
   Shub. Released November 7.
The Russia of Nicholas II and Lev Tolstoy, 1928
   1700 meters. 90 minutes. Produced by Sovkino. Written and directed by Esfir
   Shub. Released November 10.

Cuba

NEWSREELS/FILM JOURNALS

ICAIC *Latin American Weekly Newsreel*
   1960–June 1991. Produced by the Cuban Institute for Industrial and Cinematographic Art (ICAIC).

DOCUMENTARY FILMS AND SPECIAL ISSUE, TITLED NEWSREELS

Esta tierra nuestra (This is our land), 1959
   19 minutes. Produced by Cine Rebelde. Directed by Tomás Gutiérrez Alea.
La vivienda (Housing), 1959
   12 minutes. Produced by Cine Rebelde. Directed by Julio García Espinosa.
Historias de la revolución (Stories of the revolution), 1960
   81 minutes. Produced by ICAIC. Directed by Tomás Gutiérrez Alea.
Un año de libertad (A year of freedom), 1960
   27 minutes. Produced by ICAIC. Directed by Santiago Álvarez and Julio García
   Espinosa.
Cuba Sí!, 1961
   50 minutes. Produced by Films de la Pleide. Directed by Chris Marker.
Escambray, 1961
   38 minutes. Produced by ICAIC. Directed by Santiago Álvarez and Jorge Fraga.
Carnet de viaje (Travel notebook), 1961
   34 minutes. Produced by Saul Yelin (Cuba) and Roger Pigaut (France). Directed
   by Joris Ivens. Assisted by Jorge Fraga, José Massip (Cuba), Isabelle Elizando,
   and Guy Blanc (France). Camera by Ramon S. Suarez, Jorge Herrera, Roberto
   Larrabure, and Gustave Maynolet. Edited by Hélène Arnal. Music by Harold
   Gramatges. Commentary text and voice-over by Henri Fabiani. Poem by Nico-
   lás Guillén.
Cuba pueblo armado (A people armed), 1961
   35 minutes. Produced by ICAIC. Directed by Joris Ivens. Assisted by Ramon
   Suarez and Jorge Herrera. Edited by Hélène Arnal. Music by Harold Gramatges.
   Commentary text by Henri Fabiani. Voice-over by Serge Reggiiani.
Historia de una batalla (Story of a battle), 1961
   Produced by ICAIC. Directed by Manuel Octavio Gómez
Muerte al invasor (Death to the invader), 1961
   16 minutes. Produced by ICAIC. Directed by Santiago Álvarez and Tomás
   Gutiérrez Alea.
The Peace Makers, 1962
   11 minutes. Produced by ICAIC. Directed by Santiago Álvarez.

We Did Our Duty, 1962
Produced by ICAIC. Directed by Santiago Álvarez.
Crisis in the Caribbean, 1962
Produced by ICAIC. Directed by Santiago Álvarez.
Top Man in Rhythm, 1963
Produced by ICAIC. Directed by Santiago Álvarez.
Ciclón (Hurricane), 1963
22 minutes. Produced by ICAIC, Television National Newsreel, and the Film Department of the Ministry of Armed Forces. Directed by Santiago Álvarez. Music by Juan Blanco.
Fidel in the USSR, 1963
18 minutes. Produced by ICAIC. Directed by Santiago Álvarez.
First Military Sports Contest, 1964
10 minutes. Produced by ICAIC. Directed by Santiago Álvarez.
Open Way to the Sugar Harvest of '64, 1964
10 minutes. Produced by ICAIC. Directed by Santiago Álvarez.
Cuba 2nd of January, 1965
18 minutes. Produced by ICAIC. Directed by Santiago Álvarez.
Now, 1965
6 minutes. Produced by ICAIC. Directed by Santiago Álvarez. Camera by Pepin Rodriguez and Alberto Hernandez. Edited by Norma Torrado and Idalberto Gálvez. Music by Lena Horne.
Pedalling in Cuba, 1965
13 minutes. Produced by ICAIC. Directed by Santiago Álvarez.
Solidaridad Cuba y Vietnam, 1965
9 minutes. Produced by ICAIC. Directed by Santiago Álvarez. Edited by Norma Torrado
Abril de Giron (The April of Giron), 1966
18 minutes. Produced by ICAIC. Directed by Santiago Álvarez.
Año 7 (Year 7), 1966
18 minutes. Produced by ICAIC. Directed by Santiago Álvarez.
Ocho años de revolución (8 years of revolution), 1966
Produced by ICAIC. Directed by Santiago Álvarez.
Cerro Pelado, 1966
34 minutes. Produced by ICAIC. Directed by Santiago Álvarez. Edited by Norma Torrado. Music by Juan Blanco. Sound by Raúl Pérez Ureta and Idalberto Gálvez.
La escalada del chantaje (Escalation of blackmail), 1967
18 minutes. Produced by ICAIC. Directed by Santiago Álvarez.
Attack in the Forest, 1967
14 minutes. Produced by ICAIC. Directed by Santiago Álvarez.
La guerra olvivada (The forgotten war), 1967
19 minutes. Produced by ICAIC. Directed by Santiago Álvarez. Camera by Ivan Napoles and Argelio Perez. Edited by Norma Torrado. Music by Leo Brouwer and Luigi Nono.
Hanoi, martes 13 (Hanoi, Tuesday 13th), 1967
38 minutes. Produced by ICAIC. Directed by Santiago Álvarez. Camera by Ivan Napoles. Rostrum camera and special effects by Jorge Pucheux, Pepin

Rodriguez, and Adalberto Hernandez. Edited by Norma Torrado and Idalberto Gálvez. Music by Leo Brouwer. Sound by Carlos Fernandez. Text by José Martí.

Hasta la victoria siempre (Always until victory), 1967

19.5 minutes. Produced by ICAIC. Directed by Santiago Álvarez. Camera by Enrique Cardenas. Edited by Norma Torrado and Idalberto Gálvez. Music by Idalberto Gálvez. Sound by Arturo Valdes. Animation and special effects by Jorge Pucheux, Pepin Rodriguez, José Martinez, José Rodriguez, and Adalberto Hernandez.

La hora de los hornos (The hour of the furnaces), 1968

20 minutes. Produced by ICAIC. Directed by Santiago Álvarez.

Coffea Arábiga (Coffee Arabica), 1968

18 minutes. Produced by ICAIC. Directed by Nicolás Guillén Landrián.

Fastening the Belt, 1968

13 minutes. Produced by ICAIC. Directed by Santiago Álvarez.

LBJ, 1968

18 minutes. Produced by ICAIC. Directed by Santiago Álvarez. Rostrum camera by Pepin Rodriguez and Adalberto Hernandez. Edited by Norma Torrado and Idalberto Gálvez. Music by Leo Brouwer, Pablo Milanes, Miriam Makeba, Nona Simone, and Carl Orff. Special effects by Jorge Pucheux.

Despegue a las 18:00 (Takeoff at 18:00), 1969

41 minutes. Produced by ICAIC. Directed by Santiago Álvarez. Camera by Enrique Cardenas, Ivan Napoles, Bernabé Muñiz, José Fraga, and Blas Sierra. Edited by Norma Torrado and Idalberto Gálvez. Music by Leo Brouwer. Sound by Geronimo Labrada, Carlos Fernandez, and Raúl Pérez Ureta.

79 primaveras (79 springtimes), 1969

25 minutes. Produced by ICAIC. Directed by Santiago Álvarez. Camera by Ivan Napoles and Raúl Pérez Ureta. Edited by Norma Torrado. Music by Idalberto Gálvez. Sound by Idalberto Gálvez and Carlos Fernandez.

Eleven-nil, 1970

46 minutes. Produced by ICAIC. Directed by Santiago Álvarez. Camera by Arturo Agramonte, Luis Costales, Dervis Espinosa, Rodolfo Garcia, Oriol Menendez, Enrique Cardenas, Ivan Napoles, and José Fraga. Edited by Norma Torrado and Idalberto Gálvez. Music by Pablo Milanés. Sound by Idalberto Gálvez.

Piedra sobre piedra (Stone upon stone), 1970

70 minutes. Produced by ICAIC. Directed by Santiago Álvarez. Camera by Ivan Napoles and Roberto Fernandez. Rostrum camera by Pepin Rodriguez, Adalberto Hernandez, and Santiago Peñate. Edited by Norma Torrado and Idalberto Gálvez. Music by Idalberto Gálvez and Theodorakis. Sound by Ricardo Istueta and Raúl Pérez Ureta. Graphic design by Modesto Garcia, Delia Quesada, Rene Avila, and Tony Reboiro.

El sueño del pongo (The servant's dream), 1970

11 minutes. Produced by ICAIC. Directed by Santiago Álvarez. Camera by Ivan Napoles. Music edited by Idalberto Gálvez. Sound by Ricardo Istueta and Leonardo Sorrel. Special effects by Jorge Pucheux, Pepin Rodriguez, Pedro Hernandez, Santiago Peñate, Eusebio Ortiz, and Delia Quesada.

Yanapanacuna, 1970

9 minutes. Produced by ICAIC. Directed by Santiago Álvarez.

¿Cómo, por qué y para qué se asesina a un general? (How, why, and what for is a general assassinated?), 1971

36 minutes. Produced by ICAIC. Directed by Santiago Álvarez. Camera by Ivan Napoles and Dervis Espinosa. Edited by Norma Torrado. Music edited by Idalberto Gálvez. Sound by Ricardo Istueta and Leonardo Sorrel. Special effects by Jorge Pucheux, Pedro Hernandez, Eusebio Ortiz, and Delia Quesada.

La estampida (The stampede), 1971

11 minutes. Produced by ICAIC. Directed by Santiago Álvarez. Rostrum camera by Pepin Rodriguez and Adalberto Hernandez. Edited by Norma Torrado. Music edited by Idalberto Gálvez. Sound by Daniel Diaz Castillo. Special effects by Jorge Pucheux.

De América soy hijo . . . y a ella me debo (I am a son of America . . . and I am indebted to it), 1972

195 minutes. Produced by ICAIC. Directed by Santiago Álvarez. Camera by Ivan Napoles, Dervis Espinosa, and Raul Rodriguez. Rostrum camera by Pepin Rodriguez, Idalberto Hernandez, Alberto Valdes, and Santiago Penate. Edited by Norma Torrado and Idalberto Gálvez. Music by Violeta Parra, Isabel Parra, Into Illimani, Quilapyun, Victor Jara, Los Blops, Trio Lonqui, and Atahualpa Yupanqui. Sound by Daniel Diaz Castillo. Special effects by Jorge Pucheux and Eusebio Ortiz.

. . . Y el cielo fue tomado por asalto (. . . And heaven was taken by storm), 1973

128 minutes. Produced by ICAIC. Directed by Santiago Álvarez. Camera by Ivan Napoles and Dervis Espinosa. Edited by Norma Torrado and Idalberto Gálvez. Designed by Antonio Perez. Music by Leo Brouwer and Grupo de Experimentacion Sonora del ICAIC. Animation by Mario Rivas, Leonardo Pinero, and Alfredo Lio.

El tigre saltó y mató, pero morirá . . . morirá . . . (The tiger leaps and kills but it will die . . . it will die . . .), 1973

16 minutes. Produced by ICAIC. Directed by Santiago Álvarez. Rostrum camera by Adalberto Hernandez and Santiago Peñate. Edited by Gloria Arguelles. Designed by Delia Quesada. Music by Victor Jara and Violeta Parra. Sound by Juan Demosthene. Special effects by Jorge Pucheux and Eusebio Ortiz.

La hora de los credos (The hour of the pigs), 1973

30 minutes. Produced by ICAIC. Directed by Santiago Álvarez.

Los cuatro puentes (The four bridges), 1974

74 minutes. Produced by ICAIC. Directed by Santiago Álvarez. Camera by Ivan Napoles, Pablo Martinez, José Tabio, Guillermo Centeno, Julio Valdes, and Sergio Fajardo. Edited by Norma Torrado and Migdalina Vega. Designed by Delia Quesada. Music edited by Juan Marquez. Sound by Juan Demosthene. Designed by Niko. Special effects by Jorge Pucheux, Eusebio Ortiz, Pepin Rodriguez, Alberto Valdes, and Adalberto Hernandez.

INDEX

JOSHUA MALITSKY is Associate Professor in the Department of Communication and Culture at Indiana University. He has published on documentary film in the *Journal of Visual Culture; Cinema Journal; Culture, Theory and Critique;* the *Journal of Linguistic Anthropology; Screening the Past;* and *Studies in Documentary Film.*